The Shaman's Stone

Two boys, one stone, two frightening coming of age events…240 years apart

H. S. Dunham

To Jamie, Jesica, Erin, Jordan, Sam, and Katie

Table of Contents

Chapter		Page
	<u>June 1761</u>	
1	The Longing	8
2	The Shaman Awaits	22
3	The Medicine Bundle	30
4	An Untimely Diversion	44
5	Somewhere Along the River	51
6	The Capture	63
7	Words of War	76
8	A Warrior's Vow	94
9	The Struggle to Escape	109
10	The Water Spirit's Will	126
11	The Upward Climb	139
12	The Council Fire	161
13	The Shaman's Plan	178
14	A Truthful Eye	189
15	Destiny's Answer	214
	<u>June 2001</u>	
16	A Different Journey Begins	222
17	The Challenge	243
18	The Find	252
19	A Fisherman's Luck	271
20	A Stormy Night	295
21	At the Water's Edge	317
22	The Cabin Window	333
23	The Search	349
24	Deliverance	374

"Fear and courage are brothers."

—Proverb

June 1761

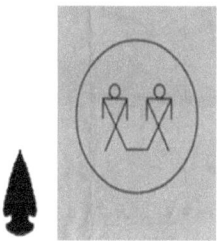

Chapter 1

The Longing

To be a warrior-brave was all Little Turtle ever wanted. That yearning was always present in one way or another, even as he sat cross-legged and idly watched over a small herd of ponies grazing together in the stillness of a nearby meadow near his village. The yearning pulled against his duty to be ever diligent in guarding the herd. Today he had to struggle against it so hard, he barely noticed any other movements nature was providing all around him.

Like the ever-present ants—both black and red, big and small—busy scurrying and savaging nearby, and the multicolored dragonflies darting about. The frequent bees, even those who buzzed too close, did not concern Little Turtle. Nor did the woodland sounds coming from a few squabbling crows and blue jays.

All these creatures living their lives in the warmth of the morning sun paid no more attention to Little Turtle than he did to them. Normally, he perceived the varied sights, soft sounds, and rich smells permeating the meadow, but today they had become invisible. Little Turtle was lost deep in his thoughts centered on his persistent longing.

That remained so until a solitary red-tailed hawk revealed himself high above, gliding upon a slow-moving breeze, the undercurrent barely ruffling its outstretched wings. Little Turtle wouldn't have noticed the soaring bird if it had not suddenly screeched repeatedly in a high-pitched tone that grabbed his attention.

Looking up and squinting his dark eyes against the brightness of the sun, he first interpreted the sighting as a welcome messenger from the spirits. Because of the hawk's power of vision and range of observation, Little Turtle's people associated it with the tribal spirits. In keeping with his search for a sign that would foretell his chance to become a full-fledged brave, it was only natural for him to believe the hawk's voice could be speaking straight to him. He began to wonder: *What messages does he carry from high above? Could it be my signal the spirits are watching me? Then again, is this a warning of some kind? Is an enemy hiding beyond the fringe of the open meadow?*

Little Turtle considered these questions more deeply as he now carefully checked all that was worth watching—first, the ponies, and now, all along the edge of the wooded fringe. With measured haste, he stood up, drew his trusted dagger handed down to him from his father, and made a more thorough visual check as he moved all along the meadow's edges. He was on high alert and more than ready to let out a series of mighty shrills to warn any nearby villagers.

Horse thievery between tribes was on the rise and was considered a serious but dangerous crime for anyone caught. The resulting punishment for those captured usually meant death. Relieved, when he affirmed to himself the potential of danger didn't exist after all, the hawk's signal quickly became a good medicine. Instead of an imminent threat, his curiosity about the ways of the spirits and his wanting for something not yet reached returned.

Within moments of the hawk sighting and his reassurance that the ponies were safe, Little Turtle thought: *Will this finally be the day the spirits consider my wish to become a brave?* It brought about a new vision of himself winning a hard-fought hand-to-hand battle with a rival. Then his vision featured a heroic role riding in the middle of an imaginary buffalo hunt with his war lance's aim reaching its deadly mark also returned. These types of yearnings brought him warm feelings of great tribal worth and were among his favorites.

Despite knowing he had to keep a careful watch on the ponies grazing before him, he was conflicted between these kinds of dreams and his absolute duty to help keep the ponies secure.

When Little Turtle was much younger, long before his pony-watching, most of his time was spent playing games in racing or arrow shooting competitions with his friends, but later, he gradually spent more time alone observing nature and interpreting her many lessons. As he grew a little older and began to take on the larger responsibilities of watching ponies and learning more skillful ways of hunting small game from his father and his many uncles, the more his time was also spent dreaming.

Of course, the safekeeping of the ponies was important, made more so after another recent rash of successful nighttime raids by unknown neighboring suspects. The most recent losses were several ponies in another clan's herd within the boundary of the village. It could mean many more losses in the future for others, including his own if he weren't careful. For the time being, Little Turtle felt confident he could easily do both—watch and dream.

Currently, it was the older boys' duty to watch during the day. Older and more seasoned sentries watched by night. Little Turtle knew his turn was important, especially since his tribe had found that ownership of horses in general had attained an immense value, once they had been brought into their territory more than ten winters ago. Over the many seasons since their arrival, the tribal ponies had become more than just novelties as overgrown dogs or a new wintertime food source. That's how they were originally treated, but his tribe quickly learned of a much greater value.

Ponies helped make Little Turtle's tribe many leaps stronger by increasing their nation's chances for survival, not only by supplying a greater ease of transportation, even carrying or dragging heavy loads, but also by giving their riders a bigger advantage in armed skirmishes over those who did not. More important, they contributed to greater and quicker successes in hunting the distant roaming buffalo or nearby elk. Now, ponies were coveted by all, be it friend or foe.

    Little Turtle understood all these things. But his dream of being recognized as a brave to fight and help provide with those crucial hunts on behalf of the tribe—not just being a solo observer of ponies grazing in the sun—was becoming a powerful force to resist.

    On this warm summer day, as he kept a careful eye on the herd, he knew many of those within his tribe and from other villages, including the white settlers, had also found a growing need to keep a vigilant watch on their stock. Except for those from within his own tribe where thievery was rare and punishment always severe, horse envy and thievery from all outside fronts was growing.

    For Little Turtle, this group of ponies of several dozen was even more special than their inherent value, wealth, or status. They required his undivided attention, far beyond just an opportunity to daydream from time to time. All the ponies in this meadow belonged to his father, Big Turtle—the Miami tribe's great and honored chief.

    The Miami people were a strong tribe led by a strong leader, but had been forced to relocate their village habitation site many times northward as the many armies of the white man continued to capture, give away or sell pieces of their lands to settlers moving in from the south and east. The land the Miami occupied was fertile and rich, and more foreigners sought it for their own.

During those confusing times, it broke Little Turtle's young heart every time he saw his mother forced to gather up everything she had, including her tools of work for the crop harvest, the daily food preparation chores, and for day long clothes making, and then, with a heavy heart leave everything else behind. It meant all the village huts would be destroyed and new ones made again.

Little Turtle had an enormous amount of pride in the work his mother and all the women of the village were able to accomplish to keep the village alive and well, and then pack everything up and start all over. Each time before the tribe's relocation, there was always a conflict in which his father and many warriors would resist these foreigners, first with meetings, and then usually with force. The last skirmish inflicted serious wounds on several warriors and led to the deaths of many others. To this day, there were several warriors who still had not recovered from their long-standing injuries from many moons ago.

For the sake of those women and children in his tribe, as of the last treaty signing, Big Turtle was forced to re-settle their village on the fringe of another tribal area, which not only harder was to hunt and gather and filled with worries of uncertain future crop yields, but also meant continuing to prevent new hostilities from erupting from time to time with those new neighbors. Consequently, the tribe's renewed feelings of homesickness after these forced relocations generated a general sadness. For Big Turtle, whether it was fighting or village moving, it was always on behalf of saving his people in the best way he could.

Little Turtle wanted to help be a force to help his father fight off this ongoing bad medicine, but he and his two brothers were still too young. For now, his duty to his father and his village belonged in the meadow as a vigilant pony watcher.

Despite the importance of horse-watching for Little Turtle, this day was rapidly becoming like any other summer day in the territory referred to by local area traders as "Michigan." The hot and muggy midmorning sun made his watching the herd uncomfortable, trying to keep his floating dreams alive while a few pesky deer flies became more bothersome, buzzing incessant circles around his head. Unlike the hawk, they were doing their part to slow down his imaginary heroics. Along with the flies, the smell of himself was also becoming noticeably more powerful. Yet it remained his honored duty to help watch the group mill about the meadow searching for their favorite grasses. Still, Little Turtle was past his fourteenth spring, and he was itching for so much more.

As the day advanced, Little Turtle managed to return to his visions of seeing himself breaking away on a moment's notice and hopping on one of those grazing ponies and riding along with the tribe's most elite riders and experienced warriors known as the tribe's "dog soldiers." Sitting in his place among the variety of the wildflowers' fragrant scents along with those renewed dreams of glory brought gladness about his future, sure to come one day. To share it with one of those animals before him would be even more special.

The fact was, he loved the ponies' spirit: their drive, their endurance, their sheer power. He admired their gliding grace on the run. Even at his young age, he knew their instinctual essence well. His emerging wartime confidence, galloping full speed, knew no bounds. At one time or another, he had physically practiced those dreams on what he considered the most spirited ponies. He was a good rider already, but it was the wanting inside him to be better, like his father, that had become his own way of learning. Bringing one of those ponies to a full-speed lather had become a skill lesson unlike all previous hunting lessons that he had come to learn. Riding was a special feeling he had come to cherish.

When the sun-warmed field finally began to scorch, which only encouraged the deer flies' persistence, Little Turtle got up and retreated to the relief of the shade. The promise of the tall cottonwood trees and the hope provided by the hawk's sighting spawned the thought: *How will I know the tribal spirits have taken an interest in me? How much longer must I wait? Where are they now?*

Once he was safely under the great spread of the overhead branches, he reached for a nearby cluster of pungent onion stalks, topped with their soft white blossoms. The fresh-picked onions' strong aroma diminished all the other smells around him, including the offensive ones of his own. It was a nice diversion from the flying insects, and the taste had become one of his favorites. After chewing on the stalks and blossoms, he rubbed what was left on his face and bare chest. He felt good. For Little Turtle, his idle time, whether in the direct sun or the shade, was never completely done or boring work. It gave him the time to help stimulate his visions of many more important contributions for the tribe. He wanted to be a provider for them just like his father was already doing every day. The hawk sighting helped.

    Little Turtle and his father had talked about his personal dreams together late at night in his father's dwelling, along with other basic fatherly talk. Mostly they talked of sharpening Little Turtle's hunting skills, like where the best wood types for bow making could be found, the importance of shaping perfectly round straight arrow shafts, and stories of the affairs of the tribe only a few of the other villagers knew. Those talks were never long, but they were frequent and always encouraging. No matter the subject, those moments were always special times where Little Turtle hung onto every word his father spoke.

    According to Big Turtle's way of encouragement at the end of their one-way talks, he usually reminded his son that the only thing that prevented Little Turtle from helping the tribe as a valued brave was a mystical transition with the spirits that had to take place beforehand. This was an important coming-of-age ritual that provided a path for all the boys to become men.

    Little Turtle felt his wait had gone on far too long, much more than his memory could hold. He knew his heart was ready, and as the recent days blended into his days of those long past, he grew more impatient and restless. His longing had only grown worse when his father, at another memorable talk, recently hinted that his time for the miraculous change might be near.

"Your path to be a brave begins with patience. It isn't up to me or you to decide. It is up to the spirits. They will alert you in some way."

Little Turtle hoped today's sighting of the hawk circling above would be that alert. His anticipation was already large enough; it was his patience that was cracking.

There were other hints, but much less personal. Little Turtle could see for himself that the tribe was experiencing even more troubling times. First, the white man's encroachments were becoming more frequent, confusing and violent. Little Turtle wondered: *Why do those people always want things? With my many friends, we will be needed to help rid our tribe of the bad medicine they are always bringing. Surely the spirits will call to me soon. Then I'll show them how I can help.* Second, more stories of enemy tribal attacks were also on the rise, lending Little Turtle to believe: *The tribe will surely need me soon. I want to help.*

Lost in his string of mental urges, he noticed a few horses lift their heads in unison and shift their ears to make sense of a disturbance. Was it a noise in the distance, not heard by Little Turtle…something moving? The direction they were looking with ears erect was across the meadow toward the village site. Something unknown to Little Turtle had been detected by their keen senses. It was made more noticeable as other ponies followed suit, paying close attention, their nostrils flared wide.

What is this? Is more danger approaching?

Little Turtle stood up to take a better look, stepping back into the light. *Oh, it's good...it's the chief. What is he doing out here?*

The bothersome deer flies took their opportunity and resumed circling once Little Turtle was again fully exposed in the sunlight. Swatting them away, he wondered what would bring his father out this way, when there were always so many other things the chief had to do.

Big Turtle turned and headed straight to where Little Turtle was standing. Once the two were finally together, Big Turtle looked over his ponies, and when he was satisfied with what he saw, he said, "An important change is to come for you. I have spoken to you of this before...today your time is near. Gray Tongues is ready to meet with you...before the rising of tonight's near full moon. He is ready to reveal the strong teachings the spirits have waiting for you. With his words...you will obey. Only then will you know the path you will have to travel to become a brave. You must hear them well. I will come again and take you there when I know he is ready to help you and the spirits join together."

With that short notice, Big Turtle raised his large, callused hand, signaling he was done, and abruptly turned and left his son alone to continue with his watchful duties.

Little Turtle could hardly contain his excitement, but he held his tongue and emotions. He did not want to appear to be a boy any longer. His father's mood was serious, and Little Turtle tried to reflect the same with his outward look, but inside his heart was leaping.

    Little Turtle managed to restrain himself a few minutes more, until he was certain his father had returned closer to the village, then he exploded with an extended victory whoop. The ponies stared transfixed as the extraordinary Little Turtle began his own version of a medicine war dance, chanting alone at the meadow's shadowy edge. Up and down and side to side, his knees and hips became a whirl and a blur.

    In his celebration, he embellished a brand-new dream, which included his own special muddy handprints along the neck of one of the ponies nearest him, signifying an image of a war pony's readiness. He even imagined adorning it with several eagle feathers woven strategically into the top of its mane to denote its bravery, like he had seen the tribe's experienced dog soldiers do before a serious battle. As he danced and sang, he tried to imagine what more would happen once the sun fell behind the trees.

    His vocals matched the rhythm of his happy feet moving in all directions among the leaves and grass. As he moved, he thanked the spirits, his ancestors, and especially the hawk's sharp penetrating message. And even though his father's revelation had been brief, it did not dampen his desire for anything more. He knew his father's careful words were true. Even those who rarely spoke to Big Turtle knew his deeds and actions spoke much more than his extended periods of silence. If Big Turtle said Gray Tongues and the spirits were ready, it would be so. Little Turtle would be ready, too.

    As Little Turtle continued to dance, he thought of his

father's words: *Today, you and the spirits will join.* He became amazed by the day's sudden turn of events. One minute he'd been idly watching over his father's grazing ponies, immersed in a variety of his long-standing dreams, and the next, his life was about to be changed forever. All he knew, this was to be the day he would come face to face with Gray Tongues, who carried an important spiritual message aimed only for him. It was all Little Turtle had ever hoped for. He was unable to stay still—dancing on until he was out of breath, panting, and drenched in dripping sweat.

While Little Turtle stood and rested from his high-stepped rhythms, he focused on Gray Tongues. He knew this particular medicine man carried his skills with honor and secrecy, well beyond the village. Gray Tongues not only was the tribe's esteemed and revered medicine man; he also was well known to have great powers within the unseen world. He could communicate directly with the spirits. Because of that, he was also their revered shaman.

So, for Little Turtle, strapped with many hard winters longing for this special lesson to come, his father's words left him stunned. At last, his father and the shaman both must have believed Little Turtle's heart had grown strong enough for a dramatic change to begin. Only now, his heart was bursting; he couldn't contain himself.

Out in this wide-ranging meadow, his father's promise that would answer his pursuit for a dedicated purpose had been delivered. Little Turtle could not wait for his father's return. Together they would find Gray Tongues. With the last of his heavy breathing done, he gave out one more great whoop. The ponies seemed to understand his joy, for they stood their ground. At least for the moment, all of nature's other living things listening within earshot also must have taken notice of that last big vocal eruption. If they hadn't, they missed an important moment, for Little Turtle was about to enter upon his path to fulfilling a long-standing and treasured dream.

Chapter 2

The Shaman Awaits

Little Turtle knew his teaching lesson would be his alone; he had been told that many times by his father. This initial lesson would become the beginning of a secret bond between him and the tribal spirits, interpreted by the tribe's mystical shaman, who would be the only one able to reveal the sacred methods for that to happen. As with all the other boys before him, there would be no exceptions to go about achieving this change, and it would require an extraordinary sacrifice. Big Turtle likened the lesson to that of a young snake shedding its confining skin. Little Turtle knew of such tribal ways of change. To free oneself from the hard casings of childhood by way of the spirits was the only recognized path through which the tribe enabled a boy to achieve his full ripeness. The teaching Little Turtle received would be the first step toward his transformation.

    It would start at the end of the sun's light and come as a dramatic flow through the tribe's mystical mouthpiece, Gray Tongues. Knowing his time of importance was near,

Little Turtle trembled with excitement as he remembered this was exactly as his father had foretold many seasons past and repeated only a few days ago: "One day, my son, you too will visit our tribe's great shaman—face to face on your own."

Not only was Little's Turtle's spirit more than ready, but also there were physical changes that had come in his appearance, which enhanced his readiness. While the summer had made him darker and more weather hardened, the oldest son of the chief had changed in more dramatic ways.

He was growing stronger and could run faster than last summer. Even though he continued to carry his hair short in front and loosely cascading midway down his back, just like his father's, he wasn't scrawny anymore. Despite standing only shoulder height to his massive-looking, invincible father, his arms and legs had thickened. They gave him a stocky appearance, but Little Turtle felt they made him stronger. He was able to ride faster than ever before, and thanks to his developing leg strength, he could stick to a galloping pony with no hands. Even his long days shooting practice arrows were becoming more accurate and penetrating with the growing power in his arms. All this and hours spent hurling his crude blunted lance much further than ever before proved to him he was ready.

These improved skills made him proud. Now he could bring home more fresh game to his mother, White Sparrow, to help feed his family. His newfound skills said to him: *Yes...I am ready. My dreams will hold true.* Now he was able to take part and help supply the tribe with the much-needed bountiful amounts of big-game meat, or, just as important, successfully ride upon the treacherous warpaths, if called upon. This lesson was to be his chance to show everyone, especially his father: *I can shed my spiritual skin when shown the way.*

Little Turtle's most pressing problem with his father's revelation was the way it suddenly caused time to slow down—down to a stop. All he could think about, while waiting for the sun to fall and finally touch Mother Earth, was his meeting with Gray Tongues. Not knowing what else to do, he passed the time by talking to and grooming a few of his favorite ponies. His hands became sweatier as he brushed and removed tangled burrs and clumps of dirt from the worst of the manes and tails. He even momentarily began to doubt himself, but was able to quickly rebound by reflecting upon his newfound abilities with his self-made weapons. *No...I am ready! More than ever!*

In his attempt to refocus away from the stalling of the sun and any more slivers of worry, he turned his attention outward to the sounds of the meadow. The late-afternoon rustling of the white-throated sparrows returning to their hiding places for the night was one. The soft cooing of a pair of mourning doves perched together in the distance and the calls of a pair of wood ducks maneuvering overhead were others. Then it was the rustling sounds of the common reed grasses swaying in a steady, late-afternoon cooling breeze. All these things he tried to dwell on and absorb to help speed up what remained of the day.

Just when the sun finally touched the edge of the earth, out of the corner of his eye he saw his father approaching. This time he was with Little Turtle's younger brothers. He pretended not to look, not wanting to disappoint his father by letting his extreme impatience show. However, it was about time. *I don't want to be late for the spirits. I can't keep Gray Tongues waiting.*

As his father and his brothers came close enough for Little Turtle to hear their moccasins sliding against the thick and rough grassy undergrowth, he aimed his glance up to his father. When their gazes came together, Big Turtle motioned for his son to come and follow. The other boys remained to carry on with the necessary watchful duties. Big Turtle escorted Little Turtle along a narrow path through patches of waist-high canary grass to the edge of the tribe's village toward a small, isolated hut known to be used by Gray Tongues. As they neared the hut, Little Turtle felt his confidence faltering.

Questions raced through his mind as they stepped closer to the shaman's hut. Not only questions, but also many unfamiliar emotions. However, no matter what, one of them was not going to be fear. He stashed those thoughts away. He desperately wanted to help his tribe fend off their new and mounting enemies, and to help hunt for the elusive buffalo. His most worrisome thoughts were: *Will the great spirits speak to me and help me begin my quest, or not at all? If they speak, what will they say? How much stronger will I become? What will the spirits look like? How brave will I become after the spirits bring their messages?*

With dusk now upon them, the pesky deer flies began

to fall away one by one, only to be replaced with the familiar hum of tall spiraling clouds of tiny black flies. They represented Little Turtle's building tension. Even though the village was large, including many hundreds of people, the remaining distance from the pasturing ponies was only a short walk. However, it gave ample time for Little Turtle to build up even more of his strained feelings and questions. Moving slowly toward a remote edge of the tribe's encampment, he was wide-eyed and secretly biting the inside of his lips. His face had stiffened and paled. He had become a little weaker, a little less confident.

Finally, his father stopped and pointed to the shaman's hut, situated only a stone's throw away. He motioned for Little Turtle to go ahead and approach it. A large fire was already burning outside the dwelling, clearly illuminating the destination, and supplying a barrier against the hordes of flying insects that were accumulating.

Little Turtle knew his father would not help him any further. But before they parted, Big Turtle gave his son a pat on his shoulder as a subtle sign of encouragement and said, "Watch with strong eyes and listen hard. Your heart will become larger today. The spirits above you will know this."

Big Turtle knew this day had been a long wait for his eldest son and an important time for his initiation. With that fatherly pat and his chosen words of encouragement, Little Turtle realized, despite the serious challenge ahead, the great chief had silently acknowledged he would remain with him in spirit.

Reassured, Little Turtle forgot his weakness. With Gray Tongues waiting and without further delay, the chief departed.

Once alone, Little Turtle took a deep breath and walked slowly and rigidly toward a small dome-shaped dwelling standing just within the growing shadows of the woods. It was made in the same manner as the larger family huts of tightly woven reeds, long bent sticks wrapped horizontally around the circumference for support. The familiar long strips of bark weighed down with bowed poles protected against the rain. That's all he could make out in the diminishing light. Little Turtle guessed the medicine man was inside.

As though he had sensed his arrival, Gray Tongues stuck his head partially out of the dwelling's entrance and motioned for the boy to come forward and enter. Even though Little Turtle was only a few more steps away, he found himself well within Gray Tongues' direct eye contact. His heart skipped a beat, and then another. *Now is the time to be brave*, he told himself. *If I can't be brave here, where can I?* He took an extended deep breath and stepped closer.

In one respect, Little Turtle was fortunate, because the other children of the village rarely saw Gray Tongues. Fortunate, because Big Turtle was the tribal chief, Little Turtle had occasionally crossed paths with the spiritual leader before. However, they had always been incidental. Gray Tongues was an old man and active mostly after dark. He was a solitary figure, who walked stooped over and took his steps in a measured way, using his walking stick for stability. When he mingled, it was exclusively with the adult leaders who needed his relished advice and wisdom the most.

    Nowadays, it seemed Gray Tongues' range of magical powers had widened, and he was being searched out by many others. After all, not only was he a wellspring of nature's curative ways as a medicine man, but also, he could interpret the will of the spirits. So, it was not simply illness that brought many to him. Most of the bad medicine in the tribe was being derived from new faces entering and claiming portions of the tribe's territory. Frequent confrontations were raising a need for more spiritual answers.

    For a long time, Gray Tongues had kept a good balance between his wisdom and his unexplained magic that most of the tribe did not understand. But more recently, the tribe had become uneasy with the continuing news of the white man's forceful intrusions and the ever-increasing deceptive encounters with them. It didn't matter whether it was for simple trading purposes or a serious fight; the white man's desires weren't always readily understood, or, for that matter, fair. Fortunately, Gray Tongues' words offered many answers for understanding the problems that now dominated each day. For those reasons, he had become an important and powerful man. No wonder Little Turtle's wait had been so long.

    Little Turtle knew of Gray Tongues' power throughout the village from secondhand stories, mostly from his father. Anticipating being face to face with him, he was sure he was about to see the shaman's magic among the spirits firsthand. To make him more nervous, he had never stepped inside, much less been anywhere near Gray Tongues' isolated structure since the tribe's relocation only a few winters ago. He'd had no reason. Little Turtle was never sickly, nor had he been threatened by any strange demons. To lurk around Gray Tongues' space without a purpose was considered bad medicine.

Most of the time, it was his father, the chief, who enlisted Gray Tongues' advice during a council meeting. Council meetings were held in a large central hut built in the same manner as the villager dwellings, only much larger to accommodate large groups. All other personal concerns, health or otherwise, were conducted by Gray Tongues with the one affected, alone at their living site.

Gray Tongues' one-man hut, conversely, was simple enough and kept from the rest of the tribe's dwellings for more intimate interactions with the spirits. It wasn't a place made for habitation purposes or group decisions. It was built as a special site to allow the revered shaman a better focus, to be alone, avoiding distractions. Little Turtle's special lesson qualified in that respect.

Little Turtle held his breath as he looked inside. There he could readily see...the shaman was waiting.

Chapter 3

The Medicine Bundle

Little Turtle entered the hut slowly and paused, stooping over inside the low-ceilinged hut. Gray Tongues was already sitting cross-legged, with a look that said he was beginning to enter a trance or a prayerful ritual. Out of respect and not knowing what to do next, the boy stayed as he was and waited for a sign from Gray Tongues.

    He didn't have to wait long. Gray Tongues looked up and motioned for him to sit directly across from him. A smoldering fire lined with stones lay between them in the center of the dwelling. Gray Tongues had smeared wood ashes across his deeply wrinkled face, around his small dark eyes, and all around his bare upper body. Little Turtle was impressed, but remained silent.

He knew that Gray Tongues was an old man, but up close he looked ancient. The wrinkles on his face were a web of deep crevasses. Time had eroded his skin without mercy. His two thick side braids were woven tight, gray, and adorned with long whitish streaks. They were held together at the ends with wrapped fur. His nose was broad, and his head carried no ornaments or feathers. The way he looked, so full of intensity, assured Little Turtle that this man held much knowledge.

Both remained seated quietly. Little Turtle followed Gray Tongues' lead and stared into the flickering flames, each occupied with his own thoughts. With neither one uttering a word, Little Turtle became aware of the larger fire outside the hut, which still burned bright and flickered just enough firelight through the entrance opening to project odd, distorted shadows along the inner dark walls of the hut. It was another intimidating sight for him to ponder.

A quick glance revealed that most of the rest of the shelter's interior was littered with what looked like dried animal parts, bright feathers, and an unusual collection of fresh-picked plants, small rocks, and colored beads nestled in various types of crudely woven baskets. Little Turtle also smelled a strange, unfamiliar smoke rising from the smoldering embers inside the hut. The little fire created enough smoke to produce an alluring light-blue haze. However, if it weren't for the hut's open smoke hole in the ceiling, the haze would have made it even harder to see clearly.

Sitting across the fire with such an imposing figure, Little Turtle had much to consider. The hut's interior was already becoming powerful to his senses, coupled with the fact the man sitting across from him was known to be hard to understand with his mysterious ways and his deep, gravelly voice. Little Turtle tried to put it all aside. He would not let his nerves get in the way; his special instructions could come at any time. *I am ready.* He knew he was on the verge of learning how he was going to be converted from a village boy to a brave. His only concerns now were: *How would it be done? Will there be a flash like lightning? Will it hurt? Will there be more?* Little Turtle was not sure of any of it, except to follow his father's instructions to watch with strong eyes and listen as hard as he could.

After much delay, including Little Turtle's uncomfortable period of being sized up, Gray Tongues finally broke the spell and turned his head to the ceiling. Thereupon he began to strike a large stick across a buffalo horn and to hum, then half chant in his unique voice. Little Turtle listened and patiently watched the slow rhythmical pattern as best he could to understand the chant. His forehead beaded with sweat as he reasoned Gray Tongues was communicating with the spirits. *What are they saying?*

Little Turtle remained quiet and took it all in, but it wasn't easy. The process was painfully slow, and the aromatic smoke made him feel dizzy and peculiar. It seemed like a great length of time had already passed before Gray Tongues abruptly stopped and his glance returned to Little Turtle. Then he spoke to Little Turtle directly and without expression.

"The ancient spirits beyond the sky are now

listening...and they have agreed to lead you to your path of change."

Gray Tongues moved his arms to create a more dramatic emphasis, saying, "I will help to start the process with the spirits...It will be they who will guide you across your inner bridge into manhood. But...to become a complete man and provider for those around you...you first must have a vision. Your vision will be a story of personal courage. It will be your bridge to the future. To cross it will take a great sacrifice on your part. Your vision...will carry a strong message and become your path to understanding the great spirits' will for you. Do not become lost on the bridge. Listen to the spirits. Trust them as your guides...they will be lodged within your heart. With their knowledge, you will understand the story they will have created for you."

He paused, then emphasized, "It is the way of the tribe."

Finally Gray Tongues raised his shaking voice and stressed, "The knowledge from your vision will be a powerful life event. This will only come from the supernatural...and not on your own. This vision could take much time...over many days and many nights...or longer. You will have to suffer. How much...the spirits will decide. However, once you walk within the spiritual world...you will see yourself as a new person. You will be able to understand their messages given. In the end, your knowledge will reveal what it will take to become an equal...among all other warriors in this tribe...upon your return to the real world. With your quiver loaded with this newfound message...and with much unbroken practice and many hunting travels...you may become a great leader like your father. None of this will be possible without the spirits' help and counsel. You will have to understand much more on your own after this private vision while remaining completely alone. Little Turtle...be strong enough and you will cross your vision's most sharpened path."

Gray Tongues stopped speaking for the moment, but he was not finished.

All this information was revealing and important to Little Turtle. He wanted nothing more than to be like his father. Even though he was sweating from the warmth during his time in the hut, Gray Tongues' final words reminding him of his father's leadership gave Little Turtle chills of mounting goose bumps, and his eyes watered. His father was the steady force of a large Miami tribe in a new territory the white man called the "Great Northwest Territory," or occasionally just referred to as "Indiana" or "Michigan." Even though the white man's calendar said it was 1761, the maps of the day still weren't precise. Little Turtle only knew his homeland as "Mother Earth."

One thing was for certain: Settlers were arriving in great numbers for their chance to grab cheap land, and this period of new faces and conflicting ideas had created difficult times for his tribe, causing much discussion between his father and the many villagers. To make matters worse, the many trappers and settlers who were entering their fertile region were also fighting among their own kind. There were stories of much blood being spilled. Despite these circumstances, his father had led with a steady hand and a straight tongue. Little Turtle wanted to be like him.

During Little Turtle's and his father's alone time together, Big Turtle had referred to these white men either as "French" or "English." Most of the time he called them French. To Little Turtle, the words were confusing, because between their different spoken tongues, Big Turtle and others said they both acted the same. All the trappers who visited the village to trade dressed similarly. Between the two, the problems they brought the tribe were becoming identical battling for favors within the tribe's sacred territory and spreading bad medicine with disease, alcohol, and physical force.

Because of these territorial struggles, Little Turtle's tribe had lost many to the increasing warfare between newfound enemy tribes, the settlers, and, from time to time, the white man's armies from the two foreign-speaking countries who roamed freely claiming territory between themselves. The worst of those struggles was the constant fear of ambushes, attacks, and loss of hunting, trading, and planting grounds. Gray Tongues recollected a few of those lost ones who were close to Little Turtle, following his vision instructions as he chanted to the spirits and inhaled the smoldering smoke. In Little Turtle's young life, he knew all these things to be true.

As recently as only a few moons ago, a small hunting party of three young braves traveling near the river were found murdered and scalped by an unknown enemy. No evidence was found—not a trace. There was not a trail sign to find or even the arrows of the destruction to be had. These were villagers Little Turtle also knew, who were only trying to provide more game for the tribe. No one had come forward yet with any answers, but were fresh reminders of the frequent and more sorrowful tribal times. This part of Gray Tongues' preparation for the spirits was uncomfortable to relive.

As Little Turtle struggled to keep listening to the old shaman's scattered stories of the lost ones in his tribe and the importance of the vision to come before him, many more memories of those villagers' faces, including those of his own clan members lost to death and suffering, returned before him. Fresh thoughts of moving the entire village west and northward several times during his young life to avoid the continual fighting and obeying unclear and slanted treaties written in the white man's tongue was a difficult concept for Little Turtle to understand. Many of his clansmen were still homesick for the lands they had already lost. Little Turtle hoped one day he could help stop all the troubles. They had been going on as long as Little Turtle could remember, and he wanted to forget.

One day, as a strong and wise warrior fighting side by side with his fearless father and the tribe's other warriors, they might find a path of true peace and happiness that he had heard his elders speak of during many previous tribal bonfires and ceremonies, recalling those peaceful years that had long passed. So, despite his anxiety sitting alone with the old mysterious one, he hoped that his visit with the spirits would eventually make his life better. He was more than ready for that.

As the night wore on, and the larger campfire's embers grew faint for supplying light outside to the immediate area, Gray Tongues reached for a woven basket staged behind him. He placed it in his own lap and positioned it squarely between his crossed legs. To Little Turtle, it looked at first to be filled with nothing more than small, underdeveloped green pine cones, early clippings from an enterprising squirrel.

Gray Tongues resumed chanting, then abruptly stopped, and raised the container. Then he reached across the flames and placed it into Little Turtle's lap. He gestured for Little Turtle to reach inside. He did as he was instructed, moving the cones aside to touch a soft, oblong object about as big as his fist at its bottom. It was the only object other than the pine cones in the basket.

The shaman nodded his approval as Little Turtle withdrew what seemed to be a rolled piece of tanned deer hide. Little Turtle wasn't sure at first. It was hard to tell because the smoke was getting thicker, but the hide felt familiar despite being wrapped with a strong length of woven horse tail strand. He felt something lumpy inside and looked at Gray Tongues with a furrowed brow. Gray Tongues nodded again and motioned for Little Turtle to hold the bundle over his head and chant along with him. Little Turtle obeyed.

After Little Turtle hummed his absolute best, the shaman explained.

"What you hold…is your medicine bundle. You will need it to help greet the spirits on your vision quest. Your father will take you to a sacred place when he is ready. There you will be left alone until the spirits come, but the objects in the bundle will help you. They hold great power. When you carry it with you...it will keep your heart full and strong. The bundle's power will help you call and know the spirits. Together, the objects will supply the good medicine of...great courage. You will need it to face difficult hunts or battles. With it, the good power of the spirits' messages will be yours."

After this brief insight, which invoked great wonder in Little Turtle, Gray Tongues instructed him to lower the bundle, place it on the ground, and gently stretch the horse tail binding until it broke. Again, Little Turtle obeyed. Inside the pouch he found a variety of small bird bones, aromatic dried mint and sage leaves, a few sharp porcupine quills, a small amount of brightly colored elongated beads, and one finger length pure white spear-shaped stone.

Even though the darkness in the hut made it hard to see, Little Turtle couldn't believe his eyes. *What does this all mean?* He was particularly struck by the color of the elongated stone. Little Turtle placed it in his hand and turned it over repeatedly. Such an object he had not seen before, and his father had never spoken of such an item to him. Although he had seen many bundles before—all the village warriors carried one strapped to their loincloth or around their back—he had never seen their contents. *Is this bundle my connection to the supernatural world?* He was stunned by the unseen force he held in his hands and the lesson he had heard. His hunger and desires were being filled; they tasted sweet.

The shaman resumed chanting. With the hut growing darker, Little Turtle wanted to get a closer look at his bundle but didn't move. Gray Tongues paused to explain, "There is much power within each of the objects before you."

Little Turtle listened intently. He was especially intrigued by the quills and the stone projectile.

Gray Tongues declared, "All these objects are necessary...They will please the spirits. The dried leaves, bones, and beads will help you attract them... They are offerings. All of them will need to be replaced after summoning the spirits in the future. The quills and the one stone...are tools to bring forth your vision. The quills...you will use to draw your sacrificial blood upon the stone as another offering. The stone will be used to slash greater wounds upon yourself if the spirits do not answer to the quills. I warn you...when you are on your way to the sacred place with your father, do not eat or drink anything...at any time...not until your vision has been revealed. You must remain focused on this journey. You must have a strong-willed sacrifice to please the spirits. If these words are followed with the pain needed...with a plentiful amount of blood offered, the spirits will enter your heart and supply a dreamlike story...your own vision to you. Once the vision is over...you alone must carry its message back to the village and tell it to the tribal elders."

Gray Tongues stopped and stared into the fire. Minutes passed in deep silence until the momentary tension was snapped by Gray Tongues' words.

"Once your vision is revealed and interpreted by the elders...and they are convinced that the great spirits have come and filled your heart, and made it strong enough, they will let it be known to you, and to all the village, that you have become a brave. At another time…the spirits will uncover an additional secret object that will be meant for your bundle. It will make it unique and only known to you…not even to your medicine man. All these objects, mixed together, will help fight against the ways of the evil spirits…who will always tempt you with their treasures of bad medicine. Changing in this way will mean you can hunt and fight if you have your bundle at your side. With it…you will no longer help with the chores of children. Instead, you will practice the ways of the hunter with sharpened points on your arrows and, when necessary, discover the ways of a fearless warrior."

But Gray Tongues wasn't finished. "The hunter's stone is to always be kept in the bundle. It will supply courage against any evil that surely will come—like an untrue arrow missing its aim—but with the stone, you'll be able to draw another. Use your bundle with the power in it…when you call the great spirits."

Little Turtle could not imagine when that might be, but he was convinced the stone would be a true source of strength for him one day. He was already thankful for having touched it.

Gray Tongues' voice was weakening. He motioned for the boy to return all the bundle's contents back into the open leather bundle spread out before him. Gray Tongues leaned across the fading fire and helped Little Turtle rewind the bundle with the remaining horse tail fiber. He then signaled he was finished and motioned for Little Turtle to leave.

Little Turtle understood and got up. It had been a long

session. Gray Tongues placed the empty basket into the smoldering embers. With the lasting image of the burning basket in his mind, Little Turtle went along the same path back home to the village. Only now, instead of hostile mosquitoes and gnats, a soothing symphony of cricket sounds went with him. And instead of feeling any sense of self-doubt, the excitement of his bundle and its message made him run as fast as he could, homeward, along the moonlit path. His new gift clutched tightly in his hands would surely guide him safely from here on.

In a few minutes, Little Turtle made it all the way back to his father's hut. Without thinking about what the chief might be doing, or if he was even present, he burst into his dwelling. Fortunately, Big Turtle was tending a small central fire and readying his array of weapons for an early-morning hunt. Without hesitation, Little Turtle began to relate all that had happened with Gray Tongues.

Big Turtle was impressed that Gray Tongues believed Little Turtle was ready to become a future warrior with the passing of the medicine bundle to him. He nodded his approval, listening to every word from his excited son.

Before Little Turtle's interruption, Big Turtle had been focused on sharpening a lance point tip, expecting his participation in a long-distance buffalo hunt. A small herd had been sighted and was moving northward toward a close traveling range. One advance group had been gone for days. A scout had returned requesting more help. Big Turtle and a larger group were to join the hunt to maximize the effort. However, with his son's earnest words pressing strongly upon his heart, he changed his mind.

"Many more hunters and I were going to join in the hunt with the early-morning sun. I will inform the others of your bundle and stay behind to help you begin your quest while your gift is still fresh and most powerful."

Big Turtle wanted his son to be at his best. There wouldn't be a lot of time to waste. A buffalo hunt was unpredictable and could take many days. Big Turtle knew both his son and the bundle were close to their peaks of ripeness for a rapid vision quest completion. Now that Gray Tongues had agreed and provided the bundle, time was of the essence.

Together, they decided Big Turtle would escort his son to an undisclosed sacred place along the winding river. There, Big Turtle would leave him deep inside an isolated wooded area to meet with the great spirits—completely alone and undisturbed.

Big Turtle repeated a portion of Gray Tongues words. "Once you are left by yourself, our spirits will consider if you are ready. If so, they will show you your new way of life and add other secrets they believe will be necessary. Only then will you be permitted to return—on your own—not before."

How long that would take, Big Turtle did not know, and did not say other than, "We will go with the shining of the morning dew. Now you must go, my son…get your rest."

Little Turtle was beginning to understand that his event would be more than he had ever known or dreamed of. He was not going to fail or disappoint his proud father. This was what he had wanted—to be a great provider for and defender of the tribe. Now he had approval from the all-knowing shaman as well as his father, the great chief.

With that exchange, Little Turtle left his father and ran down to his mother's hut not far away. She and his siblings were fast asleep. With no one else to talk to, he crawled into his bed with many swirling ideas of how he would greet the great spirits. As he did so, he gave humble gratitude to the circling hawk above the meadow, who had alerted him of what was to come, and silently said a thankful prayer to the spirits: *Help me to remain calm and strong in the face of all that comes to me. Let me learn the lessons you have hidden in every leaf and rock...*

Chapter 4

An Untimely Diversion

When daylight broke the next day, the village experienced a great disturbance. Many of the first group of buffalo hunters, who had been gone long before Little Turtle's meeting with Gray Tongues, began returning with their ponies dragging heaps of freshly chopped meat and their valuable bloody hides in a steady bountiful parade-like fashion.

Word of their arrival spread fast, and rounds of rejoicing among the people soon began. The chatter among the villagers was that the buffalo spirits had been most agreeable, relieving the hunters with a relatively short time spent traveling southwards, and then, back home again, including through portions of hostile territories.

    Once the encounter had been made, many of the animals helped the warriors by willingly accepting their accurate arrows and penetrating spears. It was the buffalos themselves, after continuous searching and being able to range amongst their favorite sweet summer grasses, that had led to their generous spirits temporarily cooperating with the hunters. Together, the many fallen animals afforded a quicker than usual hunt. It also meant the second group of hunters would not have to face additional dangers and join them. However, once the animals had seen dozens or more of their immense herd go down, the remaining buffalo became collectively disagreeable and moved away on the run, well out of striking range, for any other hunting prospects.

    This great bounty represented good fortune for the village, and jubilation spread rapidly. The waking tribe had been getting down in their communal food stocks from finding previous herds, and the stores of sun-dried venison and fish, plus the supplies of nuts, edible roots, and berries, were getting low. They were more than grateful for the replenishment.

    The only exception was Little Turtle. His long-held dream to be one of those elite hunters restocking the tribe would have to be postponed.

    As the leader of the tribe, Big Turtle was more than pleased and thankful because he knew firsthand that hunting the wandering buffalo was never an easy enterprise. Even though long ago the herds were many, their spirits could easily become contrary and dangerous.

During those earlier buffalo hunts when the tribe lived deeper in the southlands, the buffalo were easier to find in their own spacious territorial grounds, and the hunts weren't as treacherous as they had become in recent years. Even Little Turtle knew the stories of rampage and stampedes, but now, with the shrinking herds and the animals' more wayward western travels, the tribe was becoming dependent upon the quality of the prairie grasses not disturbed by the white man's horse-drawn plows and their widespread grazing livestock.

Those changes created hazardous instances when the tribe's most important food stock was encountered beyond the Miami territory, roaming in and out of neighboring tribal lands. Those tribes generally felt that for the short time the buffalo traveled and fed in their territorial hunting spaces, the buffalo not only belonged to them, but they also represented "good medicine" given to them directly as a reward from the spirits.

When buffalo such as these were harvested, derived from those other tribal lands, both the meat and the associated good medicine were believed to be stolen away from them. If discovered, those other tribes usually retaliated in a most hostile and violent way. Consequently, there was always the possibility of a long-term fight, and many deaths could result from skirmishes with once friendly bands. In this case, however, the buffalo harvest had gone unusually quick. Not only was the meat plentiful, but there also were no disputes and no warrior losses. All these factors were worth celebrating.

With a bountiful and successful hunt achieved and word of it understood throughout the village, today had become an important time for a renewed and loud celebration. First, and foremost, it was a time to thank the tribal spirits. Second, it was time to celebrate the generosity of the buffalo spirits themselves. Because of these two occasions coming together, it would be a long-lasting and joyous ceremony.

Unfortunately for Big Turtle, there would be no time for his anxious young warrior-to-be today. Little Turtle's future visit with the great spirits would have to be postponed. Even Little Turtle, despite his strong desire to get started on his vision quest, understood what a bountiful hunt meant. He would have to swallow his disappointment. For now, for the good of the tribe, a great ceremonial thanks for the village's good fortune always came first. This was not a time for satisfying any personal long-held dreams.

By midmorning, a great fire was roaring in the center of the village and many drums were beating a steady rhythm for dancing and chanting. Both were done in full force. A small part of the meat was at once cut, prepared, and set to roasting by the village women. Many people didn't wait and ate it raw and fast.

Little Turtle was intoxicated by the sights of his people's smiles, their voices recounting successful hunts of the past, and the smell of searing meat. He was thrilled to hear fresh details of the chase and the downing of so many animals fleeing. The stories were fresh, exciting, and vivid, riddled with wild-eyed danger like being trampled by the herd that stretched into the distance as far as the eye could see. He was happy to see and feel the tribal joy. Nobody needed the cheap whiskey that the white man kept trying to sell them in order to become delirious.

In the interim, Little Turtle kept his disappointment hidden, and instead traded stories with a few of his friends about visions, the spirits, and Gray Tongues in particular. These friends were also anxious about the plight of the tribe and the tensions their families were feeling. Their dreams were important too, for nothing about their lives was predictable and nothing could ever be taken for granted.

By late in the day, all the villagers had taken part in one way or another and settled back with full stomachs and a glowing satisfaction with the spirits' temporary generosity. In the upcoming days, the rest of the meat would be divided equally among the families and the many hides preserved and made into new robes and blankets to shelter against the winter's bitter cold, sure to come in the passing of a few more full moons.

After his visits with his friends and later with his younger brothers, and joining in with the festive dancing, Little Turtle had almost forgotten about his late-night experience with the old shaman. That was, until his father, full of pride with the great productive hunt, came over to him and said, "I will meet with you when the big fire burns low, and the spirits signal our thanks for their good medicine has been received."

Little Turtle furrowed his brow and nodded. Despite the multiple distractions of noise and temptations all around them both, he had a strong force of mind to question his father. "What do you mean…where should I be? How am I to know when?"

Big Turtle was direct. "Stay by the fire. I will find you."

Little Turtle didn't have to wait long. Big Turtle was also eager for his son's transition, and when he felt he could leave his celebratory duties as chief, he found Little Turtle near the big fire as instructed. Big Turtle approached his son from behind and put his hand on his shoulder and hand-signed, "Come with me."

Little Turtle followed his father until they arrived at a quiet place away from the bonfire and the festivities. Without emotion or fanfare, Big Turtle said, "When tomorrow's sun brings its first light, we will travel to a sacred place near the river where you will begin your journey to become a man. There your spirit will be given the chance to grow the wings of change. On your journey, you will begin without sight. Together, we will ride to where the spirits gather and will speak to you—if you listen. There, you will be alone without the help of weapons or food. All you will bring is your loincloth, moccasins, and your new bundle. You will stay at this sacred site…no matter how long…until the spirits speak and reveal their intentions to you. It will come through your vision. Use your bundle to appease them. Once they have spoken to you with their message, you will carry it back to the village and reveal your spiritual story to our tribal elders."

After a pause for emphasis, he concluded, "You must not fail."

Big Turtle then raised his hand showing he was finished, turned, and departed.

The meeting was another exciting surprise for Little

Turtle, but his father's last words—"You must not fail"—were sharp and strong. Dumbstruck, Little Turtle considered all that he heard: *No sight, no weapons, a vision with a message from the spirits…all alone.* He scraped his fingers through his dark flowing hair and took an extended breath, wondering: What *if I don't get a vision? What if it isn't strong enough? What will my father do?*

Little Turtle had many things to think about.

In full obedience, he ended his participation in the festivities and returned home to his mother's hut without consuming another shred of food or a drop of water. He crawled into his bed trying to predict what kind of vision he might see and the message it might hold. He still believed he would shed his boy-like ways, but to leave his childish shell would take a tall price. *I can do it. It will be done…all of it.*

Slowly, but gladly, he tried to drift asleep, but it was a struggle. It had been a long day with much to imagine. However, beyond the tribe's current good fortunes, soon it would be Little Turtle's turn. No matter the possible hardships of his upcoming quest, there could be no failing his chief or the tribe.

Chapter 5

Somewhere Along the River

Long before the first rays of the sun had broken the horizon and the sound of a robin's sparkling morning melody could be heard, Little Turtle began to stir. Despite the hour, it was warm and humid inside his mother's thatched hut. He stretched and wiped the sleep completely out of his eyes, and once fully conscious, he lay silent and listened to the rhythmical sounds of his mother and younger siblings still asleep. No sooner than he knew it, he was again daydreaming. *What will this day bring?*

Before he could fully dive into the question, his father slipped into the hut and roused him out of bed with a solid shake. There was no noise associated with his father's action. There weren't any other disturbances.

Little Turtle knew what was expected.

While his stoic-looking father stood and waited beside him, when Little Turtle's feet were flat on the dirt floor, he had the presence of mind to quietly smear a handful of rendered bear fat, readily at hand, all over his naked body. He knew he would need relief from the hordes of flying insects that would surely find him once again. As previously instructed, he dressed only in his essentials: his loincloth, versatile moccasins, and his prized medicine bundle strapped tight onto his loincloth belt. Once Big Turtle was satisfied his son was ready, he left. Little Turtle promptly followed.

Outside, the wind was still, and the grasslands were moist with a blanket of emerging dew. A great many passenger pigeons were already sounding their soft mournful coos overhead, setting up a fluttery feeling in his empty stomach. Without any further words, Little Turtle found himself blindfolded and doubled-up with his father on horseback, trotting down one of the open village trails.

There were many more things that Little Turtle thought about as he held himself close to his father. They were no longer fantasies; instead, he was full of anticipation for his encounter with the spirits.

Little Turtle had eagerly wanted this journey, but the fact that he was not able to recognize the immediate surroundings along the way was straining his mind, as he tried to determine where he and his father were headed. With his eyes blindfolded, Little Turtle was already beginning to believe his initiation into adulthood could be a challenge. Not only that, but he was becoming more confused with the direction of the trail. The morning light had carried a strong beginning. His father was continuing to make it so.

One of the joys along the beginning of the ride was being mounted atop his favorite pony, a gray-colored mustang stallion named Many Winds. The horse was temperamental enough that he could only be cared for and ridden by his father. Despite being highly spirited, Many Wind's intelligence afforded an ease to understand his father's slightest leg and hand commands. Little Turtle couldn't imagine how his father and the horse blended so well. It was as though their two souls had merged and become one whenever they raced along with their hair and mane flying straight back. Little Turtle wanted to blend with a pony like that one day.
    This mustang was not only fast, but also strong and fearless, like his father. The little stallion carried himself with a noble look. His spirit emitted confidence. Many Winds had come to the tribe as a young colt, from a place far beyond Little Turtle's grassy northern flatlands home. The colt had been a personal gift from the chief of the Potawatomi to Big Turtle, along with his name. Many Winds and other ponies were given as a token for Big Turtle's aid in driving away an army of the white man's approaching foot soldiers. Little Turtle had been told the army wore bright red coats even in the warm summer air. No one knew why.
    As Little Turtle grew up, he had ridden and raced his father's other ponies. Some were old and worn out, destined now to be no more than pack carriers, but good

enough as early training for Little Turtle and his brothers. As Little Turtle grew older, he learned his next level of riding on those ponies used for everyday casual hunting or for racing and tricks. A few of the others in the herd were reserved as long distant travelers and were referred to as "buffalo ponies." These he tested only on rare occasions. He knew their strength was needed for the long distant search and chases.

All of these he had befriended one by one at some time, but not Many Winds. This stallion was the only pony he was denied permission to mount by his father under any circumstances. This special horse was the chief's war horse and used only for battle or for special events. There was one other exception. Big Turtle promised to hand this pony over to Little Turtle once he became an established brave. To be able to ride this pony, on his own, would be an added honor he relished and aspired to. Perhaps that day would be today. For now, just being mounted upon this spectacular horse with his father positioned in front and Many Winds striding gracefully under him made Little Turtle feel as if he were floating with his long hair flopping up and down off his back. With every stride Many Winds took, Little Turtle grew more confident this day would surely belong to him.

Without a solid reason, Little Turtle felt his father would follow the usual trail out of the village toward the river where he and his young friends had spent countless hours. So, he naturally felt he'd have no difficulty finding his way back home when he was finished following the spirits' wishes, whether he was blindfolded or not.

Unfortunately, he was wrong. When the chief abruptly

leaned right and deviated Many Winds in a direction away from what Little Turtle thought was the proper path to the river, he wondered: *Why can't I be sure of this direction? This ride feels different. Is the chief playing tricks? He said my path would be difficult...I will do this.*

Little Turtle's whole being was on high alert as he tried to piece together the invisible landmarks, sounds, smells, and assorted clues that might help with his return home. The effort was rapidly becoming more confusing as they moved along.

After a little more distance on an unknown trail and before his chest tightened any more, the trail's different direction and purpose became known to him all at once. It turned out not to be an added hurdle to overcome or any trick. Innocently enough, it was a short divergence outside the village, meant to meet up with four more of the tribe's most hardened and experienced warriors, the dog soldiers, waiting on their own ponies. The sound of their voices and the additional pony noises gave it away as Big Turtle greeted them.

At that moment, Little Turtle knew what the beginning of this journey was meant to be. It was well known in such turbulent times that his father rarely traveled far without the company of more braves acting as his bodyguards. *I should have known better.*

This ride to the spirits was not to be a strict father–son experience. In that respect, it was no different and his father was acting in a normal functional way. True to his father's no-nonsense approach in all that he did, Little Turtle realized his father's sole intention remained to deliver his son to the council of the spirits as safely as possible. Relieved, Little Turtle's common sense returned. There should be no reason for any other diversions or major worries.

Judging from the brief greeting, and a long, steady ride thereafter, Little Turtle believed his original guesswork of traveling down an unknown path would disappear. All Little Turtle had to do was settle in and listen.

On they rode at a steady gait, like a prideful parade of the tribe's best, with Little Turtle holding on. He was certain he would meet the spirits with a happy heart. Even with a blindfold tightly covering his eyes and face, his only remaining concerns were when and where the trail would finally end.

On they rode, deeper into another stretch of turns, where Little Turtle felt the rough underbrush scraping his bare legs. It was obvious the trail was narrowing. Reflecting on his father's firm intentions with his accompanying braves calmed him. Nothing more would prevent them from reaching their unknown destination, no matter how remote he felt the trail was becoming. Little Turtle reassured himself: *The chief knows his way. I will, too.*

Despite these moments of continued good medicine, Little Turtle knew deep down that danger and periods of future weeping and sadness could still be lurking around any bend in the trail. But for now, he put that all aside. Just knowing the tribe's best and most revered were traveling with him kept him at a certain level of continuing peace.

As the group moved along, Little Turtle had plenty of

time to consider other possibilities. With this vision quest, he was concerned about not being armed. He and his friends rarely left the village without protection. Today, his hands carried no weapon, not even a small knife. In a sense, living during these times without the necessary tools of a hunt, or self-defense, was like being reduced to the level of the wild animals, who ventured in these same woods. Even the hunted required an elevated level of alertness for impending peril from any direction. Little Turtle would have to rely solely upon his wits for survival to return. He would be powerless against any major attacks, no matter the source. His survival and path home would be further complicated by not having any true sense of where he was.

    The longer they traveled, the more time he had to consider creeping doubts of being able to satisfy all the spirits' expectations. *What will they ask?* And the more time spent moving along the trail, the more difficulty Little Turtle had controlling this confidence. Those tiny slivers of doubt were once again trying to force their way into his heart. Those feelings vanished when he heard a faint sound of rapid water passing over a group of rocks. Gratefully, he focused hard on the new sound. *This must be the river.*
    As the ponies moved along, the flowing sound grew stronger until he was sure they were near the river. *Yes! I am right.* Somehow, he figured, the group must have circled back toward the water. He didn't know how or when, but it had to be true. He admittedly had been lost ever since the ride's beginning steps. This new and

growing sound reassured him.

Wondering more about their current position somewhere along the river, Little Turtle was caught off guard when Many Winds suddenly whinnied, snorted, and stopped. The normally reliable stallion must have seen something or reacted to a sudden silent command from Little Turtle's father. *What was that? Are we here?* Little Turtle, who was genuinely startled, found another cause for concern on this long-darkened journey. From the lack of movement, he knew the whole group had stopped for an unknown reason. Fortunately for Little Turtle, it turned out to be an opportune time for Big Turtle to reach behind himself and remove the blindfold for his son to capture what was now before them.

Unbeknown to Little Turtle, the group had been moving along the top of a rocky granite bluff, positioned within earshot of the riverbank. For all the group, looking downward, the scenic overview captured the forest below in its entirety. The outstretched land was thick and lush. It looked like it extended forever outward, unabated.

With his vision restored, Little Turtle was amazed by the emerald-like sight before him from the top of the massive flat-topped bluff. The expansive view was an open area just below a tall tree top canopy, abundant with plant life, but one he was not familiar with. Looking out and down, high above an area shaped like a cove, he saw the river on his left. It gave him a small sense of orientation, but that was all. Little Turtle knew this river was long and rich with uncertainties, but this place suggested an embarrassing gap in his knowledge and familiarity with his new homeland.

Big Turtle leaned back to his son and said, "We have reached a sacred place where the spirits will eventually come, my son, and you will stay down below this high rock and learn. You must not speak. Do not disturb this place with your voice…but listen hard."

Without any more instruction, the five adult tribesmen dismounted, and each led his pony in silence down a rocky trail to the river's edge. Little Turtle was left upon his father's mount.

Once at the river's edge, they moved further down the bank for many more steps until they could see the base of the bluff rising skyward. The stone's massive form had created a wide semicircle of solid rock reaching nearly treetop level. In effect, the bluff was shaped like a large showground, hidden from view from almost any direction. Many tall pines also surrounded it. Inside the cove was an open place where the sun could break through for the spirits to freely move about without disturbance in the open sunlight or, if desired, the mellow shine of the moon and stars.

To Little Turtle, the stately pines surely must have helped keep the area concealed from foreign river travelers as well, protecting the area as a safe harbor, satisfying the need for privacy of the spirits. The sacred ground was set apart at the bottom of the bluff like an enclosed circle. Once the group reached the base of the bluff, they loosely tethered their horses to tall tufts of grass and motioned for Little Turtle to dismount. From there, they all moved on foot as a sign of respect for the living temple they were about to enter. Each leader stepped lightly with reverence and respect. Little Turtle followed behind them in the same manner.

As they moved into the heavily wooded area, away from the shore, the inner area of the open fern-covered cove came more clearly into view. There, Mother Earth had supplied a vast home to several wide-spreading mature and stately hardwood trees, shading the open expansion. Below their outreaching branches, a thick carpet of dark leaf humus on the forest floor spread outward in all directions. The site was made more captivating with several rotting logs, and many protruding multicolored boulders dotting the immediate area, lush with either patches of thick green moss or multicolored lichens extending all along the massive and ageless trunks and rocks.

Overall, this sacred place was a naturally dark and forlorn place, and the lusty aroma of the massive amount of moist leaf mold was strong. There were many islands of giant ferns and other shadow-loving plants among them obscuring other rocky outcrops. It appeared to Little Turtle to be an ideal location where the spirits could better focus on his tribe's largest concerns, and today consider Little Turtle's immediate quest to become a worthy brave. Here, he felt a different kind of peace, an unusual calm where changes could more easily take place. *Here, I will shed my skin and become a brave.*

Little Turtle could barely breathe from the radiating awe. He felt a chilling sensation as tears welled up in his eyes. He had never seen such a place before in all his wanderings. *Thank you, Oh Great One! Thank you.*

To him it looked as though the boulders and decaying logs could have once been thrown over the bluff by a strong and powerful spirit. The place's mystical power was so daunting even the sun rarely dared to visit except at the site's central opening where no branches stretched over. This private glorious cove radiated complete reverence, and Little Turtle was convinced it truly belonged to his tribal spirits. It was theirs alone. He understood why no pony should tread upon it, fearing they may soil this unique and pristine part of Mother Earth in all its dazzling glory.

When all the members of the group were settled in place, Big Turtle motioned for his son to come and sit on one of the large flat-topped rocks situated near the middle of the sacred site with the most unfiltered sunlight. With an added firm hand signal, Big Turtle signed for all the others to remain silent.

Aiming his full attention upon his oldest son, this proud father spoke with complete authority.

"You will wait here until the spirits come. You will use your bundle to urge them to you. If they are agreeable, they will provide you with a vision with their hidden messages. Once they leave, you will travel on foot carrying your story back to us. You will have no helpers. Listen hard for the spirits along your path...for it will be only them who will provide to you...your way back home."

Little Turtle listened to his father's words and surveyed the area. He thought: *Surely, this rock is the spirits' roost—dropped upon Mother Earth straight from the sky.* From the way things appeared, Little Turtle was assured his father knew the habits of the spirits. *It won't be long, once they find me sitting alone; the spirits will shine their light and show me everything.*

    Little Turtle was ready and anxious to get started. All his doubts had evaporated. His heart was full. It was engorged and gladdened. This truly was the perfect place for his soul to be touched and be stretched forever outward. *How could anything be better than this?*

Chapter 6

The Capture

Little Turtle and the group basked in the stillness of the tribe's revered area no more than a moment before the distinct sound of an unusual movement interrupted the scene. It was clear to all that the sound did not come from their immediate area, nor was it a normal one. It was too abrupt, too provoking, and out of place—a sharp crack. From where the chief and the four warriors all stood, this sacred ground was a sound-absorbing moss-lined forest floor that extended a great distance. Under normal circumstances, the silence should have remained deafening, but the sudden change of the adult facial expressions made it clear to Little Turtle that the sound did not mean the spirits were approaching. Little Turtle hoped it was only the weight of a large animal's misstep or just a heavy branch breaking loose overhead and striking a rock. Whatever it was, it came from the direction of the riverbank, not in sight, and the others instinctively knew called for an investigation.

All five of the older men drew their hunting knives and long daggers. With wide eyes, scanning from side to side, they listened intently. Nothing more came except a prolonged silence. Big Turtle motioned the escorts to fan out and look for the source. If this was danger, it had to be discovered quickly. Little Turtle still clung to his hope it was a sign the spirits were on their way, but that didn't last. Before the four warriors had moved a few more steps away from the boulder Little Turtle was perched upon, the unidentified source became obvious.

Big Turtle was still standing closest to his son when several unfamiliar warriors stepped out from behind a tight mix of trees and shrubs. They were close enough for Little Turtle to see the dark river mud smeared all over their bodies and their odd-looking feathered headcaps. Plus, they were boldly displaying their fully drawn bows already aimed at them all. Big Turtle hand-motioned for his son to be silent and to quickly run low, while he shouted to the others, "Iroquois!"

Little Turtle recognized that name, giving him speed as he broke away. The Iroquois had become a common subject throughout the village. He knew they were a tribe from a distant territory, friends of the intrusive English-speaking traders and settlers. He also knew the Iroquois spoke an unfamiliar language of their own and were becoming more active in the northern part of the "Ohio" and "Indiana" territories, making surprise raids and looting random habitations throughout their neighboring tribes. Judging from his father's late-night stories, huddled close to the warmth of the fire inside his hut, Little Turtle trusted his words and knew the hostile actions by the Iroquois were made to reinforce their advancing westward territorial ambitions and claim more fur-harvesting sites.

Big Turtle had no more than finished his signal to Little Turtle when he returned his glance to his fellow tribe members advancing toward the intruders. Shocked and confused, Little Turtle stopped and witnessed his father's bodyguards' realization that their knives would not serve as a useful defense. They tried to return the sporadic fire with their own arrows. Instead, they stumbled and fell from several of the intruders' well-aimed arrows.

The enemy had the advantage of complete surprise, and their steadily released shots all went true. Big Turtle also had no time to fetch a clutch of arrows from his own quiver, much less time to draw his bow. His priority had been with Little Turtle. As Little Turtle turned to flee, he saw his father's only reasonable protection, and last resort, was the large hunting knife and dagger he was already holding.

Shocked and continuing to watch as he moved away, Little Turtle saw at least six of the enemy invaders. There could have been more, but the ones he spied before resuming his way through the thick undergrowth looked well-armed with iron firesticks strapped to their backs. They charged, bellowing fiercely from the cove's edge. Little Turtle stopped again to see if he should intervene, but then he saw the Miami braves lying mortally wounded. Dazed, he stood frozen, and when he saw the Iroquois charging his father, he did all he could from the distance. He screamed, "No! No! No!"

Little Turtle instinctively ran back while the enemy took a running aim at his father with their redrawn bows. Distracted by his son, Big Turtle was hit by one of the attackers' arrows. It tore through his raised forearm as he moved forward. Little Turtle desperately wanted to help and continued to advance toward the battle and screamed again, "No!"

The attackers looked but paid no notice for the moment. They were intent on the last vestige of the direct resistance. Before Little Turtle could continue any further, he saw his father take a direct hit in his lower ribs from another arrow. In an act of doomed defiance, the chief stood his ground and pulled the bloody shaft out of his side with one strong pull, snapped it in half, and threw it down. Realizing Little Turtle was still in view, he screamed, "You must run!"

Big Turtle then let out an ear-shattering shrill of his own to his enemy and charged toward the surprised group with his raised knives, while bleeding profusely.

The last Little Turtle saw of his father, the Iroquois had already dropped their bows, slung off their guns, and were charging in retaliation. They must have relished a direct fight. Big Turtle lunged and successfully stabbed the first two to arrive. Then two more quickly tackled him. With the struggle, Little Turtle realized his father's courage was providing him a brief sliver of time to escape. Breaking out of his shock, he reluctantly ran as commanded. The image of the others already fallen with no chance to retaliate pushed Little Turtle away from the river's sacred cove and deep into an unknown portion of the forest. Crashing through the underbrush, Little Turtle was mortified with what he had seen and fully aware the enemy recognized their work was not done. There was one more victim to be had.

He heard a series of horrifying victory yelps as he rushed away from the ambush. The woods around him were thick with shrubs and undergrowth that tugged at his legs. There was no room for a sprinted run. His effort to get away was painfully slow and loud. Plus, he knew he had been seen. It wouldn't be long before the attackers regained their senses and came after him to finish their grisly work. He had only a short head start and was struggling just to think and control his panicked breathing, fighting to maintain his balance as he forged his way along. He shook and beat his head with his fists to try and clear out the images he had just seen. Despite the immense pain he was experiencing reliving the dreadful shock of the incident, he knew he had to keep moving. With no idea how many would be coming with the chase, he knew they eventually would.

Little Turtle continued to try to run, but he was unfamiliar with this area and the brush consisted of wayward briar vines and patches of prickly ash. It was too thick. There wasn't a clear path to be seen—except for a short remnant of an abandoned deer trail blocked by downed trees and branches. The more he tried to hurry on, avoiding the large patches of unpassable vegetation, the more he realized the noise he was generating was becoming a dangerous threat to himself.

As he gasped for air, his mind cried: *No, no, no!* He stumbled at times. Other times he stopped when the dry sticks crunched under his feet and tore at his legs too much. All the while, he was trying to make sense of what had just happened and was beginning to believe his own death was coming.

He knew the enemy intruders were more than likely skilled men, and with their knives and hatchets would have an easier time plowing their way through the same brush Little Turtle was struggling against. It would only be a matter of time before they would be able to quickly gain ground on him. His thrashing movements had to be only an earshot away from those following him by now. He was already lost and only making himself an easy prey. *I have my medicine bundle. Do the spirits know this?* The strength in his legs was beginning to fade. In a moment he'd have to stop and fight or drop and hide before it was too late. *But where? Spirits, guide me!*

Out of breath, he stopped, stooped low, and looked around. Behind him, the piercing shrills of his followers, hot on his trail, were getting closer. Where he stood, besides the continuous underbrush, he saw more hardwood trees, a few struggling pine saplings interspersed in between, and a continuous blanket of shrubs. This area had no full-grown pines where he could hide inside their low-sweeping branches. Bewildered, he hastily made up his mind. He'd have to climb into one of the trees or lie flat, right where he was. There would be no more trying to run. He was exhausted and had to hide right now. There was no other choice. With that in mind, he spotted a massive oak close by, with an extended lower branch at a ground level no more than his height. Without help from the spirits, that branch would be his only chance to save himself.

A gut-wrenching savage yell came from behind him. Before he could leap onto the extended branch, he was seized from behind and struck on the top of his head with a club. Finding himself face down in a heavy mix of rotting leaves and moist soft dirt, he prayed. *Help me, spirits. Help me!*

Little Turtle felt the warmth of his blood pour from a gash in his head, but realized he was still alive. He tried to turn over and fight them off with his feet, but there were three. The most aggressive one grabbed him by the shoulders, jerked him up, then kicked him down again. This time he just lay there on his back staring up at his enemy, hoping the spirits would come. But before he knew it, another one flipped him over and lashed his wrists tightly behind his back. Next, he heard them bend down a nearby pine sapling, furiously chop its base, and slash its branches away. Once they had a sturdy pole, they placed it under his arms. After another hard kick, they pulled him up by using the pole's ends and dragged him all the way back to the first bloody encounter site. Little Turtle kicked and resisted the entire way, but to no avail.

When Little Turtle saw the gruesome results of the ambush, his mouth dropped open, his eyes narrowed, and his face turned ashen. He was weak and riveted with shock. Before him, the area was rank with pooled and splattered blood.

Several nearby tree trunks and patches of tall grass

blades that were once dry and light green were now wet and bright red. The once dark-green logs of moss were multicolored and forever stained in Little Turtle's mind. His heart ached as he saw the lifeless bodies of his tribesmen torn apart—grimly mutilated. He tried looking away but couldn't. He could only let out a prolonged, anguished scream.

Without thinking of the consequences, he jumped and kicked, exploding in rage. Not only were his fellow tribe members destroyed, but his beloved and invincible father lay lifeless among them. Even though his father's bodyguards were all scalped with their bodies desecrated, strangely his father's body and head were not. The Iroquois must have sensed an ample amount of bad medicine associated with the chief and his courageous reactions. Little Turtle hoped his father's soul was resting in the Great Spirit's invisible hands, but he couldn't be sure. His knowledge in this respect was weak. One thing was certain: His own previously gladdened heart was now deeply pierced by an explosion of a blazing hatred for these Iroquois people.

Despite his tribe's several hostile encounters with the white man, and occasionally with their native neighbors, Little Turtle had never personally seen so much death laying contorted before him. He could not believe his tear-filled eyes. Terrified, he expected to be next and struggled with all his might to avenge his fallen father and the others. Instead, the two Iroquois warriors holding the ends of the transport poles lifted him higher, so his feet were suspended off the ground, while another one of the attackers standing behind him drew his knife and slashed it across the entire width of the boy's back—from side to side—as a warning of what would come if he continued.

At the command of the group's leader, they lowered him down, removed the pole, and forcibly bound Little Turtle's arms tightly against his bloody body, pushing him backward toward the nearby shore while his blood flowed, freely soaking his loincloth and on down the back of his legs. Each time he resisted afterward; he was struck by high kicks to his ribs. As they continued their hostilities, moving their prisoner to the river, Little Turtle painfully wondered what would be next. *How can this be? Am I to be drowned? Will I be buried alive...or saved for a sacrifice? Why have the spirits let this happen? Why am I still breathing? Was this massacre my fault?* His rapid-fire questions burned and tortured him with a different kind of pain.

Continuing back to the water's edge, one of the more severely wounded warriors that Big Turtle fought, who looked to have been stabbed several times, was grimacing, gasping for air, as he struggled to keep up. Two other wounded warriors were using the moss from the rotted logs to help stop their own bleeding. Despite the seriousness of their multiple wounds, the Iroquois leader hand-signed for all to return to where they came from, even the most seriously injured one, who had to be lifted at one point and carried to where they had first entered the cove.

When they reached the water's edge, Little Turtle could clearly see there were eight of these people and instead of any of them pushing him into the river's current and easily drowning him with his wrists tied and arms bound behind him, they all moved a little more downstream to an isolated wooded entrance. There the group pulled out four canoes that had been lying hidden in the underbrush.

    They took great care in moving these delicate vessels made of long sheets of birch bark, sewn together with pine root strands and sealed with dark pine tar. They looked to be skillfully built, able to swiftly move long distances and with rails high enough to carry heavy loads. These vessels were also long enough to carry two or three paddlers each. Little Turtle's tribe's traditional canoes were much smaller, not meant for extensive travels or heavy loads.

    Once the first craft was launched into the water and in position parallel to the water's edge, Little Turtle was the first thrown in the middle and secured with two guards—one in front and another behind him. The most gravely wounded warrior, resting on his knees, waited on the shore. Leaving no one behind, that brave was then picked up and placed prone in the middle of the next craft. After all the others were settled and ready to launch, the leader raised one of Little Turtle's fellow tribesmen's blood-soaked scalps skyward and let out a great victory scream. The others followed suit. It was spine tingling and joyous for the enemy, horrifying for Little Turtle. His empty stomach lurched. He shook his head in denial. *No! No! No!*

    It was at this moment that a thoroughly demoralized Little Turtle realized that he, along with the four freshly taken human scalps, had just become another prize in this brutal raid. Now he was a dazed war captive of a foreign evil force, with his mind swirling and numb as they set off into the river for parts unknown. He was convinced he was being saved to be tortured and killed at a more convenient time, or, worse yet, be enslaved and outcast forever in an unfamiliar land. All Little Turtle knew, between his rasping breaths, was he had become wild-eyed with hate and remorse, and a captive victim, holding the excruciating pain that he was leaving his beloved father, who was lying in the hidden sacred place behind him.

As Little Turtle lay in the Iroquois canoe, exhausted, severely bruised and bleeding, with blood still oozing from his back and his head, he wondered how his life had become filled with so much bad medicine. He was suffering a great physical pain, but the pain of losing his father was the greatest of all. All he could do was think of those left behind. How could such a satisfying life, watching and learning from his beloved chief, be twisted so quickly?

His wide, expanding, grieving thoughts took him to a time barely a summer before, when he'd first heard of these marauding Iroquois—ironically to become one of the last words his father would ever say to him. So here he was in a canoe with two of these same treacherous people, with no more knowledge about them than a few random stories he had previously heard from Big Turtle himself. With a single-minded emotional focus on his father, he wondered what he could do based on what he had heard from a man who now was gone.

The Iroquois stories from his father had first started

when one of the neighboring tribes had a similar encounter with a mysterious native group, also called the Iroquois. That name and a series of related stories originated from the Erie tribe, who lived in an area east of the Miami homeland. Despite Little Turtle's physical horror, the memory of his father's story of the Erie attack had now become a much more vivid and sorrowful one.

    Big Turtle had briefly explained that the confrontation with the Iroquois had become a large bloody affair and the reason the Erie's tribal council had declared a defensive warpath afterward. Any trespassing Iroquois were to be killed on sight. Despite the Erie tribe's decision to become more watchful in their day-to-day lives, the Iroquois raids continued. The Erie decided to alert and try to enlist the help of their neighbors, including Big Turtle's tribe and the Potawatomi, before a full-scale warpath took over.

    As a result, even though there had been previous problems with pony theft between the neighboring tribes, a small group of Erie braves assembled with the intention of traveling the great distance west to each of the two tribes' villages. According to Big Turtle, the Potawatomi were more reluctant for such a meeting at first, but they too eventually agreed to meet with the Miami at Big Turtle's council fire, fearing the same kind of attacks. The leaders of the two neighboring tribes hoped to convince the Miami to form a loose three-way alliance without committing to a total warpath against an enemy that was perceived as a superior and more experienced force. However, if the tribes could overcome their sporadic feuding and band together, they might curb the violence and, if necessary, better supply an overwhelming response.

   Not only were the Miami neighbors concerned, but Little Turtle's father and his elders had previously heard other stories of the Iroquois' aggressions from other sources, usually the passing French fur traders. All this information helped solidify the idea that a united force might prevent future raids. In a sense, from what the Miami had already heard, Big Turtle had told his son he was agreeable to helping protect and keep all homelands safe despite any other disagreements. As Little Turtle sat hunched over in the canoe, he could still hear a few more of his father's strong words resonating from the end of one particularly frightful story.

   "You must remember, my son…never stop thinking of our tribe and our people. One day…you will be called upon to defend them with all your heart…even when you think the spirits have left you…even after faraway war drums have called. Act like a leader and you will become one. You are a part of me…and I am of you. Our hearts beat as one. You must be worthy for our people…only you…can make this so."

   Those foretelling words now echoed far beyond the young captive's agonizing physical pain and tortured heart. With bloodshot eyes from many freshly released tears, Little Turtle resisted the pains of his open wounds by slumping over, hiding his clenched fists, and clinging to his father's memorable words about the importance of their village as the Iroquois feverishly paddled their crafts further up the river.

Chapter 7

Words of War

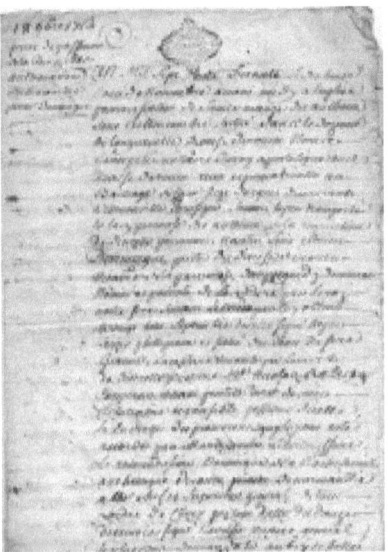

During that same fateful summer of the many Iroquois surprise attacks upon the Erie tribe, and the prospect that a meeting was about to take place between the Erie, the Potawatomi, and the Miami, a dedicated and faith-driven French Jesuit missionary, a few native Hurons and a small group of French traders from Fort Detroit, were making their way to a tiny fur-trading outpost called Fort St. Joseph.

The Jesuit priest intended to help enlist people into making an informal agreement with the local French military stationed at the fort to start a new mission somewhere within that geographical portion of the western frontier. His secondary aim, coincidently, was an attempt to help form a coalition to ward off any stray Indian attacks based on what he had seen during his former missionary work in Canada's eastern territory, referred to as "Quebec." This area was known to be the Huron Indian nation's homeland. More importantly, the priest also hoped to alert his fellow Frenchmen, whomever he met and wherever he met them, about the ongoing disputes with the British currently spilling into those same western Canadian frontier lands. His former residence in Quebec had already become a long-term mix of French, British, Huron, and Iroquois clashes. Because of the ongoing turmoil, the priest had to reluctantly flee and move on.

This missionary who arrived at the St. Joseph post was a well-educated French priest named Father Jean-Joseph LaFleur. His personal and primary undertaking was to show people of all levels of society and all races the righteous path to heaven to save their souls.

When he first arrived with like-minded Jesuits in the new world, referred to originally as "New France," he began studying the Aboriginal languages in Quebec, where their headquarters was set up. After several years educating himself in the primary language of those natives in his immediate area, referred to as Algonquian speakers, he traveled with a group of other Jesuit priests, teaching Christianity's principles, recording the events of the times, describing the tribes he met and their culture, and interpreting their languages.

Over the years, while immersed in this new society,

enlightening all those he met by introducing the ways of God, he became aware of the history and importance of the French fur trade. Because of his teachings, he was brought into direct contact with many native villages, most of which were of the Huron people. They were the most prevalent tribe in the New France territory, and he specialized in their language until he could speak it fluently. It was with them he spent most of his time spreading the holy word and recording what he saw.

    Later, as conflicts between the French and British continued to increase, he decided to go out on his own to focus more on recording his historical accounts. In the process, he compiled a language dictionary of Huron words and hoped one day to settle down and set up a small mission for the benefit of those poor "uncivilized" natives. Because most Indigenous people were considered "savages," Father LaFleur decided to focus more on helping the Huron come to God, and it was with them he often visited. Despite rising threats of war from two different fronts, primarily the British expansionists and various Iroquois tribes south of the St. Lawrence River, he became sympathetic to the Huron and embraced their culture. He remained in their villages for longer periods until he lived among them full-time. Despite the danger, he had finally become fully prepared to die for their salvation, if necessary.

    Unfortunately, the Huron got caught in their own struggle with multiple groups of ferocious Iroquois tribes over the control of the well-traveled St. Lawrence River thoroughfare. Aside from the possibility of setting up his Christian mission within the Huron territory, Father

LaFleur hoped he could enlist the help of his French compatriots toward warding off the advancing British influence. The French provincial government agreed and helped support a future physical structure for his new mission if he could keep his adopted tribe as trusted allies.

Father LaFleur was a determined and dedicated Jesuit, and he immersed himself within the Huron people and remained with them for an additional year. While he was there, his dream of a mission was built and it was where he spent countless hours teaching his adopted tribe Christianity, documenting their daily lives, as well as helping as best he could in their struggles against more frequent Iroquois attacks. It was a perilous time, and many priests moving through the land confronting hostile tribes such as these lost their lives in horrific ways, but it was all in the name of God and country.

Consequently, Father LaFleur witnessed the Hurons' rapid destruction by the wide-ranging Iroquois tribes during the struggle for fur-trading dominance. He was devastated when his newly completed mission structure was burned to the ground during one sweeping Iroquois raid. It was only then he became convinced his mission's plan could not survive within the once powerful Huron nation. Like his simple structure, the Huron nation was rapidly becoming thoroughly ravaged. Father LaFleur himself was barely able to escape the violence and terror occurring right before his eyes. With only his long black robe on his back, his personal Bible, and a small travel trunk full of his historical records, manuscripts, and writing instruments, he narrowly escaped and made his way westward, deeper into less disputed territories, explaining the events of the day to all who would listen and praying for those who wouldn't.

With a firm resolve, he believed he would find more opportunities to convert more tribes toward Christianity and help pacify their suspicious attitudes toward the French trappers along the way. In addition to his desire to introduce Christ's teachings to a whole new group of native people, he felt it was his duty to alert them about the impending dangers of an ongoing and spreading war. It was the Iroquois who had embodied a warlike arrogance toward whomever they met in their quest for new trapping territories. But he also believed the British would be sure to follow with their own type of terror.

During his travels, Father LaFleur moved by boat south to Fort Detroit and then westward by buggy across the Michigan territory down the eastern shore of Lake Michigan with his supporting Huron assistants in search for a new mission site. He happened to stop at the Fort St. Joseph riverside location, which he subsequently learned already had an assigned priest and established mission. His purpose there was only to replenish his dwindling food and supplies and enlist a military escort for protection.

At that time, the leaders of the Erie tribe, along with the Potawatomi, also happened to be at the fort, enlisting added protection and requesting their own trading supplies. This was when Father LaFleur first learned of the recent raids upon the Erie and their wish to form an association with the Miami and the Potawatomi. He was more than happy to offer his help. In his view, it was a calling.

With firsthand knowledge to aid their intentions, he offered to travel the rest of the long distance to the Miami village. Along with his assistants, a few trappers who were there, a couple of representatives from the fort, and the tribal leaders present, it became an opportune time to meet with three tribal chiefs all at once. He felt the coincidence of his presence with the meeting was a direct message from God, and an opportunity for a new mission somewhere in the region.

The commander at that time was an able military man, Captain Lewies Charpentier, who was concerned with the Erie leaders' fears and their effort to enlist help to quell any more threats of bloodshed. Since the captain had been commissioned by the French government to counteract the British influence in the area and support French trapping interests, he was attracted to the idea of getting more warrior allies to help fight any potential intrusions and help keep his country's established source of beaver in the area.

Father LaFleur was more than willing to act as an interpreter and hopefully contribute to the demise of those responsible for inflicting harm on his adopted Huron. He believed these meetings would also help solidify his safe travels throughout this new territory as he spread the word of Christ while warning those along the way of the foreseeable advances of an already long and agonizing war.

According to Father LaFleur's notes, he and several Erie and Potawatomi leaders and the small contingent from the outpost's supportive military group left by horse and wagon and traveled eastward to the Miami village. They arrived two days later on June 16, 1760. During the daylong meeting and a later peace council between the tribal leaders and Captain Charpentier, they reached a momentous agreement. It came after Father LaFleur, being a knowledgeable witness to the recent history, was able to inform them all in a passionate and convincing way what he knew about the tragic events that had occurred with the destruction of the Huron. He verified most of the rumored stories about the Iroquois' recent atrocities and the extent of the threat both they and the British represented.

    For Big Turtle and his elders, who were also present, the priest came across as a man full of a mysterious spirit but one who spoke with a straight tongue. Big Turtle was convinced the priest knew the Iroquois and their ways well, as he was an experienced educator who had spent many years in dedicated missionary work in the other Indian territories. Father LaFleur had already been successful in his primary goal of informing the captain of the joint threat the English and Iroquois represented. His task was to explain that same need to not only form a unified resistance but also help protect the French flow of goods westward, far out into the bush, for the mutual benefit of the tribes. By the end of the day, all present agreed.

    After their firm agreement to form an alliance was made, and prayers to the spirits were given, all the outsiders present in Father LaFleur's group returned to the safety of the fort's small stronghold. Once there, the priest felt compelled to formally record what had happened during the council meeting. He had been forceful with his spoken words, and all agreed he had been instrumental in helping to guide the three tribes together as one. His impassioned words had prompted the three tribal leaders to raise a meaningful white plume of smoke skyward from their shared peace pipe.

With a trained eye for recording whatever he saw, Father LaFleur felt history had been created and his impactful words should be converted into a tangible form on parchment; first, to be destined for the Jesuit superiors headquartered in Quebec to compile, and then to be redirected to French governmental officials. Even though the task took him three days to complete several copies, he felt his earlier persuasive words, plus other facts blended in, would serve a much greater purpose. At this point, he felt God had led the way. All he had to do was to record the results.

He believed the love of God was directing him to warn and report the specifics of the recent ravages left behind in the Huron territory. He felt once the fateful meeting was preserved, the results would be used as an aid in persuading other key military leaders and his compatriots, whom he had yet to meet, of the dangers and undesirable changes he foresaw. His aim was to save as many souls as possible, including those innocent natives who could find themselves in harm's way.

The following is the document he personally framed—in full. The events that he described were those that led up to the new alliance's current threat. The conflicts back east were commonly referred to as the French and Indian

War by all those already tangled in its web, but they had not yet slipped into this distant region. This personal plea from Father LaFleur presented a firsthand warning to all Frenchmen who may have had the privilege of reading it and had a strong desire to venture deeper into the lands of the Miami, the Erie, and the many others far beyond them.

A History of French and Indian Relations and the Threads of War

Greetings, my dear brothers and sisters. For the greater glory of God, I come in peace and walk in the ways and teachings of our Lord, Jesus Christ. Several items have happened before us this year. I thought it proper to extend to you what I know of a common native enemy. These are the Iroquois and as a group are an advanced tribe in many respects. Years ago, they formed and are a part of a large federation of neighboring tribes in the American territory commonly known as New York. They are unique as they have one strong centralized form of tribal rule. These tribes are known as the "Nation of Six of the Long House," which include the Seneca, Mohawk, Cayuga, Oneida, Onondaga and Tuscarora tribes—all of which speak a common language. Even though they are referred to as Iroquois because of the name of their spoken words, they all have kept their own tribal customs.

This federation of tribes had originally been neutral toward all forms of white foreigners, because they were distracted and generally involved in competing with the other surrounding native tribes in a constant war of trapping territories, mainly with those directly to the north of them, such as the Hurons (of which I had lived with for many months), and their group of allied tribes, namely the Ottawa and Algonquin, all residing in territories now known to be in the southern portion of our New France.

This long-term war between the Indian tribes began as a continuous battle for obtaining and supplying beaver pelts to the emerging white fur traders of all origins. These struggles for trapping rights went on for many years prior to the white man's gradual influence, and ultimately, has now become known as the Beaver Wars occurring during the 1600s. The results were the destruction of a great many Great Lake tribal people on all sides. However, it wasn't long thereafter, the Iroquois began an off and on mutual coalition with the English fur traders which ensued more Indian conflicts to the north.

From what I have learned from meeting with my fellow Jesuits and other Christians elsewhere, there have been many reasons for this merging alliance, which has also included other white settlers. First, the Iroquois Federation is a large and powerful group, but they have wanted more guns in their ongoing stalemate with the tribes to the north. The primary tribe in the Iroquois warmongering were the Mohawks, but they have been weakening after being the first to meet our common contagious diseases, most namely, smallpox. Later, it became the Seneca, as they are now the most populated and strongest of the other tribes in the Federation, but they couldn't overcome the Huron nation on their own.

The Iroquois not only have been against their northern enemy tribes but have an ongoing concern with the heavy flow of colonial settlers moving into the New England area from the East. At the same time, while the British were becoming more prevalent in the southeastern Canadian region, they also happened to be getting into frequent conflicts with the Hurons. As the Iroquois and the British began to find themselves fighting a common enemy, they eventually became more cooperative, and gradually appeared as new trading partners.

The early Indian conflicts with us have been directly in relation to the intrusion of the permanent settlements in most of their territories, which has included all Europeans to a certain extent. In this respect, we Frenchmen were also involved, but our interest in the New England area was centered mostly on the fur trade, which has become the fashionable rage deriving from all of Europe. Further, we have still not yet proved to be as reliable trade partners with the early Iroquois tribes, as we commonly have taken offense with their frequent associations with our British foes.

A second factor for the Iroquois hostilities for anyone French has been our refusal by law to trade guns to any Indians, including the Iroquois tribes. Therefore, without access to guns from us, we have never been considered as equal trade partners like the British, who have no qualms trading such items.

Now, I give the story of one of our famous explorers, Samuel de Champlain, who noticed Indian women grinding maize in the villages he visited. He began trading European raised corn for furs with the Huron, who at that time also controlled the expansive St. Lawrence seaway. The Hurons were active traders with a wide array of northern tribes and with this new source of readily available grain, overnight, made Indian crop raising efforts in that area unnecessary. Thanks to the access to an abundant and reliable source of corn, trading became a windfall for the Huron, and later their associated trading allies. As a result, we inadvertently became their preferred trading partner.

Trading for goods with the readily abundant source of furs has become a new source of wealth for the tribes within that region, which not only includes an assortment of new goods, but more importantly the reliable source for guns, whiskey, and horses. Most of those valuable commodities have come from the British and even those called "Dutchmen."

These new trade items—guns in particular—have become important in the constant tribal warfare, and the Iroquois braves, who now own them from the British, obviously have a great advantage over those who do not. While the flintlocks are effective to a point, a good brave can accurately usually shoot five or six arrows at short range long before a flintlock can be fired, reloaded and fired again. Despite that fact, most Iroquois braves carry both, if practical, making them twice as deadly.

Later, it was the forged metal products, knives, kettles and hatchets that are now in high demand, because they are proving to be the best value for improving the Indian way of life, not just warfare. Those that can't trade for items of need including the occasional horse simply must steal them whenever and wherever they can. Thanks to the new European goods, and from what I have heard, Indian thieving is becoming a secondary and skilled enterprise.

    Finally, besides the access to furs and gaining an advantage over the French and the Hurons, the British have been impressed with the Iroquois Federation's style of warfare. In the few of the early conflicts that the Redcoats have had with them, they have been no match with their use of the element of surprise, their extraordinary bravery and aggressive "dodge and hide" style of battle. The British have been quick to understand the military success of this type of warfare and it has been their policy to be avoided, if possible. From my perspective and for all the reasons written here, the Iroquois and the British have become preferred partners.

    Additionally, due to the vast geological area the Huron traditionally traveled throughout the northern Great Lakes region, and at one time were able to control the trading pathway up and down the St. Lawrence, an immense number of furs was available to them from their northern trading partners. For our part as Frenchmen, we have felt it more helpful to trade exclusively with the Huron—grain for furs. Consequently, we gradually formed with them an exclusive and strong trading relationship.

    When the beaver supply started to dry up south of the Great Lakes region, within the Iroquois' own territory, it wasn't long before the Iroquois began more frequent and aggressive raiding parties against the Huron and today it is the Erie and other western tribes. Being much better armed, they have found success, as those pursued tried in vain to paddle their fur laden canoes to our trading posts along the seaway. Since we Frenchmen were proven trading partners with the Huron, and the Dutch and British have often allied with their Iroquois partners, the conflict spilled over to the competing European fur traders and their respective suppliers.

Speaking for our view, it has been about the fur trade mostly and the protection of the free access of the remaining trading routes with the building of protective forts along those waterways. However, for the British, I contend it has been not only about the fur trade, but also the land, treaties, and permanent settlements, plus promises to the Iroquois they would help clear out any other white settlers, including the emerging American colonists.

The Huron and the many other neighboring tribes aligned with them have been defeated and are in disarray. This once strong tribe has been nearly wiped out by not only the Iroquois tribes' superior aggressive pursuits and destruction of their tribal villages but also by the introduction of the many diseases that are becoming common. Those last remaining Hurons that have survived and captured have become useful as slaves. With the Huron defeated and beaver supplies severely diminished, our French partners have vacated those depleted areas of earlier wealth and moved westward, where the British steadily have transitioned our collective losses into more settlements and protective forts.

Because of the ever-increasing pressure of the colonial settlements advancing westward, the earlier successes of the Federation have helped encourage the Iroquois to also move westward with raids to the neighboring tribes in the quest for more pelts. This is where our compatriots and our alliances of a wide variety of remaining Indian trading partners must decide to make a stronger stand against both the British and the Iroquois. This conflict, which has been expanding since 1753, in the year of our Lord, must be stopped. To do so, we must unite throughout the occupied lands.

These years have been a turbulent time for these Iroquois, both good and bad, but they are known to be a savvy group and have come to believe the British will help them regain lands already lost in the colonial east with their developing disputes with the "Americans." Not only that, but it is believed the British will help them open more productive hunting lands to the west. This is an area commonly referred to by us as the great Northwest Territory and is the place of my most recent meeting with the great leaders of the Miami, Erie, and Potawatomie.

From what I have seen, the key to the Iroquois tribal struggles and to their ventures into new homelands is they must control more beaver fur territory, which is the same as generating another great abundance for whomever has the means to reach those new beaver populations. For the Iroquois, to continue their dominance with the fur trade, they will have to follow those fresh beaver supplies however westward that will take them. We must be vigilant, because the ultimate key for the British with their underlying shrewdness is why they continue to support their current Iroquois relationship. It is to increase their land ownership for the *crown through more conflict and with more favorable treaties as time marches on.*

For those mutual endeavors, the English will continue to encourage the help of the Iroquois, and they have been more than up for the task. The Iroquois are shameless as they try to open more areas of their own for more territorial influence. For these times and on many different occasions, they have bumped up against other Indian groups such as our newly allied natives known as the Miami and their neighbors, the Erie and Potawatomie. Peaceful villages such as these I have visited throughout the new world, and as God as my witness, will soon be in peril.

That's because earlier Iroquois war accounts flowing from neighboring tribes near the Hurons that I have previously visited have been those that tell accounts showing the Iroquois to be aggressive warriors. As their reputation has been beginning to grow westward, I would expect the associated stories told in councils across the Great Lake nations, and even spilling into this land of the Miami, to continue.

It is already known to those neighboring tribes, the threat for any of those who may be allied or sympathetic to our French ideals in any way is real. All those invaded tribes may soon find out these Iroquois warriors' frightening reputations do exist, particularly when there is ample time for torture and their accompanying atrocities. According to settlers' tales, sadly from whom I have already visited, those unfortunate people who accidentally crossed into the Iroquois' path, either as a Frenchman or as an ally, their discovered remains looked as though they were the victims of work that may have been guided by the skillful hand of the devil himself. With a firm resolve and steadfast faith in God, I have seen this work myself. Although I have seen atrocities from other tribes, including the Huron, these actions were inflicted by invaders. Those by others were not derived from purposeful aggression.

Therefore, you must heed my words. It is clear the tainted threads of war have already been pulled through a wide needle's eye and its sharp point of great harm is being pressed deeper into the Frenchman's soul. Our enemies' only purpose is to forever stain the colors of our lives and all that we hold dear. With God as my guide, I trust these written words will provide you with the knowledge for a safer haven.

In union with the sacred hearts of Jesus and Mary,
Signed: Father Jean-Joseph LaFleur
On this day: June 20, 1760

The post commander first reviewed the letter, and he confirmed it was comprehensive and as convincing as those impassioned words spoken only a few days before. The lower-ranking officers, those who could read, were also impressed with the priest's formal report.

Now fully forewarned, all were in a unified agreement. The captain gave orders to busy themselves refortifying their quarters and bracing themselves for the worst, no matter the origin, or risk eventual annihilation from these potential invaders. In that respect, the coalition established between the men occupying the fort, the Miami, and their threatened neighbors had become practical and necessary. It was up to all of them to follow through to allow the trappers and traders to keep the flow of the pelts moving in exchange for reliable goods and a mutual protective effort from all sides. But they had to be diligent and brace themselves primarily against their newly suspected approaching foes, be they the British or the Iroquois, or perhaps both.

With the written words returned to him for the next stop in his travels and his most basic travel necessities restocked, Father LaFleur was satisfied his search for a new mission for the safe advancement of Christ's teachings could continue somewhere within the nearby vicinity. He had laid the groundwork for a workable agreement with the natives and the French representatives within the immediate territory; and with the help of God Almighty, they might all be able to move on, supplying a stronger barricade against the growing westward tentacles of an intrusive and wasteful war. It was Father LaFleur's way of extending a safe path for salvation at the gates of heaven to open for all who would listen and to all who wished to remain free to believe in their faith-driven redemption.

Chapter 8

A Warrior's Vow

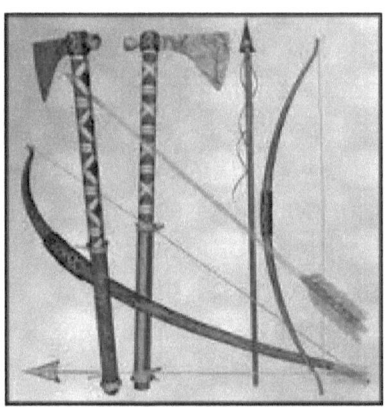

For Little Turtle, the insightful warning from Father LaFleur that had filtered its way to him through the chief's fireside stories, starting only a summer ago, came forward into full display right in front of him. His father and the others now lay dead within the cove at the hands of the Iroquois, and he himself had been brutally captured and was on his way to a destination for an unknown fate. Thanks to the ambush, he had already seen the Iroquois' handiwork, and the priest's warnings of future Iroquois' bloody advancements had rung true. Even though the Iroquois were the trespassers, and could have misunderstood the Miami intentions, the outcome was devastating, nonetheless. Little Turtle wondered: *But why have I been spared?*

Back at the sacred cove, the Iroquois had lived up to

their reputation, reacted quickly, and much Miami blood had been spilled. Now a wounded prisoner, Little Turtle lay slumped and tortured with his mind racing. *How can I be of any use to these evil people? Will I be forced to try and guide them to my village? Will I become their slave or an object of unrelenting torture?* He fumbled for answers. He looked skyward but saw no hawks or other answers there. He was alive but beyond that, he and the sky were empty.

Despite the storied ruthlessness of the Iroquois warriors toward their adult male victims and verified by those who knew, like Father LaFleur and Big Turtle, it was a harrowing thought that this invading enemy—or any tribal nation, for that matter—would go further and torture or cannibalize women or children. At least, it wasn't spoken of, not by anyone Little Turtle knew. According to the priest and passed on through the words of others, depending on the number of casualties suffered by the onslaught of war or deaths originating from the white man's diseases, the Iroquois would occasionally forcefully adopt replacements into the tribe, or just as easily trade them away.

Is that it? A future slave? Little Turtle also suspected these Iroquois were creatures who could quickly adapt to any difficulty, and a swift captive disposal would not be out of the question, either. As each minute passed by, the more he saw of them, the more he was sure of that. He also knew he was at their mercy based on their slightest whim. Whether or not he was kept alive depended upon how his captors viewed him. Was he half a man or was he still mostly a boy? Judging by the speed of the four canoes moving further west in the direction of the sun, headed for deeper waters and an unknown destination, he knew he would find out soon enough.

    The Iroquois moved quickly, and after a short travel time reached a remote river site that was also unfamiliar to Little Turtle. It was another heavily wooded area along the river, elevated and rocky. The band deviated into its shallow waters and came ashore. Little Turtle was thrown out onto the wet sand. Behind him the canoes were sunk under the water's surface and weighed down with small nearby rocks to keep them from being discovered. Further inland, they retrieved hidden fur pelts that had been curing in the sun. The skins looked fresh, with a few more carcasses remaining to be skinned. They must have been abruptly interrupted and had to abandon their work to risk spoilage of even a single fur.
    While one of the group was left to menace Little Turtle at the water's edge, the others, excluding the most injured, began cleaning the remaining ripened carcasses at hand. Two Iroquois promptly lit a small fire composed mostly of grass and leaves. It only lasted enough to create a few large puffball-type clouds of light-gray smoke, signaling a message for eyes unknown, and then it was quickly snuffed out. After a discussion among themselves and their leader, they abruptly returned to the shore laden with all their furs, which included the extra-aromatic sun-ripened beaver meat for a later time.
    Little Turtle believed now was the time he would learn his fate. The Iroquois moved fast, removing the canoes' weighted anchors, and it wasn't long before—one by

one—the canoes were floating, ready for transport and loaded down with all the furs. Little Turtle was pushed into the closest canoe, and they all were again on their way. When he realized he had a little more time to be alive, he decided: *I must act. I must get away before all my chances are forever lost.*

So, when only a few hours earlier his heart was full of hope to greet his tribal spirits, now his grief was full of a desire to destroy something, even if it meant himself. He was fighting his newfound guilt for being alive.

Demoralized, and forgetting about his village, he made a desperate move to lean over and flip himself out of the craft, where death by the hands of the great Water Spirit would be welcome. Then he could rejoin his father. His futile attempt was stopped when the alert brave behind him grabbed him before the canoe could be tipped enough for Little Turtle to lift himself up and over the canoe's gunwale.

At that same instant, and without any hesitation, the brave drew his knife and slashed Little Turtle across his back with a cutting force that penetrated his skin deeper than the time before. If that slashing wasn't enough, he struck the back of the boy's head twice with the butt of his bloodied knife for good measure. The pain from the blows was intense, dishing out a clear and violent message. Little Turtle's life was nothing, absolutely nothing, compared to the canoe's tipping into the flowing river and losing its load of immensely valuable furs.

The blood from Little Turtle's back once again poured freely. Barely conscious, writhing in severe pain, and dizzy with unrelenting anguish, he wondered how he could have angered the tribal spirits in such a terrible way, even to deny his own watery self-sacrifice. Now, more than ever, he was trapped in a canoe filled with an overabundance of bad medicine that continued to haunt him unabated.

Barely able to return his thoughts to those of his loved ones and the imperiled tribe he might never see again, Little Turtle's eyes swelled with fresh tears. After all, no matter what the Iroquois thought, he had not yet been declared a man and there were many tears remaining to be released from deep within him. Recovering his grieving emotions, and enduring his pain in total silence, was difficult, but he managed to dwell on his recent experience with Gray Tongues and the promise of an eventual visit by the spirits. *What about the power of the medicine bundle?* Up to now, he had thought of it but only once. *Where is it and its power?*

He glanced downward without moving his head, not to tip off his captors, who were confidently racing their heavily loaded canoes downstream. Though the bundle encasement was soaked with water and diluted blood, he still had it. The bundle had shifted inside his loincloth belt and was covered. Only now, it was more centered within his groin area and concealed under the cloth. With that relief, he tried to refocus his mind by calling to any spirit that might be near, trying to resist the overriding pain coming from all directions that was squeezing him tighter like a mighty fist. *Hear me, spirits!*

Without Little Turtle's attention, the captors again veered toward the shore, and those situated in the bows each jumped out into the water before they landed, so as not to damage the canoe's inner framework or the outer bark covering. Recovering his awareness, Little Turtle saw that the shore around this location was rocky and hazardous, but open. He suspected his captors had been here many times before. Each canoe was stopped just short of touching the rocks, even the submerged ones, as though the warriors knew the terrain.

As soon as the boats were landed, Little Turtle was dragged out of his canoe. All the boats were then emptied of their prized cargo, weighted down, and sunk once again.

While his enemy was busy, Little Turtle stood and focused on the background sound of a pair of doves perched overhead. Their soft coos gave him a rush of hope for a peaceful ending. His body had already been wracked with multiple pains and his heart pierced with a gaping hole, but somehow, he found an instant of escape. Here was where death would come. Here, he expected the Iroquois to make their inevitable end of him. As he stood on the shore bound and weak, waiting for what was to come, his knees suddenly buckled. Seeing him collapse, two of the closest paddlers grabbed him before he hit the ground. They held him up until the leader of the group came rushing over to him.

Without a word, the leader signaled the two holders to move him over to a solid part of the shoreline and release him, while keeping his wrists and arms bound. Then, without warning, the leader stepped up and struck him in the face with the back of his hand with such force, it knocked him over. Restricted with his bindings, he was unable to break his fall and his face struck against the hardened shoreline surface. The strike rendered him unconscious. The fall was bad enough, but the force of the hit twisted his body into a chest-down position. Fortunately, this prone position concealed his bundle, situated underneath his full deadweight.

Little Turtle had no previous knowledge of whether any band of hostiles would ever take or destroy another's bundle given an opportunity. According to Gray Tongues, these items were highly personalized and could be considered non-effective for those for whom there were not intended, especially with the secret ingredients. Consequently, most tribal people believed possessing another's bundle was bad medicine.

The Iroquois may have also believed Little Turtle was too young for such a thing. Regardless, when they carried him off, they hadn't spotted it, because when he awoke, it was approaching dusk, and the bundle was still attached under his soiled cloth. It was then he also found himself tied to the base of a sizable pine sapling in a sitting position. The warm mist of a beginning rain may have played a role in his revival and had begun to dampen the bloody remnants from his many wounds.

His awakening, however, did not supply any measure of relief. From where he was placed, he could see most of the invaders out of the corner of his eye, and they could easily see him in return. He wasn't much of a distance from them. From what he could tell, at one time or another, he could see all eight of them. Even the wounded few were idly moving about in the open area between the river and the woods. Later, a few of the others began covering up the piles of dried beaver pelts with fresh cut branches to protect them from the rain, while the leader busied himself consuming one of the many pungent carcasses they had brought along. It wasn't long before the two most seriously injured had stopped what they were doing altogether and looked to be tending to their lingering individual wounds suffered at the hands of Big Turtle. As they did, they focused their attention on his son. Their long menacing stares made Little Turtle wonder even more when and how soon their vengeance would arrive. For the moment Little Turtle played it safe and did his best not to challenge their stares. He was too dazed and weak for another encounter. Instead, he locked his attention at the number of skins they had stashed away not far from him. He wondered: *Why so many and why are they here?*

    The unsorted pelts Little Turtle had seen earlier, when spread about, showed to him that this group was a dedicated hunting party, focused solely on beaver. Judging from the large number of pelts, they must have been undetected for a good while. With the amount of time and effort they had spent on this harvest, they could have thought that someone might eventually discover their bounty and they hid their treasure at the earlier site. However, mistaken or not, when they discovered Big Turtle's group, they certainly didn't ask questions and reacted accordingly.

    Little Turtle reimagined a variety of reasons why they were prone to such an extreme reaction. *Could they have already been scouting my tribe for an upcoming raid? What were the smoke signals for?* Despite his questions, he knew his speculations and deep concerns for his tribe were pointless. Little Turtle was tightly bound within clear view for all to see. One thing he was sure of: it was time to somehow stop thinking of pain and misery. He had begun to think of all the others he had left behind and the danger that could come to his family, his clan members, and his tribe. If he were ever to save all the others at his village, he'd have to somehow save himself—first. He had to think of anything that might keep him alive a little longer.

More questions followed. *What am I to do?* Little Turtle's mind had become soft and mushy, filled with the same kind of wandering thoughts as during his ride in the canoe. *How much longer before I know if I'm to remain alive? Do I even deserve to be?* And worse yet: *Am I to become reserve food…like those remaining spoiled beaver? Am I to become a discarded pile of bones?*

Those kinds of questions persisted. *And, if I am to be tortured later, will I be able to endure the pain and stand up to it without cowering like a frightened bird?*

Little Turtle's battle deep within himself torched his mind without mercy.

Little Turtle already feared the Iroquois' every move. At each passing evil glance, he shuddered. After multiple physical blows, a clubbing, and a couple deep slashes, the prospect that his brutal end could come at any time was real. It might even become a welcome one, given his current condition. The outcome of this wide-ranging danger was out of his control. Even the few shreds of any rational thinking were fast fading from his soul, rendering the possibility of saving his tribe more distant. One thing for sure, the despair in his heart was increasing.

Now that Little Turtle's fellow tribesmen only hours ago had been discovered and disposed of, his misery worsened with the reemerging and haunting notion that his whole village could come under siege next. *What will become of my dear mother...brothers...and friends? What will happen to Many Winds? Did he and the other ponies free themselves from their loose tethers and return home as a dire warning of their riders' peril? If they didn't, will my people all be driven out of their huts and slaughtered by a much larger, unsuspected force I have not seen? Will my village become nothing but ashes—the surrounding grounds charred, and blood soaked?*

Although Little Turtle had never seen such extreme savagery, thanks to his father's foresight, everyone in the village knew of those things. The continual village relocations were reason enough to know why. But, no matter where the tribe settled, it wasn't long before there was an ample amount of danger that resumed around the territory, be it near or well beyond. It had been heightened even more after the passing of the peace pipe between his father, the Erie, and Potawatomi tribal leaders. On that special occasion, the imperative of group survival had been dramatically reinforced by the words brought forth from Father LaFleur's tongue, but peace still could not be completely assured.

Little Turtle himself could understand and accept when death was delivered by the hands of Mother Nature with her late-winter animal starvations. Those occasional aspects were acts of a natural cruelty. But the cruelty Little Turtle had witnessed by people upon one another earlier had been a different kind of viciousness; the indiscriminate kind of death that only comes with the ravages of people at war. So, there he was, shaking and trying to make sense of what was happening derived from the horrific ambush and amplified by the force of every single paddle stroke that had transported him to this isolated place, bound to his tree, and facing an unknown fate.

Hurting as he was, his heart was still beating, and it was becoming consumed by the terror that his village could be in imminent danger. Those thoughts again reminded him not only of what Father LaFleur had said earlier, but also what his father had spoken directly to him:

"Never stop thinking of our tribe and our people…even when you think the spirits have left you."

As also instructed by his father, Little Turtle desperately tried to listen hard for any spiritual responses, but he was weak, hungry, semiconscious, and feeling hollowed out from his bodily wounds. His ribs hurt so bad he could hardly breathe. Worse yet, he was continually thinking of his slain father. The image of him lying motionless brought Little Turtle much sadness and heartache, which he had not been able to fully absorb. Only now did he come fully conscious of a tightness deep within his chest that would not loosen. His heart was heavy, barely beating, as he remembered and cherished his father's words. They were everything to Little Turtle.

His longing turned to wishing he could see his father once again, and as he did, time slowed down to a trickle. So much so, he felt he wouldn't be able to bear the approaching darkness. *But what could I have done? Should I have obeyed my father's signal to run earlier or have stayed longer and helped in the fight?* He choked back more emptiness and guilt, wishing he could change what had happened. Wet eyed and trembling, he knew he would have to physically get away or die trying to avenge his decisions. He would have to find a way to muster his strength, defy his enemy captors, escape, and make his way back to the village to alert his elders. He decided he would suffer all consequences in so doing. *Should I let death come willingly from my enemies? No! My father was a fighter. He was strong until the end. He lived for our many others. His heart and mine are together. I will fight, too.*

    No sooner had he resolved to continue with his will to fight on, hovering in and out of his mental numbness, he heard a faint voice that was clearly not human. It eventually grew stronger until he surmised it must be a spirit.

    The voice grew stronger as it approached Little Turtle, as if appearing from a fog-like mist. Then came the sound of a few black crows cawing back and forth to one another, as if trying to draw attention to a newfound source of fresh flesh to be devoured among themselves. Little Turtle was curious as to what this could mean. *Am I to be food for these wanton crows other than my enemy captors? Or am I stepping into the afterlife and becoming a part of the Great Mystery?* And then he saw the crows start to flutter. An extraordinarily large bird, almost as tall as Little Turtle would be if he were able to stand, dressed in an eagle-feathered body, wings and tail but with the head of his tribe's sacred bird—the sandhill crane—had come into view.

Its beak was bright yellow, longer than Little Turtle's stumpy arms, and sharply pointed. The top of the creature's head was cherry red, with shadowy eyes that were focused on him. With outstretched wings, it hovered before him and shrieked a repeating call like a noble trumpet. When it stopped, it looked as if it were about to strike its imposing beak directly into each of Little Turtle's dark, blurred eyes. Instead, it landed upright a few feet away from him. It paused for a moment. After sizing him up, it spoke in a bird-like language that was strangely known to Little Turtle.

"Wait until dark."

The bird spirit had many stone-pointed arrows in its talons. It bent down and plucked one with its beak and raised it up as a show of force before the boy. The spirit then replaced the arrow and spoke again.

"You must avenge your father's savage death by returning home. This is urgent! Your father's spirit has become disturbed and will not be able to rest in peace until you face this challenge and help your people. This will be a test of your courage and prove your future bravery by returning to your village where I and my fellow spirits originally agreed to receive you with Gray Tongues. Once your father is returned peaceful unto the Great Mystery in a proper manner, you will be able to claim your courage as a new brave. You must be worthy! Without this courage…you will never be able to remove the fear of death that will try to squeeze the Miami way out of you. Without revealing this courage…you cannot be received as an honored brave. Without it…you will never return home."

The Crane Spirit then turned away from Little Turtle, and motioned for the crows to leave, and raised his talons, still clutching the arrows as they obeyed and disappeared. He returned his gaze to the boy and uttered, "Use the soft strength of the white pine…It will have much to teach you."

The sacred bird did not say anything more and abruptly vanished as the fluttering crows returned. Realizing the Crane Spirit had finished and was already gone, they too flickered out of sight.

Little Turtle believed the spiritual vision revealed that he must use his courage to lose all fear of death and use his inner strength of will. It would require a great strength to be able to help release his father's spirit—one that was severely troubled from not being able to save his own son and fellow tribesmen from death or capture; a tormented spirit that also abruptly left his family and fellow tribe members without a leader. For Little Turtle, his will to succeed had been laid out before him.

He weakly opened one eye to confirm that the spiritual bird and accompanying crows were really gone. All he could see was that the rainy mist had returned, but the strong message the spirit had left was clear. He would have to look death in the eye and escape its dark shadow in any manner possible, no matter his miserable condition, no matter how many Iroquois he faced. But the advice had given him a glimmer of hope. The tribe's sacred spirit had spoken directly to him. He would have to stop wavering with his weakened thoughts, defeat his lingering fears, and somehow return to his village in one piece.

    During Little Turtle's darkest moments, one of the most revered spirits of the tribe had finally come forward with a strong message. He now knew he must be trustworthy enough to become a committed warrior against all the bad medicine he was facing, and rise above it, to save the spirit of his father and the rest of the people in his tribe. He knew this was possible because a great spirit had come to him and made his heart beat stronger, despite his wounds, waning confidence, and mounting hunger and frustrations. Without a plan of any kind, he had to overcome the persistent doubts in his heart and fulfill the spirit's commands and expectations. Despite his damaged ribs, he drew a determined breath and vowed to make it so.

Chapter 9

The Struggle to Escape

The Iroquois invaders were still milling about or conversing quietly among themselves as the shadows of dusk were growing, unaware that Little Turtle's will power was on the rise. Despite the casual movements among the enemy group, at least one of them managed to keep a steady eye on him. Even with the constant attention, they were oblivious to his inner uplift brought on by his forceful spiritual adviser.

The steady warm mist turned into a light drizzle. It not only helped to keep the remaining flying insects at bay, but also caused more of the group to busy themselves securing their valuable beaver pelts and flintlocks. While they were preoccupied, Little Turtle's mind began to stir more rapidly. Although he had become numb to the pain of his wounds from his ongoing terror, he managed to question what he should do while he still had a chance to consider how to get free. It would have to have a high possibility of working. *What can I do? I am getting too much attention.* He wasn't being harassed, as the drizzle was rapidly turning to a steady rain, but Little Turtle knew if he got caught doing anything suspicious, the answer to his questions about any uncertain outcomes would be rapid.

As the Crane Spirit had advised, he decided to wait until total darkness. As soon as that happened, he would have to put his leather bindings to a test. *If the patter of the steady rain against the leaves and ground continues, I might start sooner.* His plan was simple. He would start with a gradual leaning from the tree to test the bindings' strength. *Will they stretch?*

He waited patiently, staying still. He was tired, but eager to get started. With partially cracked-open eyes, he studied his enemy's patterns. Now that the rain was falling, would they continue to watch him or not? During this time, he was also fighting sharp hunger pains and a deep raging thirst. He raised his head and let the rain rinse his face and moisten his parched lips. It felt good.

Just sitting, staring up at the rain and watching the camp, was difficult to endure, but the spirit's words and images of his loved ones kept him hopeful. When dark shadows began to creep into the camp area, he couldn't wait any longer. Bolstered by the spirit's passion, he was ready to try out his dangerous plan.

First, he pretended to slouch, as if asleep. As he eased forward, he discovered the bindings did stretch, but only a little. The Iroquois were sure-handed and had bound him tight. Next, while slouched forward, he decided to try shifting from one side to another. He reminded himself: *I must be careful.* Then he began moving to his left side, ever so slowly, to avoid detection. It was only a slight shift. He also had to avoid scraping his fresh wounds against the tree's jagged bark. There would be no compromises for any additional pain.

The results of his first bit of a side movement revealed that the rain might have softened his bindings. The side movement allowed him to stretch them a little better. He was encouraged, but he decided to wait another short period before he tried it again. He was afraid his pounding heart would give his movements away.

So far, the enemy group was busy keeping to themselves, mostly devouring the available beaver meat, and he wanted them to stay that way. It was bad enough they were scattered all around him and still moving about the area. The rain hadn't made that much of a difference to them. Despite his eagerness to continue, he knew the darkness was not where it needed to be. Thanks to the Crane Spirit's inspiration, he had become more daring, but not foolish.

When he felt the darkness had increased enough, he slowly shifted his position from his left to his right side. As he did, he realized he still had the medicine bundle with him. It began to press against his inner left thigh as he progressed. With all his suffering and worry, he had once again forgotten about his newly gained prize from Gray Tongues. *Great Spirit! You are here with me!*

In that instant, he reconnected with the invisible world. Refocusing on the shaman's stone reignited the memory of what had been said in the modest hut about how the bundle provides "great courage" in "difficult hunts or battles." With Gray Tongues' solemn words ringing in his heart, Little Turtle began to silently chant the way Gray Tongues had done. It awoke in him the feeling he could make something helpful begin to happen.

The spirits seemed to encourage him to put more pressure on the bindings. If he could stretch them enough, he should be able to get his tethered hands down into a position for his outstretched fingers to touch his loincloth strap. Then he would be able to grab it and shift it around his waist. His idea was to move the bundle from his groin, around his side, toward his back to get a grip around it. For Little Turtle, the spirits supplied an ambitious prodding to continue his plan. All he needed was the will to make it work.

When he was ready, he closed his eyes and prayed as hard as he could: *Oh, Great Spirit, whose voice I hear in the wind, whose breath gives life to all the world. Hear me! I need your strength and wisdom…*

He cracked one eye open, checked on the enemy's current positions and waited.

Despite the weather and increasing darkness, to him it looked like they were finally finished with their feedings and preserving their valuable bounty from any unnecessary pelt spoilage. He hoped they were ready to dig in for the night. They had to be too exhausted from their extensive beaver activities, their deadly ambush, and later escape to be overly concerned with him harnessed to a tree. *Maybe their watchful eyes will finally fall.*

After a long pause and a deeper, more painful breath, he managed to slowly shift to his side again, away from his hands. He stopped and waited. Now he could move his fingers more freely. He slipped his index finger further down his back toward his loincloth and when he felt it, curled his finger under and around the strap. Then he pulled up with continuous tension, sucking in his belly as he pulled his belt toward the left. It moved. He pulled harder—and not only the belt, but also the bundle, shifted away from his groin and around toward his side. With the spirit's help, his escape effort was beginning to work.

He tried once more with the same amount of tension, and again it moved, until after several more tugs he could feel the soaked leather pouch in the middle of his back. Beads of nervous sweat raced out his every pore. Little Turtle recognized this good fortune had to come from the grace of the spirits. He paused and gave them his ample respects. *Hear me! Make my hands respect the things you made. Bring me your strength and wisdom...*

With the major feat of being able to grasp the bundle achieved, it was now just a matter of maneuvering the bundle into the center of his hands. His heart pounded, he felt cold all over, and time stood still, until he finally was able to squeeze the pouch enough to clutch the tip of the stone between his bound hands. All the other contents originally in the bundle were missing, but the act of holding a portion of the main content was a profound achievement. His escape became a real possibility. While he feverishly thanked the spirits, he continued to listen for footsteps from a curious enemy, who might be beyond his view.

A few of the visible ones were sitting and still gorging themselves with the very last bits of the leftover raw beaver meat or chewing on their remaining bones. Others were stretching and headed further away from him. One by one, they took their turns walking down to the water's edge. The rest of the group remained stretched out on the cold ground, impervious to the wet weather.

These Iroquois looked to Little Turtle to be a hardened lot, tough enough to withstand the rigors of long travels, existing only on what they could find and survive on from day to day. Their nighttime behavior reinforced his notion. Weather such as this must have simply been a part of the life to which they were accustomed. It gave him more reason to believe there could be no room for a mistake on his part. He would need more of the spirits' help to get past these well-seasoned strangers.

The rain continued to fall. It made the wait longer. He had to make sure the rest of the group had finished their business and were settled in. When he felt the time was right, Little Turtle moved his hands more firmly around the leather bundle and tried to stretch it open while holding the stone tip, but both were soaked in blood and slippery. His first attempt to clear the stone failed. With a sigh of frustration, he tried using the tree and was able to push the bundle against the trunk to force the pouch open a little more. It was a long process, without being able to see what he was doing and relying only on his sense of touch.

Another eternity passed before he succeeded in pushing the pouch just enough and could feel the rest of the stone beginning to emerge. With a little more force, he got a firm grip on the whole stone with one hand. It was an amazing victory. *The spirits have guided my hands!*

Before Little Turtle could use one of the stone's sharp edges to cut a strap, two of the enemy hunters sitting on the highest rock got up and began to move his way. *Uh-oh...*

With stern faces, the two approached him quickly. Little Turtle's pulse began to race. *Have I been discovered?* His heart was ready to make its final leap as the hair on his arms stood straight out. He stiffened and gasped. *Is this the end?* He closed his eyes, fearing the worst.

One of the Iroquois came all the way over to him. He stopped directly in front of Little Turtle and pushed him on his shoulder with his wet moccasin, but not hard, and then backed away. Little Turtle squeezed the stone and played like a frightened possum as best he could.

When the other came forward and took his turn, he kicked Little Turtle much harder in his tender ribs. Little Turtle let out a deep moan and opened his eyes. Accepting an unknown fate, he stared at the braves as a last act of weakened defiance. The two returned his stare, but did nothing more. They looked to be satisfied he was still alive and securely bound. Both responded with no more than grunting and nodding and returned to their stations to keep a careful watch over the site. Little Turtle breathed a painful sigh of relief and remained motionless, aside from a continuous trembling in his lips. It had been a close call and an ample reminder that the enemy had not forgotten him.

    Little Turtle tried to collect himself while he waited before daring to try using the stone. When he was finally able to calm his heart down, and all the other Iroquois were lying still, scattered around the site, he silently called to the spirits. *Great Spirit!* No response. Again, *Great Spirit!* Despite the silence, he believed they would eventually come. Meanwhile, he wasn't going to give up, but the death-defying scare had convinced him to be even more careful. For the sake of his tribe, he was determined to pursue the course of the work he still had to do.

    Little Turtle stayed stationary for as long as he could stand it, despite mentally dwelling back and forth in a rocky state between terror and hope. Even though anxious and suffering the effects of a dry mouth and headache, at least he knew he had found a measure of courage in his brief act of defiance with the two sentries. Little Turtle believed his inspiration had to be derived from his grip on the stone. The feeling gave him a sense of clarity that the spirits would remain with him from afar. That helped him return to his plan. With renewed motivation, he squared his jaw and mentally repeated his vow to get back to his people over and over—*I will return…I will walk with you!*—while he waited for his opportunity with the stone's sharp forefront still held firmly in his hand.

    Much more rain fell. He wanted to stick out his tongue

to catch some drops but, remembering his shaman's words of requiring a great sacrifice, dared not. Then, with his courage renewed, and denying his urges, including sleep, he resumed his risky attempt to escape. He leaned forward as hard as he could to stretch the bindings again. He repeated this effort several times. Because the bindings were now thoroughly wet with the rain and diluted blood, the uppermost loop eventually stretched enough so that when he leaned back, it fell a few inches down his chest. By rotating the stone blade upward, he could touch one of the straps with the sharpened edge. When he moved forward again, he was able to hold the blade firmly against the taut binding. He was barely able to move the stone back and forth against it, but that achievement was encouraging.

Little Turtle worked the blade slowly at first, making sure not to drop it. Plus, the stone's position wasn't at an easy angle, but if he remained in his forward position, the blade could at least stay consistently pressed against the binding. Up and down, back and forth, he tried both, but the effort didn't get easier. The location of the binding made the awkward cutting motion limited and frustrating. Even so, knowing it was his only chance, he stuck with it.

Leaning forward also aggravated the pain in his ribs from the multiple kicks he had received. The situation forced him to concentrate as hard as he could to ignore the pain. During these moments, the dark world of exhaustion and his unrelenting grief kept a tight grasp on his heart. But he had to make certain he didn't lose his hold of the wet stone and drop it. That result would be unthinkable.

Solemnly, he continued his strokes. Just when he thought the binding would never give way, the same overpowering Crane Spirit returned with his crows. This time the spirit repeated a loud shrilling chant over and over. Little Turtle feared the screeching could be heard, but not an Iroquois stirred. Amazed, he listened hard and watched.

As he did, Little Turtle began to see the strength of a soft white pine, mature and tall, as it appeared and swayed in a strong summer wind while the Crane Spirit hopped and chanted. Then he saw his father walking away in the distance. During a few more screeches and chants, he saw a blurry view of his village burning as the spirit turned angry, flapping his huge wide-spreading wings. Without a further sign or even a spoken message, all that Little Turtle could see faded away.

Little Turtle opened his eyes, bewildered. Looking around for the spirit, all he saw was the dankness of wet vegetation, and all he heard was rain dripping from the pine needles extending above him. No sign of the two sentries, but the night had become pitch dark. He hoped they were sleeping or watching somewhere else far away. He knew not where.

Is the spirit angry because I'm not doing enough? Does the spirit want me to hurry the blade against the strap and not give up? That must be it. As soon as he could muster enough energy to stop his feverous trembles, he leaned forward and moved the blade again. As he did, the image of his father and his village burning to the ground remained.

Energized, he continued his off-and-on strokes as best he could. But when he was ready to stop and rest one more time, the strap partially gave way. Encouraged, he gave another great push and leaned away from the remaining restraints—and the upper loops around his chest loosened and fell to his waist. *What good medicine! Thank you, Oh Crane Spirit!*

Quietly, he leaned forward enough to touch the side of his face and his shoulder all the way down to the wet pine needles next to him. He guessed, if he possessed enough strength to move to his knees, without more injury to his back, he might be able to stand upward against the tree. All he needed was enough room to free himself from this bondage. *If I remain silent, will I be free?*

The rain came down harder, but it felt good against his many wounds. Little Turtle tried to visualize what he should do next. He rested in his face-down position with his hands still bound, fearful of moving. He felt his heart pounding again so hard he thought the sound in his ears would make them burst. It was all because Little Turtle had become half free, and could be seen as such, amid his enemy's sinister encampment.

Now, it was clear to him he'd first have to get to his knees without being noticed, and without a sound. Then he'd still have to force himself to stand up and step out of the remaining loops, but he was trembling and weak. *Can I even stand?* Second, he could hardly see a thing. It was so dark in his little spot in the woods he might as well have been blindfolded again. But despite the lack of light, the night was supplying a sympathetic rain, offering him cover from an enemy's piercing eyes and sensitive ears. He gave thanks once again and asked: *Help me, Spirit! Talk to me!*

There was no response to Little Turtle's silent plea, but he knew now was the time. Opportunity had presented itself. The rain had given him a slight advantage, if he could control himself and not be in such a panic that his haste would give him away. Any foolish move—the slightest sound—or an inadvertent snap of a tiny twig would be a disaster. Little Turtle knew it wouldn't take much to raise a curious eye. The desperate urge to run was hard to resist, but the noise of sprinting to the river would put a harsh end to his escape. However, the temptation to get away as fast as he could was overwhelming, so much so, he endured an additional pain, that of holding his breath—afraid to even breathe—knowing that he could not run. It was either walk or crawl.

He reasoned walking would work better. If he crawled on his knees, he wouldn't be able to move as much with his hands still bound behind his back. He'd be forced to slide them along, much too slow. The camp was close to the river, and where he was bound was only a little farther inland. *Oh Spirit! What should I do?* With a raging feeling of desperation having claimed him, knowing his pathway should be sand and only a few rocks, Little Turtle decided, *I will step softly to the water.*

The sound of the rain was a continuing helper. Little Turtle was convinced it was brought on by the spirits after his repeated calls. He gave them many thanks, and after a successful effort to get to his knees, he made his move to stand up. As he did, he almost lost his balance. *Oh no!* His legs had lost most of their power, but he managed to straighten up. Ever so carefully, he held his breath as long as he could stand, and he stepped out of the loops. Little Turtle was free from his bounds, but his soul was now trapped in intense turmoil.

Standing and looking around the parts of the camp closest to him turned out to be more frightening than he could have ever imagined. Soaked in nervous sweat, from this higher vantage point he could now make out two more of the closest Iroquois much clearer. He was certain, given the slightest reason, they would be able to see him equally as well. With that quick glance he told himself: *This is far too risky.*

The Iroquois' nearness was already frightening but standing made it more so. Without question he'd have to get back down and stay low just to restrain himself from dashing to the river. Being this close to his resting enemy in clear view made the veins in his neck pound outward. A sharp stabbing at every nerve ending enveloped him. Even the sounds of the rain had disappeared from the feeling of fainting on the spot from a terror induced strangling with his every breath. Despite the Crane Spirit's message to lose the fear of death, those words had not completely taken hold.

Overcoming this wave of near hysteria, he convinced himself to lower himself back to the ground and make his first move to set himself free. *This is it…it's now or never. My tribe needs me. Oh Spirits, guide me!*

In slow motion, Little Turtle got back down on his

knees and closely rechecked his path. He took as deep a breath as he could manage and made his first move toward the shore, shuffling on his knees without the aid of his hands for balance. Without the ability to even raise his knees, they were to become his plows forging, bit by bit, through a sandy terrain toward the shore. The Iroquois would know the direction he went, but it was his only hope.

With each careful slide forward through the damp sand, he stopped to catch his breath to avoid the exploding panic attack that was trying to erupt as he kept his eyes trained on his captors. He had to keep his focus. He knew full well that at any second, any of one of them could stir and spot their defenseless prize.

Yet, Little Turtle was able to move forward one knee, stop, and then another. He knew from the moment he had freed himself that he had breached the point of no return. To be discovered now by one of the group's sentries, surely still out there somewhere, would result in an unimaginable nighttime slaughter. With every passing second, he expected to be knocked over and stabbed over and over. It kept him in a steady agonizing forward motion, each slide necessitating not completely losing oneself, each slide demanding control.

With each effort in his struggle, he bit down hard on his tongue and managed to stay silent. He forced himself to move in a deliberate manner, but as quickly as he thought he could get away with. Inside, though, he frantically wanted this heartless nightmare to end. *I can't believe this! Spirits, carry me out of here!*

Although he had embraced the Spirit's demands, his

fears remained. So much so, he was not conscious of where his strength to remain upright was coming from. Constantly looking all around, he struggled to breathe more than ever. With tears and rain hampering his vision, he pleaded for strength to keep going. As he held on tight to the shaman's stone, the words: *Use the soft strength of the white pine* began to echo in his mind. With those words, the welcome sound of the river's rolling current gradually grew closer, hinting he was almost there. *I hear it!*

    The closer he got with one agonizing slide after another, the shorter the periods between his slides became. All along the way, the threat of detection by one of those killers leaping out of the darkness caused him to flinch and shake his head to clear that dreaded thought away. To keep fear from gaining on him, he became riskier with his quickened pace. His stomach had already turned into a rock from the escape-generated tension. Even as he moved further away from the camp, the evil they still represented supplied no relief. Nervous sweat blended in with the rain, dripped off his brow, and down to and off his elbows. Somehow, he found the wherewithal to keep moving, hardly taking a full breath, instead inching toward freedom with a quickened panting.

    As he continued for his life, his bound wrists were proving to be a great hindrance, especially when he butted up against his first major obstacle. *What's this?* A group of rocks near the hazy shoreline was blocking his way. Frustrated to be this close to the river and forced to stop, he realized he could go no further in this crawling manner. He had no choice but to lean and roll himself over the rocks using his feet for leverage. *What about the noise?* He held tight to his lifeline to the spirits—the shaman's stone—and took the greatest risk of his young life. He went ahead and attempted to roll over the stone tops. With an ample mix of an aching ribcage, more tears, gut determination, and blind faith, his effort to move on succeeded.

After overcoming this final stretch of intensifying terror, he finally reached the shoreline and slipped into the cool arms of the moving water. He made sure it was a quiet entry. He rejoiced the instant he and the river became one. He had achieved a huge victory.

Submerged lengthwise in the river shallows, floating in water no more than two feet deep, Little Turtle dared not to move even a finger. The only sounds were those that came from the pattering of raindrops all around him. Exhausted from the intensity of his ordeal, he tried to release the immense stress from the day's events by silently speaking to the great tribal spirit with humble gratitude. *Thank you, Crane Spirit, for pushing me closer to home! I am forever listening.*

Before he made another move, he listened for a response, not only for more of the Spirit's words, but also to make sure his escape had not been discovered by his enemy capturers. He hoped they wouldn't until at least daylight. Mindful of not angering the spirits and more bad medicine returning, he dared not to even gulp a taste of the cool water to quench his immense thirst. It took all his willpower, but he did not allow himself even a quick sip.

Though he still had a long way to go to return home, his huge sacrifices for the spirits would have to continue.

At first, the safety of the water was gratifying, but as his scrapes and deep lacerations showed, he realized the Water Spirit was reminding him he was still in grave danger. The stinging pain would be minor compared to what could happen if he didn't get moving.

With the river under him, Little Turtle found himself with the good medicine of a trackless path away from here forward. So far, he had only reached the edge of freedom. He wasted no more time relishing his initial escape, for he knew there was much more distance to go before he'd find any real freedom.

With a renewed flow of tears of gratitude streaming down his face, he continued his prayer, this time thanking the Water Spirit directly for his emotional rescue. *Make my hands respect the things you have made and my ears sharp to hear your voice…*

It was a short prayer, but it had to be. His fears of remaining this close to the enemy camp were still strong and made it so.

Chapter 10

The Water Spirit's Will

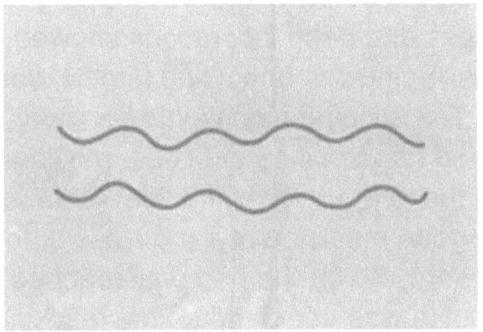

Little Turtle began to float a little deeper until he was able to stand with the support of the water. He stopped at waist-deep level. To be further out of view from the chance of a wandering eye would have been better, but being unable to swim with his arms bound behind his back made that idea too risky.

What should I do? He decided to stay submerged at this level and backtrack his captors' canoe ride. He knew the Iroquois had gotten him to this site paddling with the current, following the lowering sun, so he would go in the opposite direction and hopefully reach the cove thereafter. This decision meant a lot more effort would be needed to keep his footing against the current's flow without his arms free to keep his balance, but he was still gratified, nonetheless. He would be leaving no trail.

As he moved on through the continuous light rain, as a confidence builder he repeated to himself: *This must be the way for my journey. Soon I'll recognize this land.* His instincts also told him he had to make sure he remained no deeper than his waist, and when necessary, venture no closer to shore than knee deep to avoid any unnecessary splashes or becoming too visible. That meant not slipping on an algae-covered rock or a submerged tree branch. To fall now without the aid of his arms could also mean a struggle with the Water Spirit. While he viewed the spirit as a giver of life, he knew it could also be a powerful underwater adversary. He was too weak for any unnecessary challenges.

Carefully and diligently, he moved his feet ahead without disturbing the water's surface. He was quiet in this way. Once he was a good distance from the enemy's encampment and felt slightly safer, he tried to free his wrists from behind his back. It was a difficult effort while trying to keep a firm grip on his stone. On many occasions, he squeezed it hard, hoping for another sign from the spirits.

Neither striding along against the river water nor being exposed to the rain helped soften his lashings. His best alternative was to enlist outside help and return to the shore somewhere further along his way. *I might be able to use a nearby boulder or a fallen log to push my hands forward.*

His idea was to bring his short, stocky arms in front of him so he could chew on his lashings as he traveled. All he'd have to do would be extend his wrists under his buttocks as far as he could, sit down, and lean against a solid shoreline obstacle to push against it with his feet and slide his hands forward.

Even though it was still very dark, he soon spotted a large log near the shore to try out his plan. To use it, though, meant he'd have to step out of the river. The exposure made him anxious, but he needed the use of his hands. *I must try this one.*

Cautiously, he moved ashore. Once he was in position sitting on the log and still clutching his shaman's gift, he tried out his idea. He squeezed the stone to alert the spirits then pushed his legs out against the sand with his wrists wedged against the log. The effort didn't work at first. His loincloth got in the way; but, undeterred, he tried again. With the help of what was left of the bear grease he had applied before his ride to the cove, his plan worked.

A huge sigh of relief came out of him as he slowly and painfully stood up. His heart said: *Thanks to the spirits for granting me this help,* while his eyes glanced all around. Then, holding his breath, he stepped back into the cool water with his hands in front of him. It was a good effort and a welcome change. His only regret was he had made a new set of footprints which could easily be read. At least he would be able to chew on the wet leather bindings with each step from this point on. It was another sacrifice he had to make.

Little Turtle hadn't been in the water for longer than it would take a healthy beaver to swim across the river when he heard frantic screams and shrills of a dire alarm. *Oh no!* His shock from hearing the Iroquois' expanded uproar made his knees weak, close to buckling, as he turned to look back. It was a terrible revelation that a hair-raising chase was inevitable.

    The chaos that ensued reenergized his body but not the way Little Turtle wanted. His heart began to race wildly again, his skin tingled, and he struggled to catch his breath. He visualized the discovery of his disappearance like stirring up an anthill. Even though he had a head start, the screaming carrying on beyond his view made it easy to envision his blood clouding the water. A new kind of fear was creeping into his life. Not the fear the Crane Spirit spoke of, but a rising fear of failure. To end up unable to warn his people in time of what might lie ahead shook him. He could not let that happen. Nothing was going to stop his struggle to return home to warn his people. The thought that his village could ultimately be destroyed was something he could not bear.

    I must move faster. They are coming! I must free my hands! The combination of the distant commotion and striding through the current while frantically chewing on his wrist bands proved to be a monumental task considering his injuries already sustained. But despite his handicaps, he would not be captured again. *Never!* But he knew his pursuers would be ever vengeful to save face after being surprised and outwitted by a mere boy. These were seasoned warriors, and the bad medicine delivered by Little Turtle's escape could never be forgiven.

    As Little Turtle struggled on, looking for any way of escape, he glanced at his pure white artifact and called for the Crane Spirit to return. *Hear me, spirits!* There was no answer. The only sounds were the rushing splashes as he slogged on in shallower water. *Hear me! Hear me!*

To make his plight worse, the cover provided by the darkness was beginning to melt away. Despite the warm sprinkling rain, the typical early-morning brightening would not be far behind. That meant those angry Iroquois would be able to see more clearly any activity in the water or along the shore. That included the sighting of his footprints during his brief time trying to move his wrists forward.

Even if they missed that sign, he knew they were aware he was somewhere in the river. The trail he'd made reentering the water during his daring escape was glaring. Because he was staying in the water to avoid any new trails, he was forced to find a hiding place somewhere along the riverbank, one where nothing would look disturbed. His eyes begged to find that place.

Little Turtle's shallow rapid breaths expressed his panic. He desperately hoped the stone he still held would summon the spirits for him and show him the way, but it did not. Glancing up and down the shore, he saw nothing obvious for a safe hiding place. Wild-eyed, he gasped for more air, trying to step faster.

Then he spotted a large log lying parallel to the shore not far ahead. Part of it looked to be above the water's surface. It was one of many of the wooden outcrops he had seen along the course of the river, but this one looked to be positioned mostly in and above the water. It would have to do. As he sloshed closer, he hoped it was in deep enough water, so he'd be able to crawl under it and stay submerged.

He looked back to see if anyone could see him, but

he couldn't tell. It was still a little too dark. For all he knew, they could be just beyond the bend behind him. With the hot pursuit well under way, this log looked to be his only opportunity other than dashing into the woods; he'd have to try it. If he made it unseen and managed to get under the log, he'd hold his breath and stay submerged for as long as he could. He hoped the Water Spirit was agreeable. He needed its additional help; he was too exhausted to go any further. The way his chest was tingling, and his ongoing struggle with his ribs to breathe, he doubted he could even make it that far.

    To keep from falling to his knees, he slowed down, focusing on his chewing at the wrist straps. It was tricky while trying to avoid losing his grip on the stone. As he moved, he continued to check behind his trail to see how close they were getting. *Are they coming by canoe or along the shore?* His questions continued as he moved to shallower water straight to the log. *Are they gaining on me? Can they see me? Is it light enough? Are they on the shore looking for more signs? Oh Spirits, give me a push. I must hurry!*

    It was then he heard faint voices carrying across the water. It was the same strange language Little Turtle had come to despise. The frenzied enemy was getting closer. *They are near!* He could distinguish at least two voices, but there may have been more. He was getting confused. All he knew was they were within range. Even though he couldn't see them, he feared his chances to continue were rapidly slipping away. However, if they couldn't see him, he still had a chance.

    As he struggled in the log's direction, he could see its

stump's lower portion hidden under the surface by an extended outward ridge and the log itself. Getting closer, he saw there were other logs a little further down the shoreline, which looked similar, but there was no more time. This trunk was extended along the water's surface. Without another thought, he made his way to it. This looked to be his one and only chance. He would put all his hope into a final attempt to crawl underneath the middle of the trunk.

There he hoped to find a place of a steady undercurrent from the flow of the water, or a shady spot where a large fish may have hollowed out some sand for a wide nest, to guard its eggs in the security of the log's summertime shade. If this was so, it would now be shared. However, he had no assurances that it would be a deep enough one to squeeze under. With his complete desperation, he already knew he'd hollow out his own hole if he had to.

With the strength in his legs giving out from striding in

the water for so long, he couldn't tell if the Water Spirit had secretly attached many heavy stones to his ankles. *Turn me loose, Oh Spirit!* Again, there was no answer, just the sounds of stirring water and his own delirious grunts from straining.

When he reached the log, he managed to step up to the shadowy spot and squeeze under the tangled wooden overhang. His hunch that this site could be an ideal place for a productive fish nest or, better yet, a river current's steady undercutting, proved true: the water directly underneath the log was deeper than it looked. The Water Spirit had been generous. But without the full use of his hands, Little Turtle found maneuvering himself completely under the log more difficult than he expected. He was running out of time until the Iroquois would be upon him. His impatience with his wrist restrictions made him want to scream. Instead, he shook off his frustration and tried again.

Thanks to the river's ageless undercutting and swirling against the log's tangled branches, the watery hole was deep enough to allow Little Turtle's partial success in positioning himself further away from the danger headed his way. He was well under the overhang and much deeper into the silence of the water, but not completely out of sight. His hideaway wasn't good enough.

More frustrated than ever, with his bound wrists, he angrily slammed his fists against a thick part of a submerged branch and tried again. This time, he was able to forcefully slide himself further up the trunk toward the elevated stump and more directly above the swirling undercurrent. There he was able to lower his entire body, including his head, in a stretched-out position, well below the waterline. He had made it! He was finally completely out of sight. And even though his mind was still in furious turmoil, being anchored under the log gave him a chance to rest as he awaited his fate.

After a minute or two, he tilted his head back and raised it enough to expose his upright nose like a common painted turtle. Clinging in place, directly under the log, he brought his nose and one eye just above the waterline. This position gave him a better chance to see what was out there and still breathe. And then he saw them: two fast-moving paddlers with their distinctive headgear coming his way. *They are here! Oh Spirits, they are here!* He lowered his face.

Minutes later, while completely submerged, he heard their explosive paddles striking in and out of the water and the faint vibrations of their water-dulled Iroquoian voices. There was no doubt: *It's them!* The sounds told him they were almost upon his murky hideaway. He lowered his head even further into the water, as deep as he could, directly on the sandy bottom. There he became frozen stiff in his new watery tomb. So much so, his continuous emotional shaking from head to toe completely stopped. He was rapidly becoming dead in the water.

As much as Little Turtle tried to control it, his personal fear of death had returned and was proving to be an overwhelming adversary. All he could do, as he held his breath for as long as he could, was wait for his ultimate discovery.

For the moment...nothing happened. The paddling noises faded and were silenced. *Are they looking at me now? What's taking them so long?* He listened hard but there were no more sounds. *Are they on the shore?*

Turning blue and faint, he dared to raise himself for one last gasping breath, expecting to see at least two of them standing over him with their weapons of death drawn. But again, the accompanying shrills of discovery did not come. Instead, the water remained mysteriously quiet. *What is happening up there? Tell me, Water Spirit!*

Little Turtle could get no idea from his vantage point. However, the downed tree proved to be an ally after all, for it looked to be ordinary enough, one of a great many the pursuers had already seen along their frenzied way. They, too, may have mistakenly thought the water was too shallow even for a canoe to glide upon.

Just to be sure there was no mistake, Little Turtle waited. *Even if they passed me by, they could circle back.* Frightened beyond his imagination, he wasn't going to take any chances. He stayed in his horizontal position, crowded under the ancient overhang's slimy bark and tangled roots, until the tips of his fingers began to wrinkle. Yet, on he stayed with the "strength of a soft white pine" for as long as he could, occasionally exposing himself only long enough to breathe sufficiently and then back down. He was determined not to become careless. His distant world depended on him.

As the silence above the water's surface lingered and the sky brightened, the urgency of not being discovered gradually turned into great relief. With supreme caution,

Little Turtle moved out from under his hideaway, rose slightly, exposing only his head, and took a good look. It was good to breathe the moist air again. Feeling his chest pains return, he managed to fill his lungs several times. Fortunately, he was still alive and there were no Iroquois visible in any direction along the shore or out on the water. Instead of any humankind, he spotted a hungry river muskrat digging for roots further along the rising bank and heard a red squirrel scolding another in a nearby tree. He surmised none would be there if there were any people in the vicinity.

He gave thanks to the Water Spirit for its help in finding the haven of the great log and even the shallow hole to avoid his detection. While giving his heartfelt thanks, he thought of the power of the stone to help give him more guidance and its added spiritual strength. That's when he realized it was no longer in his bound hands. *Oh no! I must have dropped it when I was trying to keep my grip on the old log's branches!*

Believing the stone might still be lying somewhere underneath him in the sandy bottom, he turned himself face down, and with his eyes wide open tried to retrieve his direct line to the tribal spirits. As a practical matter, he was also hoping to use the stone to sever the lashings on his wrists. So, its loss was doubly crushing.

Thanks to the rainfall and the river's increased turbulence, coupled with Little Turtle's underwater leg movements, the water was murky. Opening his eyes underwater did not help. Consequently, he had no choice but to blindly submerge himself repeatedly and feel around the bottom with his tethered hands. He even extended himself more outward and felt for it with his feet in deeper waters. He did find a few random stones, but they were of the ordinary kind. *Could it be, when I lost the stone, the current carried it a little more of a distance away from where I was before it hit bottom?* He made many more attempts with that in mind using a wider-ranging search, but to no avail. *Did I step on it…driving it deeper in the sand?* Even with that prospect, his efforts proved fruitless.

    Over and over, he frantically searched. Each time he came up empty, he still had to be wary of being spotted. The other unaccounted-for Iroquois could be lurking and approaching on foot with the sky growing brighter. He knew full well the remaining warriors could discover him if he was distracted for too long. These hunters were skilled killers and not just of beaver.

    Soon the inevitable truth began to speak loudly within his aching heart. His mind cried, *No! no! Why is this happening? How can this be?* Now it was far too clear that his conduit to the Crane Spirit, and many others, was gone. Reluctantly, he accepted the fact that he'd have to abandon this spot to find his way back to the cove, and then, his village without any spiritual help. His temporary freedom from the pursuing Iroquois had come at a tremendous cost.

    Staring down at his bound and empty hands, he slowly rose out of the water. Struggling to stand up straight with his brown skin shining in the emerging sun, his long black hair emptied a steady flow of water down his back into the river, while a trickle of sorrowful tears cascaded down his chest. Little Turtle wondered: *How can anything get any worse?*

    Now more than ever, he was bewildered and alone in a place he did not know. With no plan, his hollow heart crying and a body ready to collapse, for no apparent reason, except for what felt like a gentle push and a touch upon his shoulder, he noticed an urgent pulling of something from within the woods. For no other reason, he solemnly left the security of the river and reentered the forest. There, among the trees, he knew he'd have to face whatever else was waiting for him just beyond his muddled view.

Chapter 11

The Upward Climb

Once Little Turtle was under the cover of the woods, he stopped to try to justify why it was time to leave the safety of the Water Spirit's world. Without the stone, he had no answer. All he knew was he had to fulfill a spiritual calling to save his village. Beyond that, something else was pushing him, even if his escape back into the woods meant he had left another set of prints from the water's edge. For now, his greater concern was he had to get deeper into the safety of the trees and out of sight of the open water. It was getting far too light, with the rain clouds having broken apart and the fresh colors of the dawn stretching across the sky.

Safely amongst the forest's darkest shadows, all was quiet except for the early sounds of the forest...more red squirrel chatter overhead, and chirps from a few startled chipmunks underfoot. It seemed a safe enough start, albeit a risky one. With every step Little Turtle made, he could still see his father and the others wasted on the sacred grounds, riddled with feathered shafts. He couldn't shake that terrifying image, and was filled with dread and doubt about what to do next. The imminent danger from his captors, who were still somewhere out there looking for his trail, pressed hard upon his heart.

With his strength almost gone, Little Turtle knew it would be a struggle to visually relocate the river's most striking landmark, the sacred cove. His hope was, if he found his way back to the most hallowed grounds, his village wouldn't be that hard to find. He hoped once he found the cove, the spirits would come again and speak to him. Despite his great worries, he was growing desperate to complete the Crane Spirit's original commands to return home.

If he reached the cove, he also thought he'd be able to locate traces of the ponies' presence. *It was only a day ago.* Even though the rain could have washed away most of the hoofprints on the harder surfaces, there might be a few remaining. He believed there should be other evidence like broken or bent branches, and a few of their droppings along the way. He took a deeper, more painful breath, knowing he would have to do this based on a much stronger will to survive. *Oh, to see my mother, White Sparrow, and fellow brothers again…*

Little Turtle remembered how the path they traveled had felt to be on solid earth and must have been wider than just an ordinary deer trail, having certainly been traveled by Gray Tongues and many others among his tribe who wished to honor the spirits at that same sacred place.

Little Turtle hoped Gray Tongues might have even used an alternate foot trail or two. Since he rarely traveled on horseback, that could account for his long absences, hobbling there and back for those in need. *How else did he know so much about the spirits and their invisible world?* Little Turtle was hoping for the discovery of one of those additional trails.

Having met the tribal spirits firsthand while captured, Little Turtle wondered: *Are they testing my will to return?* He knew he'd have to get his bearings for his current whereabouts to familiarize himself with this new land. Without knowing how long he had been in the canoe and occasionally losing his senses, he could be standing anywhere, or worse, become a victim of his own incorrect choice of direction.

For the time being, Little Turtle knew he was lost for the first time in his life and that the moving river still carried many more secrets for him to learn. The area where he stood was one. For a proud Miami as himself, not knowing where to turn in his own hunting territory was certainly bad medicine. If he had a pair of wings like the chirping birds all around him, he might be even able to see his village, but standing flat-footed on the ground, he had no way of knowing. Worse yet, he still didn't know where the murderous Iroquois were in their furious effort to hunt him down.

Little Turtle wasn't a bird, but he could climb, and the dawn's early light was becoming bright enough for him to be spotted even in these foreboding woods. Without any more delays, he sought the tallest tree he could find close enough to the shore. His mind was trying to recover from a continual haunting, but despite it all, he managed to visualize being high in the air where he might be able to spot the high-rising stone bluff where the cove was standing, and then locate his home further beyond. More so, if the Iroquois killers were still moving toward him, they may not be the wiser if he became like a bear cub and was hiding high off the ground. Little Turtle knew what they could do, having remembered what they had already done.

There were many varieties of trees where he stood looking back toward the shoreline. Then he remembered his vision and the Crane Spirit's strong words—*Use the soft strength of the white pine*—and looked for those mighty trees first. He needed only a few side-to-side glances in his immediate area before he spotted a massive pine standing apart from many others. It had a certain age to it, and the tree's great size proved it had weathered many storms and withstood their many mighty windswept ways. There were a few other pines in the distance, but this one was only a short path away. It was standing there calling for his attention, and so it must have been meant to be…it would be the chosen one.

Before he could get any climbing done, however, there remained a serious problem for Little Turtle to solve. His wrists were still tightly bound, and even though the lashings were softer from the long period of an overnight in the rain, and most recently hiding submerged under the shoreline log, they still were not soft enough to move apart. To scale and roost high in his special tree, he'd first have to free himself from his bondage.

I need something sharp and solid. He looked around. Spotting nothing where he stood, he reluctantly returned closer to the shoreline to see if he could find something more substantial. Fortunately, he found much better medicine in the form of a split medium-sized boulder extruding a little above the edge of the woodland soil. The rock was surrounded underneath by a variety of soft green mosses and topped with splotches of gray and green lichens, giving it a semblance to a giant bird egg cracked open by the weight of another magical great force. With the center edges looking jagged and wide enough for him to place his wrists in between the split, he felt sure the Rock Spirit had called to him and signaled it would help. All he had to do was reply in kind. *I am coming!*

    Little Turtle moved quickly in a silent and cautious way. Checking for any signs of danger, he positioned himself directly in front of the boulder. The big rock provided a glimpse of promise, and he dropped to his knees ready to try to free himself of his leather restraints. But once he was closer to the ground, he was overcome by the faint developing aroma of his most welcomed taste of summer—a small nearby patch of blueberries.
    Blueberries were surely one of Little Turtle's favorites, but these weren't fully ripe. Nevertheless, they tempted him as an easy source of raw food for the taking.
    Without any more thought of his dangerous predicament or Gray Tongues' stipulation—no food or drink—he got up, mustered a scant bit of energy, and moved over to them. They were mostly green, but

despite their unripened condition, he reached for them with his tethered hands and grabbed as many as he could—including their leaves and stems—by the clutch full. *I am starving!* First, he ate one handful, then two. *I must have them!* They looked to be plentiful, and they helped to quiet his raging hunger, and even though bitterly sour, he gulped them down.

They helped him recover his presence of mind and remember what he had to do to free his wrists. He returned to the boulder, patiently waiting nearby. It was then he heard an ominous rustle just behind him and froze. It became the sound of danger. Someone was out there, hiding and waiting, just beyond his view. *Iroquois?*

In hindsight, even though the luring green berries had offered only a brief diversion, he knew he had made a major mistake. *The spirits must know.* He remained still and lowered himself to his knees. He watched and waited as his heart pounded. His fear-enhanced tremors returned while his slightly replenished stomach tightened into a ball as he slowly turned around to see if he could locate the source.

There! Again! The sound of a rustling branch was distinct. It was a soft sound, but there was no mistake. The rustling seemed to be creeping closer his way, as though whoever it was thought they were remaining undetected before springing out. *Why have I been so careless? Why have I done this?* The threat of a great danger was upon him and only a short striking distance away. *Where are they? Oh Spirits, I am sorry!*

Little Turtle knew his predicament was entirely of his own making. Only this time, as he waited, his mind darted from one thought to another. He barely had enough time to think about how he was going to respond when he came to his decisive moment. *Is this going to be my death fight?* His answer was—*Yes! I am ready.* As he stood to face his fate, without realizing it with his defiant resolve, Little Turtle had unknowingly stepped closer to what it takes to become a brave.

Despite the fact that Little Turtle's wrists were still bound, making him almost defenseless, he waited for the inevitable as the undergrowth tops moved once more. Many thoughts circled in his head. *What if this continues? Should I leap into action first?* As his muscles tensed up, the drama suddenly ended. A weakened fawn emerged from the underbrush, struggling mightily to continue to stand and greet its brand-new wooded world.

Relieved beyond measure, Little Turtle then noticed its mother standing in the distance, fearful for her newborn. She must have come down to the river for an early-morning drink and had to give birth shortly thereafter. However, in their own special way, they both taught Little Turtle a major lesson in survival. He simply had to remain focused with no more distractions. He had to continue enduring sacrifices and concentrate on getting his wrists free and quickly. He could not forget; he was weaponless and being hunted. Thanking both the deer and the spirits for their teachings, he moved back to the split rock. The shocking message had been well received.

This time the rugged rock halves called him back with more urgency. Without delay, he returned and got into a position to free himself. The open space allowed him to move his coupled wrists back and forth freely along the rock's jagged edges.

Because he was still exhausted, he rubbed the leather bindings slowly at first, but also to make sure he didn't cause any more injury to himself. He was in enough pain already, but he was in a mental hurry in this most vulnerable position in these menacing woods. With his eyes constantly moving from side-to-side checking for the enemy Iroquois, he kept his bindings forced against the rock's jagged edge. It was hard work.

The longer it took, and anticipating a possible attack at any moment, he moved his wrists back and forth much more briskly. His patience with this overall effort was rapidly evaporating. Even though he was getting better at sawing against different portions of the split edges, the longer he remained stationary and exposed in this open setting, the more frightened and frustrated he became.

Although Little Turtle could see the leather of the binding beginning to fray, it remained stubborn. He was getting tired from the back-and-forth repetitive motions, and had to stop and rest from time to time. As he did, he looked around for any more impending danger while recalling the painful sound of his father's defiant battle screams echoing in the cove. That haunting image, and his regret at not doing more to help, regenerated his getaway efforts. While pressing against the stone's jagged edges before him, he once again heard his father demanding him to run, which reminded him he still had a village to get back to.

The horror of that atrocity drove Little Turtle to try harder to keep his wrists separated as much as possible and to keep the leather taut. Even though he could see his work was beginning to pay off, it was difficult. Just when his arm muscles were burning badly and his shoulders felt they were tormented enough, the thinnest strand let loose.

Shocked at first and then using his teeth, he was able to unravel the rest of the strands, even though many were overlapped and tangled. When he finally shed the last of them, he felt a rush of fresh blood return to the tips of his fingers. He wanted to let out a victory scream. Once again, he held his tongue and looked all around to make sure he hadn't been discovered.

Assuring himself he was still alone and temporarily in the clear, Little Turtle threw the spent bindings into the rock's deep crack and moved straight over to where the welcoming pine stood waiting. The trunk was studded with a great many brown shafts pointing outward. The tree was many times wider than Little Turtle's broad chest and daunting in height. But looking upward showed it to be straight enough, and it appeared to reach all the way to touch the highest overcast clouds floating by. At last, he was ready to see them closer himself. If only he had the strength.

Little Turtle was surely weak and tired. Fortunately, the lowest branch came to his neck. All he had to do was to grab it, pull up, and swing a foot up and over it. It took more than one attempt, but he managed to do it. The branch he was eventually perched upon was strong and thick, and the trunk it stemmed from was tacky from sap drippings from many woodpecker holes drilled higher above. As he tried to better position himself, it wasn't long before the front of his almost naked body was smeared, gooey and sticky, as he straddled the branch. Little Turtle paid no mind. He was thankful to be off the ground. Besides, he knew the sap would help improve his grip as he moved upward and keep his moccasins from slipping.

Little Turtle made the best of it all and was happy to be able to use his hands again despite the circumstances. His wrists, arms, and shoulders were all sore, but his heart was anticipating the climb. Once he was able to stabilize himself and stand completely erect on the branch, he began figuring out how to make his ascent to the top while staying as close to the trunk as possible. His heart began to pound as he glanced downward and surveyed the abandoned path below him. No Iroquois were in sight. Except for Little Turtle's heavy breathing, all was quiet.

As Little Turtle stood there and collected his resolve, he noticed this tree had a powerful pine scent. The welcome aroma overtook his spirit and calmed his anxiety, which had continued unabated ever since the terror of seeing his fellow tribesmen attacked. Just making it safely into the tree without being discovered was another one of the many big hurdles he had overcome so far. He knew there would be more because he was still lost and being pursued. However, the sweet pine smell helped his lost soul, reducing the stress associated with it all.

Little Turtle was proud of himself for having made it this far, despite discovering he was much weaker than he realized. He had made his first big step in finding his way back home with the help of his newfound friend. Even looking straight upward to the top of the tree with its smaller dead and green branches intermixed above him found him becoming less worried. For now, he was safe, but not pain free.

That's because Little Turtle soon found that even the smallest stubbles of the nearby branches managed to poke at every part of him. The constant sharp stabs reminded him of the dangers of falling as well as his recent slashings and mental horrors as a captive. All the pokes and scrapes kept him vigilant for an Iroquois reemergence. Even a broken branch falling to the ground as he moved upward was not lost to him. He knew, if seen or heard, his savvy enemy could also climb.

While he carefully continued his determined ascent further up the pine, that strange sense of calm persisted. It brought about better thoughts like the happy time when he and his father last stood together in the cove ready to visit the spirits. The soft strength of the pine was proving to be a soothing companion, speaking to him with gentle sway. It was a feeling he hadn't felt since the morning of the last big buffalo feast. The unexpected experiences that followed were bad enough, but the loss of his father and the possibility that his whole village might also be lost had taken its toll. But once he found himself moving further up in this tree, he felt a degree of recovery.

For the moment, he was free and safe—except for the unseen spirits. They, of course, could deliver good or bad medicine at any time. There would always be uncertainties, but for the time being, this huge pine was supplying him with the good medicine he desperately needed.

    Carefully, he willed himself up the tree until about halfway to the top. After the latest sharp poke, he felt a fresh gush of blood move down his back. It was a good reason to stop and rest and let it trickle until it could start to dry. It was a good sacrifice for the spirits to see.

    As he rested, he was able to appreciate the panoramic scene the Mother Provider had placed before him and into his heart. He was above most of the neighboring trees and could better see the river moving a great distance away from him and the landscape across its other shore. It was an impressive view of a contrast between the movement of the blue river and the stillness of a continuous carpet of green treetops mixed with the glow of the morning sun—a view that was not lost upon his grateful eyes–until he spotted a small billow of gray smoke, and then another. They formed two robust clouds purposely created down the same side of the river as he was positioned in the tree, but a further distance downstream. Little Turtle watched for more, but they didn't come. Even though he didn't know who created those clouds, he assumed the enemy was close and they were signals meant to be seen.

    The sighting conjured up the remembrance of his recent fresh prints left in the nearby shore, the discarded leather bindings, and the ravished blueberries. They were all valid signs of his recent presence and surely would not escape the sharp eye of someone looking for his trail. The resulting baffling sighting of the two large puffs generated nearby caused Little Turtle to worry even more. Tired or not, he told himself, *I must keep moving and find my way.*

Regaining a little more strength from the brief but unsettling rest, he muttered, "I am ready." Little Turtle moved further up, mindful to try and get a better view of the flow of the river and the general vicinity of where the signal had originated. As he struggled through the shorter-spaced branches and felt closer to the spirits, he prayed they would talk to him again. His confidence sorely needed a boost. *Oh, Spirits, guide me home.*

The more he strained upward, the more the branches he reached for and eventually stood against got smaller, until one snapped under his weight. Alarmed, he steadied himself. Beyond the noise of the crack, the branches all around him were still scraping his body as they began to sway in a growing breeze.

Even though Little Turtle was now a little more than halfway to the top, he reasoned: *This is far enough.* He knew he wouldn't be of any good for his people if, after his risky and daring escape, he foolishly overextended his difficult climb. To fall and end up splattered flat on the ground as a future feast for a passing four-legged meat-eater, or a group of stench-loving flies, was an outcome he simply had to avoid.

From his new vantage point, he felt like an eagle with a full view of all things outward and of all things far below. There, he rechecked his position. He had lost all fear of losing his grip or his nerve, despite his aching and soreness. His truthful eyes were still sharp enough.

Beyond the river sights and the recent billows of smoke, he spotted what he believed to be the large bluff of the sacred cove far in the distance. He gave it a good look and finally realized what was wrong with the image. The bluff was on the opposite side of the river!

No wonder he hadn't spotted it right away. While he lay bleeding in the canoe and suffering from advancing shock, the Iroquois had crossed the river downstream before making camp. It was obvious to Little Turtle now, but that notion had not crossed his mind until this moment. He questioned himself. *Is it really the same bluff? What am I to do?*

From Little Turtle's position high in the pine, that bluff was the only one visible. If it were the tribe's sacred place, he would never be able to swim across, not with the state of his injuries. The river was moving fast.

Little Turtle's heart fell from the tree like a dead branch. Surely, he'd have to find a floating log or continue walking upstream to find a shallow bridgeway to cross and check out the bluff.

Little Turtle's mind shattered. He was exhausted and so distraught from the realization of how far he still had to go, with the enemy still possibly nearby, he thought of giving up—but only for a moment. *I am the son of a great chief. The spirits are testing me. I will sacrifice myself even more. The spirits will see this.*

With the powerful scent of pine resonating deep within his lungs and extending far into his nerves, he snapped back his remaining strength and remembered his vow to the spirits to find his way home. *I will make it so. I cannot remain within the strength of my newfound friend.* Their time spent together was coming to its end. However, as Little Turtle had made up his mind to continue, he felt an additional soft strength begin to grow in his heart. It was just in time. He knew his journey had only just begun.

Armed with a full resolve, Little Turtle backtracked downward branch by branch, scrape by scrape. For a while he thought he knew vaguely where he was, but his village was still hidden and unseen. During his long descent, he had plenty of time to wonder: *How am I to get there? Even if I were a bird, my wings would become weary, circling above, searching for my true path.*

Now, he was confused with what the Water Spirit had laid out before him. In times past, the great Water Spirit had always been willing to quench his daily thirst or offer him enough food to satisfy his deepest hunger. And, most recently, it had provided him with a safe hideaway from his angry renegade hunters.

But this same Water Spirit had not only taken away his tangible contact with the spiritual world when he lost the stone, but also had revealed its strength with a formidable barrier. In its own way, for its own reasons, the Water Spirit had reversed Little Turtle's inner peace provided by the pine and heightened his mounting frustrations.

Little Turtle decided: *If I am to become a brave, I must finish my way downward carefully and continue onward to my suspected cove location. I must tell my story. I need to find out if my belief of the sacred place is correct. I will satisfy the spirits by returning.* All the while, the smoke signal sighting made his determination more challenging.

After dodging more stabs on the way down, he stopped. He held his grip tight and took another long look. There was no sign of anyone coming. Nothing had changed, except he was slowly getting closer to the ground. Returning to Mother Earth meant that any steps taken away from the safety of this massive pine would mean more steps taken deeper into unknown danger.

From here on out, his journey forward would need an additional mixture of courage and grit. Each step would be filled with ample life-ending peril leaping out from behind any of the shadowy obstacles placed before him, especially when ample signs of his presence remained visible on the sandy shore.

Once Little Turtle reached the base of the tree, the firm forest floor of pine needles and sporadic green woodland plants extended a soft welcome-back feel as his foot reached the ground. He carefully surveyed his surroundings. Satisfied with its look, he turned back to the pine and touched its dark reddish brown, scale-shaped bark one last time. It was a grateful good bye.

 Little Turtle then returned his eyes to the depths of

the forest before him and softly tiptoed away from the tree's protection without bothering to remove the sticky sap and bark particles from his hands. They were reminders of his adopted friend providing him with a safe place.

As he moved along, his senses were on high alert. He continually moved his eyes from side to side, high and low, and listened hard for the slightest hint of someone intercepting his path. Before long, he became frustrated with not knowing his way without the visual aid of the river's course. He was in unfamiliar territory. To keep from losing his bearings, he was forced to move closer to the water, to keep it in sight.

Closer to the water he could once again see its long shoreline distances, including the great bluff across the way. In the process of finding a safe crossing, he spotted an area that could be shallow enough. Carefully, he moved toward it with great anticipation until he reached the point where he could clearly see the water was only covering a wide sandbar and then falling deep again, shortly beyond. Despite his disappointment, he spotted several large crayfish clustered together within his reach among the dark submerged rocks.

He paused and considered a quick meal. They were a huge temptation, as Little Turtle was still experiencing unrelenting pains of hunger. He envisioned crunching a few of them whole and relieving his aching stomach, but he remembered the incident with the deer and her fawn, and the teaching they provided. Instead, he swallowed hard and tolerated his hunger as his extended shadow, silently dancing atop the water's ripples, startled the crayfish, and shooed them away. The Water Spirit's tempting lurer was challenging, but Little Turtle trusted its renewed messages. With the food source out of reach, Little Turtle regained his resolve and hoped his demonstration of another sacrifice had pleased the spirits.

Remembering his ongoing quest to find his home, Little Turtle hastily took another glance across the river, hoping to see an alternate way to the illusive cove. But there were none. With no more time to waste, he hurried back to the edge of the woods to stay out of view. Somewhere, the winding river would eventually have to become narrow enough at some other place. Even an obstruction created by a strong beaver dam, or a cluster of fallen trees would help. For now, he had to remain vigilant and press on. He knew the Great Spirit and the rest of the spirit world would continue to measure his will. They were watching.

Little Turtle trudged quietly through the unfamiliar woods, swatting away more nagging flies and staying wary of any kind of enemy sightings. As he made his way onward, desperately hoping to find his way to cross the water, it wasn't long before he spotted a well-traveled shoreline deer trail. Gratefully, he took it. The hidden trail made his movements through the underbrush much easier and helped him to become completely sound free. It also gave him time to think of his father and obsess over his tribe. The idea that these invading Iroquois could possibly remain in the area with others equal in their evil intentions became more of a threatening thought. His heart was already black with sadness and grief, but guessing what other fearful things could happen shook his imagination.

Consequently, he tried to continue to move as quickly as he could. His many pains were great. His wounds were caked with dirt, his legs were weak. At times, the trail was harder to follow. Most of the time, he had to struggle to just keep the shoreline in sight. He knew not all deer trails moved along the water. Some moved to and away from it, so he had to not only watch for impending danger, but also pay close attention to the direction of the path and avoid any noise producing obstacles along the way.

Despite Little Turtle's multiple fears, combined with his constant labored breathing, he occasionally had to stop to regain his fading strength. Cautiously, he stopped once more. At this point, while listening intently, he heard something strange. *What was that?* It sounded like several unfamiliar chirps in the distance...but not precisely natural.

His nerves and neck hairs immediately bristled. On full alert, he waited to see if he would hear it once again. The strange sound reminded him of a call that was supposed to sound like a solitary bird making a quick series of territorial high-pitched calls. However, it was not coming high above from the tree branches as one would expect, or any natural sound he was familiar with that would come from a lower ground level height. *What is this?* Still hoping to hear it again, he waited. His weak heart began to beat faster as he paid close attention.

There! I heard it! This can't be what it is. It was odd

and unfamiliar as he conjured memories of the tragic ambush. He quickly fell to his knees. Once on the ground, his body became one like the low-lying plants surrounding him. Except for his inner trembling, he became as still as a branch. *More Iroquois? Are they over here? Have they found me? Or is this a special spirit's call showing me the way to follow home?* Little Turtle was unsure what kind of medicine was out there.

Alone in the thick woods, vastly troubled by the double loss of his father and the shaman's stone, worried for his village, and finding his way to the cove, Little Turtle looked up beyond the overhead branches and prayed again. Without his stone, it was another stressful appeal for help. *Oh Spirits! Hear me! Help me remain calm and strong in the face of all that comes to me!* Then he crouched lower and waited for what was to come.

During a long pause floundering in nature's continual mystery, Little Turtle recognized another new sound. This time it was the undeniable sound of a snort. *Was that from an anxious pony or maybe a frightened deer?* Little Turtle's strained his eyes to catch a better glance as he raised himself up. Then he heard another one of that unfamiliar bird's high-pitched series of calls. Now, he was sure. *This is not a bird. Who is this?*

An instant later he saw movement, then a shadow. He stood his ground. With his continuous stare, it appeared to be the shadow of a man. Then to his astonishment, he caught a glimpse of that same man following an open trail leading a pony, coming his way. Little Turtle didn't know what to think except this was another confusing and terrifying situation with his inability to escape. *Does my enemy have horses, too?* The answer came quickly when he was able to recognize the intruder, who must have been the source of the frightful disturbance. It was one of his own people. *Yes, I am sure. I know him! He's one of my fellow Miami tribesman!*

Without thinking, Little Turtle let out a shrill and stepped out into the open. The tribesman returned an ear-piercing shrill of his own when he realized he had found what he was looking for, Little Turtle. It was a joyful, overwhelming sight for both. The scout, who had recognized him at once, jumped on his pony and turned it toward Little Turtle. He spurred his pony on as quickly as he could, and without stopping, he confidently and skillfully reached out and swooped him up, placing Little Turtle soundly in front of him. Then the successful rider leaned forward and demanded, "Who did this to you?"

Besides Little Turtle's overall battered body, the scout had obviously noticed the boy's multiple wounds and bruises. Little Turtle turned and choked back his emotions, and like his father, uttered the only word he needed to…"Iroquois."

The scout whistled another series of odd bird calls as they trotted forward through the woods. Almost at once, another village scout came into view on horseback. Before long he too yelled a mighty shrill. It was another burst of sheer joy. Little Turtle mustered the same as best he could. Both ponies reared up in response to the sudden screams, as if it were a spirited reunion by all the living in the search party. It was justified. The scouts had succeeded in finding the long-lost son of their departed chief.

It was a short-lived jubilation, though. Little Turtle immediately found himself riding headlong through the woods and into an open savannah as a close threesome. He held on tight-fisted to the pony's flying mane and had no more thoughts about his weary, drained condition or his miserable wounds. Once again, he and the two scouts let out a series of victorious shrills as they galloped through the sparsely wooded terrain toward a known narrow sandbank further down the river, an area where the scouts knew the ponies could safely cross.

Another loud series of group whoops followed when they cleared the woods and turned their ponies towards the flowing river. Far across it, Little Turtle could see an area he immediately recognized. It was the bluff. At that point, the scouts hastened their surefooted steeds through the river and onto a well-established tribal trail homeward. For now, Little Turtle's horrific nightmare appeared to be over.

Chapter 12

The Council Fire

The group had moved across the river with relative ease. Once they splashed their way to the opposite side, the trail widened, and the scouts pushed even faster—as this was familiar ground even for Little Turtle. When the village finally came into view, Little Turtle was relieved to see it was still there. He was coming home. The two horsemen began their victory cries and yelping to gain the attention of their tribal brethren. Soon the joy of seeing and recognizing Little Turtle became a continuous wave of noise and excitement. One of their own had returned...alive.

White Sparrow was one of the first to come running to him with many soft tears, carrying fresh evidence of several self-inflicted sacrificial slashings on her forearms. It was her way of demonstrating her deep grief over the losses of her husband, and presumably, her eldest son.

She was a strong and silent woman, who worked hard like all the women of the tribe, but was grieving her losses. She was Little Turtle's spiritual leader, teacher, and the head of his family's clan. Despite her spiritual strength, her heart had been severely broken, and now her emotions had turned over and were spilling out with immeasurable joy.

Immediately after Little Turtle was helped down off his lathered pony, mother and son came together and carefully held each other tightly in unity and prayer, thanking the Great Spirit for bringing them together once again amid their fellow villagers and clansmen. Despite this public moment, the embrace remained theirs alone. She had feared the worst after the searching scouts' discovery of the murders and was jubilant that her son hadn't been one of the fallen. The back-and-forth flow of emotions provided by the reunion overwhelmed them both.

While his mother openly wept, Little Turtle's festering wounds and visible bruises were becoming a concern to all who had gathered around him. A few of the other women slipped away and brought back vessels of fresh river water for his ravaging thirst and to clean the worst of his filthy cuts and gashes, along with soft green mosses. Meanwhile, many of the men were guessing among themselves as to the origins of the significant injuries. Gray Tongues eventually arrived with an assortment of his sacred pulverized herbs for White Sparrow to apply to Little Turtle's most severe wounds before any more bad medicine could arrive.

Right from the beginning and all through the early

morning, there was a great stirring for retribution, and at the same time, many offerings of thanks to the Great Spirit. Throughout Little Turtle's life, he had never been the center of this much attention before and it was already becoming uncomfortable. He had always been a humble child, as were most tribal children, responding accordingly to the strict teachings by their clan elders. All Little Turtle knew before this day, besides humility, peace, and inner silence, was nature's generosity and his tribe's widespread connections with Mother Earth and her vast spiritual world. His extended time observing and learning from his father's leadership examples or nature's abundant teachings (mostly by himself) had never been anything like this.

    Little Turtle didn't consider himself a hero worthy of all this attention. He had survived his experience with no intention other than to satisfy the tribe's mandatory sacrificial vision quest to become a faithful brave. To be able to answer that call and eventually take part in a great buffalo drive or fight on behalf of his people was all he strived to do. It was part of his teachings and his culture. However, this welcoming celebration was an honor reluctantly received. More gratifying, his village was intact and unharmed.

    Gray Tongues, after passing his medicinal aids to Little Turtle's mother and acting in his role as the temporary leader of the tribe, announced an immediate beginning of another feast of thanks to the spirits for Little Turtle's safe return. Like all traditional celebrations, this was to be a village-wide observation for the good medicine for Little Turtle's return, and would devote more time for a solemn period of mourning for those who were lost in the ambush. Many stories would be told in their honor. Gray Tongues included in his message that an important council meeting was to be held with the setting of the sun with all the tribal elders. With the reasons for the ambush unknown and a response not clear, decisions would have to be made.

When Gray Tongues was finished delivering his message, all in the tribe knew two fires would be built that day. The first fire would begin in the customary open area in the central portion of the village where all large tribal celebrations or periods of mourning were held. Any remaining nearby stockpiled wood was to be gathered and brought to the giant fire site and a rapid bonfire would ensue. Loud rhythmic chanting and dancing always followed for the benefit of the spirits. Later, more feasting would begin, as the community did their best to demonstrate their appreciation to the spiritual world for a lost villager's return and for their slain heroes' safe journey into the mystic world of the Great Spirit.

When the sun touched the horizon, all the tribal elders were to begin to gather for the strategic council meeting. There, Little Turtle would be given the opportunity to speak of his visionary travels among the spirits and reveal the source of his physical sufferings. If he were able to speak with a true heart, his monumental story before all of those who carried the tribe's greatest influence would help carry over to what would be done next. During that time, the council would also begin talks about their choice for a new chief.

Gray Tongues repeated his message several times

as he moved about the assembled tribe, so all those who needed to hear his words did. It would be an important time for the tribe on many fronts.

The second fire would be for the council meeting. It would be in a central location inside the village's meeting lodge, which was a simple but large circular hut, based on the same style and materials as a typical family hut. This special meeting place was reserved only for the wisest of the village elders and included the most courageous and honorable braves to gather for all important tribal affairs. These meetings were held in secret. Common concerns for gatherings of this type were concerns regarding tribal feuds, war party decisions, trapping and trading issues, buffalo hunting opportunities, and more frequently, airing grievances about the white man's increasing advances.

The elders' council fire was typically much smaller than the village bonfire but just as important. Its flames were primarily used as an invitation for the tribal spirits to take part in the council's decision-making. If the fire was active in this setting, the presence of the spirits was always possible. It was up to Gray Tongues to verify not only whether they had answered the council's call, but also whether they had been a part of any of the council's later decisions.

Little Turtle didn't have an overly extended time to stretch his stomach, continue to slosh down as much drink as he could hold, or completely enjoy the outside celebration on his behalf. Once the sun's light was beginning to reach the tree tops and the council fire made ready, the hut was quickly filled. There was a high degree of anticipation associated with what they might hear. And, Little Turtle would have his opportunity to reveal what happened in the cove.

It wasn't long before he found himself being helped to the hut's opening. Standing at the entrance, he saw the flames were already dancing and the most important members of the council were already in position, sitting around the fire's stone boundary. Gray Tongues was positioned where the light of the flames illuminated the hut at its brightest.

With further assistance, Little Turtle entered the hut slowly and anxiously. His trembling had come upon him again. He was tired and nervous, not knowing what he would have to do or say and not disrespect anyone, including the spirits. Internally, he was filled with as much apprehension as he had experienced during his first meeting with Gray Tongues. However, this occasion was different. He guessed there were at least forty, maybe many more of the tribe's most elite, all packed closely together. As he glanced about, he could feel their heavy stares, watching his every move and eager to hear his story.

Little Turtle had never attended a meeting such as this and knew none of this hut's settings or any of its sacred rituals. Tribal youth were always excluded, but since he was the only witness to the brutal attack and murders, he had no choice but to prepare himself for what all those faces were waiting to hear. Despite his many years of keeping to himself, today he was to become an important storyteller.

As the son of a chief, Little Turtle obediently held tightly to his father's will and approval. Even though he rarely spoke to those other than members of his clan, here he was obligated to tell his personal story to men he considered strangers. His tongue had to be straight. Unfortunately, or fortunately, the vivid images of all he had seen, and who had fallen within the cove, dead and desecrated, were still strong. He could have much to say if he could rise above that painful, dark memory and his mounting tremors in front of so many chosen ones who needed to hear his words.

Little Turtle was still very weak from his unhealed wounds and hardly able to stand. He hoped the spirits would grant him more courage and help him remember all the truth of his story as he moved further into the hut. At the same time, he was grateful to be able to speak for his fallen father and the others, who as far as he knew were still suffering in the shadowy world of the Great Mystery. He knew many decisions would be derived from the fullness of his words; most of all, he hoped by revisiting his dreadful clash, he would be able to help those he revered come to a restful stay alongside his ancestors.

As Little Turtle waited for Gray Tongues' instructions, he wondered: *Is this what the Crane Spirit meant by "You must avenge your father's savage death..." to retell my story from a darkened memory? Is reliving that attack once again before council what the spirit considers claiming my courage?* Little Turtle didn't have any time to wonder more. Gray Tongues spotted him and signaled for Little Turtle to come forward. As he did, he felt all eyes present following his every step.

Once Little Turtle was escorted and seated in a prominent position next to Gray Tongues, despite Little Turtle's mix of anxious fears and gritty determination, a cold sweat started to encompass his entire body. Sitting this close to the tribe's "wise one" was humbling. He crossed his arms and covered his eyes with his hands. He wanted to hide. Others may have believed he was retrieving his story.

All was quiet, giving Little Turtle time to peek between his fingers and take note of the variety of those around him, one by one, many with war wounds of their own. His knees and back ached as he waited, surveying those closest. Little Turtle glanced about to see if there was anyone he knew, but the faces and eyes were many and seemed to blend in together except for those in front. Most of those eyes looked ancient and weary.

A few other council members sprinkled throughout the group possessed much sterner faces. Those included the dog soldiers who identified themselves with their faces painted in a most striking way, adorned with many thin alternating red and white stripes extending straight down from the top of their foreheads all the way to their chins and completed with a thick wide black paint across their eyes and nose stretching from temple to temple. It was an effective look for anticipating the possibility of war.

All others Little Turtle could readily see had their bodies adorned with body paint in some way, including their finest collection of colorful beaded necklaces and head feathers. A few others, who were more aged and further away from the fire, had wrapped themselves in light blankets, protecting themselves from the expected damp humidity generated from the bare, hard ground. Those same ones looked slightly distracted, anticipating their turn drawing upon the sweet smoke of the council pipe being passed around from left to right. For Little Turtle, the display before him clearly demonstrated the importance of this council; all were waiting with heavy hearts to react to Little Turtle's words.

Even with the bright fire, the inner contents of the hut revealed a continuing gloomy and foreboding setting for one who, only hours earlier, had found himself in the throes of a bloody battle and a harrowing escape. He found it to be a place where the dark brown wooden walls, filled with a soft blue haze of the fire smoke trying to escape while holding in the pervasive smell of strong tobacco, at times looked to Little Turtle as an illusion. The many humans gathered throughout the floor sitting so tightly together in their wide circle–had all blended together creating an appearance of one–a powerful force for Little Turtle to overcome.

Worse yet, he was still wrestling with the growing grief from such a quick and violent episode that turned his whole world upside down. The loss of his father was particularly devastating, and that reflection kept urging him: *Do not be afraid…be not afraid.* For it was clear Little Turtle's decisive moment was near. While he hoped he would be able to stand tall, he clung to his father's cherished words: "You are a part of me…and I am of you." Those few words helped the most.

Gray Tongues, as the ceremonial leader and helped by another elder, slowly stood up. Hunched over, he pulled out his most fragrant scented dried herbs and fresh green tobacco leaves and dropped them into the flames. They flared and crackled as they cleared the heavy air and signaled to any spirits hovering nearby the importance of the upcoming council meeting.

Next, he reached for the sacred tribal ash-filled gourd in his medicine basket. The ashes from the sacred vessel began every council meeting ceremony. It held the tribe's sacred ashes over many generations of council fires. These were the revered remains of the spent wood burned and preserved from countless important council fires over the years. This was a symbolic opening ritual that physically connected the tribe's many council meetings over the ages, uniting the tribe's ancestors with the present-day elders. Gray Tongues carefully sprinkled a couple of small handfuls of these ashes into the flames.

As they were added, the memory of many more faces and voices, which virtually tied together the tribe's long and colorful history into this one fire, all came alive again. The offering was a visual hand-me-down connection binding the pages of the tribe's unwritten past, from the long-standing past to the present. It was an honored tradition to keep their ancestors' identities and memories alive and set the tone for the importance of this day's council hearing.

Once Gray Tongues finished the ritualized introduction and tucked away the sacred ash container, he began a simple rhythmical chant in which the others eventually joined in, as their spiritual leader took his place back down on the earthen floor. While the chanting continued, Gray Tongues picked up a pair of deer antlers and held them high in his outstretched arms, to draw any reluctant spirits into the hut. Once satisfied the tribal spirits were indeed receptive and present, he motioned for the chanting to stop, whereupon he began to softly sing a special solemn song only he knew. Little Turtle perked up and watched in awe. Since he knew the tribe did little without the spirits' guidance beforehand, he thought Gray Tongues must be reciting their very words.

Little Turtle remained quiet and spellbound throughout his leader's serious tone and rhythms. After being mesmerized by the shaman's actions, he hoped he would be able to remain strong and still remember all the words of retelling his story to the others. This brand-new council experience was particularly unnerving, as Gray Tongues' chants were intimidating enough.

After Gray Tongues finished his last chant, there was a brief period when no words or sounds of any kind were made by anyone. Little Turtle felt the rising tension within the hut's walls as he looked upon those within his range of view. The whole place had a feeling that the force of war and great revenge was about to be unleashed. He saw the excitement and heavy breathing and nodding in anticipation of what was to come next from the great shaman. Gray Tongues then broke the long pause with an inspirational story of his own in the now smoke-filled hut.

He told of a brave forefather, with the likes of Big Turtle's character, who was wounded in battle and unarmed due to tending his serious injury resulting from an enemy's arrow. The brave was still physically able to prove his courage against the one who inflicted his injury by grabbing and breaking off a low-hanging branch from a nearby tree and charging the one responsible for his suffering with only that harmless piece of wood. Before his enemy could redraw another arrow and shoot again, the tribal warrior was able to achieve "coup" by tapping the enemy on the shoulder with that simple branch in defiance of death before he was able to escape without receiving another shot.

This extreme feat of courage, a brazen defiance of the fear of death and seen by many who returned safely from that battle, was used by Gray Tongues as an example of a strong future chief, one the tribe would need to keep safe in these turbulent times of hostile interferences. Gray Tongues knew in his heart that Little Turtle would have a strong story to tell once given the opportunity. He knew the tribe's future depended on a wise decision afterward for a new leader, while appraising those responsible for the loss of the current one.

After Gray Tongues' captivating story, there was silence again, except for the soft sounds associated with the passing and drawing upon the tobacco pipe. A great tension was rebuilding within the hut. Gray Tongues added more dried leaves and herbs to enhance the embers with the scent that would surely continue to please the present spirits. He then passed his remaining tobacco to the others and motioned for Little Turtle to stand and speak.

All eyes became trained upon Little Turtle, as recollections from the recent frightful hours quickly enveloped his darkened heart once again. Strangely, he could feel the warmth of his father's spirit entering his pores as he reluctantly tried to straighten his legs before they buckled from his weakened state. Remembering his father's encouraging pat on his shoulder before entering Gray Tongues' hut gave Little Turtle confidence that he could face this current challenge. Taking a deep breath, he knew he had to move away from his prevailing sadness, overcome his physical condition, face his elders with conviction, and repeat the horrifying truth in all his words and for all those before him to know, forevermore.

    Little Turtle stammered with his first words. Then he stopped, trying to hold in his tears as his elders waited. Never had he been called upon to recount a story as important as this. But his nervous stumbling was only momentary. His anger at failing to reveal a great personal wrong overtook his temporary weakness. Nothing else mattered now, and he found an inner strength to brush away this awkward feeling. He was speaking for his father and the others. He used their voices to remake a start.

    Recovering from his emotional stranglehold, Little Turtle retold the details of the ambush, including the only word his father said of the attackers—"Iroquois!"—before he motioned for Little Turtle to run. Gaining a little more confidence, and discovering that the more he spoke, the more clearly he could speak, Little Turtle proudly recounted his father's courage and even of his own capture, incurring his most severe wounds while resisting being forcibly taken to the enemy's camp. With a wavering voice and a swelling of his eyes, he spoke of the two visions he had during this time while captured, most notably with the tribal spirit, the sacred sandhill crane, dressed as an eagle and escorted by his many crows.

He paused in silence to collect himself, and then spoke of the Crane Spirit's message to stand tall with the strength of a soft white pine and continue to fight for his freedom. He told of his escape with the help of the Water Spirit, who hid his trail and guided him to a deepened fish hollow to evade recapture, and the loss of his stone. He told of the help of the Pine Spirit who upheld his weight and supported his difficult climb to prevent being lost in his own territorial land by showing where the sacred bluff was concealed. He even included the split rock who helped free his hands, the berries who tried to nourish him, and, more important, the crayfish who tempted his newfound resolve.

But most of all, he thanked the shaman's stone that stayed with him in his darkest hours and filled his empty heart with courage to stay strong as he sneaked past his enemy captors on his dangerous and frightful crawl to freedom. While there was much to worry about with the intentions of the Iroquois, the stone had provided proof that the spirits were with him. He was ever thankful for its sharp cutting power to help him break free from his bondage. Finally, he said he would go back and ask the Water Spirit to help him bring the stone back to him when and if the elders said it would be safe to do so.

Of course, the final rescue was recounted, then Little Turtle stopped the story because there was nothing more to tell. It was a long and complete story, but the elders and the others listened intently without interruption. Many nodded as if to approve of his words because they knew the tone was coming from a straight tongue and an honest heart. They could see that for themselves as his story moved along. It became strong medicine.

When Little Turtle was finished and relieved from the strain of reliving the ambush, he sat down and was quiet. The experience had made him numb. Others in the group took their turns approving of Little Turtle's courage and honor, and respect of his visions with the Crane Spirit. Others told stories of war with other marauding peoples who had violated their great tribe before and of the need for retribution now for the horrendous crime that had resulted in the loss of their great chief.

Little Turtle sat still and listened intently as the discussion went on while the tobacco pipe continued to be passed. A few elders told of historical times, stories handed down from long ago, when the buffalo and the elk were plentiful, and of war times, both good and bad. Others reminded the younger ones present that much blood would be spilled during war time and much sadness would follow, when so many loved ones would inevitably leave and enter the afterlife.

Still others reminded the group how many times the tribe had to move northward to find more peaceful ways and how many times the spirits were slow to help win back their tribal losses. The Miami people were a proud and powerful tribe, but it was hard to please all the spirits; and they reminded the others, it was becoming harder to call the spirits to answer for all the suffering and enduring pain of the lost braves, including the women and children, to the white man's diseases, forked tongues, and iron weapons.

The session lasted far into the day with much still unresolved. However, many spoke of Little Turtle's actions and felt he had passed into manhood and achieved true warrior status. As a tribute, when the pipe came around once again to Gray Tongues, he handed it to the courageous young speaker. Gray Tongues nodded in approval, and Little Turtle was ready for his first taste of its full effect. Little Turtle hesitated, but responded by partially inhaling his first puff and passing the pipe on, while listening to many others wanting to find the Iroquois who made this attack and remove them from their hunting territory. Thanks to Little Turtle's words, the group had become passionate and hungry for action.

The consensus within the council became that if any of these people were found, they would have to be destroyed. And if after battle, any were captured alive, they would be brought back to the central village for a harsh torturous public display of justice served without any mercy for their vile trespass and wanton murderous acts. The elders knew the youngest of the braves, not present at this council meeting, but learning of the truth, would call for the most violent blood-riddled retribution possible. That would certainly mean almost any ingenious public torture and long-term sustained pain imaginable would be justifiable, and a good share of the elders voiced agreement.

A couple of the more visionary warriors soon spoke up and invoked their battle wisdom to suggest a basic plan to continue actively searching the forest and patrolling the waterway for signs that this treacherous Iroquois band was still in the area or returning to increase their beaver bounty. They knew that satisfying the white man's needs was not easy and the beaver harvest was getting scarce elsewhere. However, despite the evil desires of groups like the Iroquois and many others, the beaver were still plentiful in the Miami territorial waters. The rivers and shoreline evidence proved the beaver here were still many, and it was understood more invaders would eventually come.

    At the end of the council, although a new chief had not yet been chosen, the tribe had declared war upon this group called Iroquois and would meet again later to request the help of the spirits of the forest and water to find this evil band and grant their aid to win their battle for a just vengeance.

    Gray Tongues gave a final solemn prayer to the Great Spirit, then all present exited quietly. Most went to the ongoing bonfire and informed the others that not only was Little Turtle now to be considered a tribal warrior, but also the tribe would follow upon a narrow warpath aimed at the select Iroquois group. Proper wartime chants quickly ensued. Little Turtle was the last to exit his first council with a fresh taste of tobacco on his lips and a swelling in his heart. He felt proud of his storytelling and the decision of the tribe. While a new chief was not yet decided upon, he felt his time as a new brave would be time well spent. As far as he was concerned, there would be no more apprehensions. Better yet, he felt this would not be his last council fire as a brave new warrior.

Chapter 13

The Shaman's Plan

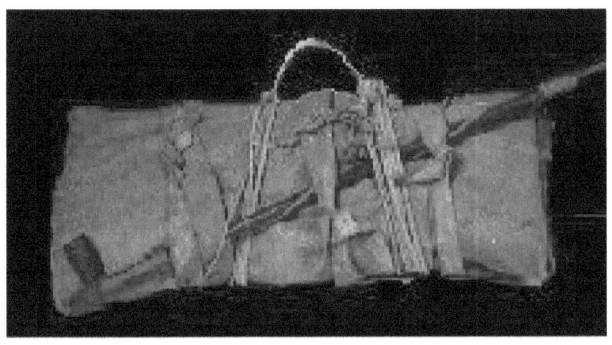

After Little Turtle's story and spiritual visions were revealed in front of the council fire with the elders, he was back at the great bonfire and enjoying, as best he could, the benefits of the feast and a tireless ceremony honoring his return and news of the warpath. Many others were also calling for a signal from the spirits for their help with the tribe's choice of a new chief. The Miami tribe was large, and with hundreds of seasoned warriors, there were bound to be many candidates to choose from.

While the earlier council's choice of a new leader had been indecisive, it was a good beginning. However, they had been diverted by the mystery of the murderous attack and circumstances. Little Turtle's words had been well received, but did almost nothing to help come to a clear conclusion for the tribe's replacement of its chief.

After many more bonfire stories, it had been agreed—

tribal wide—that there was much yet to consider. Even all those in attendance in the decision-making hut, aware that these were perilous times, knew there would have to be at least one more council fire, maybe more, until an overall majority agreed on who the new leader should be. During these anxious times, the calling for a powerful and gifted leader was paramount.

Little Turtle was savoring his own testimony of the events he had experienced and thankful the group had accepted his heartfelt words. At least they had a clear idea who was responsible. At the great village bonfire, he tried his best to help take part, despite his limiting pains and lingering sorrowful images, with the chants sung by his fellow warriors and the food and drink provided.

At one point, while he was resting with his grateful family and many friends, he noticed Gray Tongues hobble away from the group. Most of the time he was a solitary figure, an aloof participant in these types of village affairs; that is, until his wisdom was needed. His social distancing during this celebration, when he had been acting as a temporary leader, got Little Turtle's attention.

Later, when the ceremony's rituals were winding down, one of the elders from Little Turtle's own clan approached him and said, "Come…follow me."

Little Turtle, although puzzled by the request, did as he was instructed. The order came from none other than Spotted Bird, who was his mother's eldest brother and was still ailing from wounds suffered long ago while taking part in a disastrous buffalo hunt. It had been filled with bad medicine. Spotted Bird survived a serious trampling from an uncooperative and temperamental herd. If this well-respected member of his clan wanted anything of Little Turtle, he would be more than happy to comply, despite his own present handicaps.

As they moved slowly from the village, Little Turtle realized they were following the same path that led to Gray Tongues' medicinal hut.

Spotted Bird stopped and paused in a sad reflection. With the look on his uncle's face, Little Turtle thought it might be a silent reverence of the many days gone by when Gray Tongues, with his strong medicine, helped try to heal a few of Spotted Bird's most severe injuries. All the tribe had worried about his recovery, and when his bad medicine continued, it became his last hunt. It was an awkward moment for Little Turtle, but he understood.

During this short pause, Little Turtle wondered why he was even here. *What have I done?* It was enough time to recall his own pain, still lingering within his heart and throughout his body. However, the sad stillness was brief. Without any other words, the aged elder pointed to the simple hut and said, "Go inside, young warrior. Gray Tongues is waiting for you with messages from the spirits."

Little Turtle didn't know what to think. *Are the spirits angry with me? Were my words inside the council not strong enough? Was my story believed to be forked? What could these new messages be?* Little Turtle was confused, but said nothing in return as he watched his once strong uncle begin to make his way back to the village.

Gray Tongues was indeed waiting and prepared. Inside, his small fire was already burning, and the aromatic plants were emitting a strong, vibrant smoke as Little Turtle cautiously entered the hut. Gray Tongues signaled for his tribe's newest brave to sit across from him as before with the fire burning directly between them.
    Once Little Turtle was in place, Gray Tongues did not wait long before he added more magic on the fire, making it sparkle and flare. Little Turtle only had time to believe the spirits were nearby before Gray Tongues began to chant. When the great shaman was satisfied the spirits indeed were present and listening, he began a low-pitched song as if he were telling them another story.
    Little Turtle waited patiently in honor of Gray Tongues' manner of communicating with the unseen world. It was a style like he used at the council fire of the elders, except it was for an audience of one and much more dramatic.
    With the spirits fully attuned, Gray Tongues took a long look at Little Turtle, as if sizing him up, and began to speak to his young brave directly.
    "You have suffered much…and survived a violent capture from a hostile group of intruders. You have seen with unfailing eyes as your father fell along with the others in battle. Your father was brave and received many grave wounds before he breathed his last and discovered the sacred air of the Great Mystery. Our scouts found their desecrated bodies, and we helped prepare and ready them for the afterlife. Your mother and Spotted Bird will take you to where they are resting when you have more strength in your body."

"When your father fought, he struck many of the enemy with his knife. The scouts found much blood on it that he left behind. These intruders did not take your father's hair or knife. He must have shown much courage. They ran like frightened squirrels and left his things behind."

As Gray Tongues spoke, Little Turtle's eyes welled, and he began to slump. His heart was already heavy, but he listened hard. "Our scouts found your father. They said besides being wounded with arrows, he was clubbed and slashed with the enemy's knives. Eventually our chief stopped lashing his blooded blade. It was a quick death."

Gray Tongues noticed Little Turtle's reactions to his words of his father's death and added softer words to help lighten his heart.

"Your father's body remained undisturbed...without being disrespected. Despite our enemy's methods of war, these daring Iroquois must have had a great deal of respect for strong courage when they saw it. Your father and others like him who fearlessly give themselves up in a spectacular way are considered privileged to most tribes. It is believed to be bad medicine if disregard is given to an enemy who defies death in this way. For those like your father…a quick death is in recognition of their bravery. Even this battle-hardened group, these Iroquois must have understood your father's undeniable display of unusual courage when they saw it."

Gray Tongues paused and added more dried plants to the fire. With great deliberation, he picked up an eagle's feather, and then his pipe, as he pondered words he had yet to speak. Both watched the small flames flicker, and then Gray Tongues continued.

"I will give this…your first eagle feather…to you for your bravery among your enemy. You have earned it. You will wear it well, and with your strong heart you will earn many more."

Little Turtle's heart swelled, but he had lost his words. Instead, he continued to watch Gray Tongues light a twig from the embers and draw on his pipe bowl filled with fresh tobacco.

"The Water Spirit is great and powerful and a provider of many things. It knows much. You spoke of the Great Sandhill and the Water Spirit, and together they may have tried to tell you that the bundle was not meant for you any longer. Others may benefit from its lingering power."

Gray Tongues paused again, but only long enough to turn and reach for another object near where he was sitting. "Here is another medicine bundle, which I give to you. It is more powerful than the other…it belonged to a great chief. It has provided much courage and power in guiding him through troubled times and reaching the spirits."

As Gray Tongues held the bundle, he fell silent. When he continued, he calmly informed Little Turtle, "This bundle…was your father's."

Little Turtle looked up in disbelief as he brushed his watery eyes.

Gray Tongues patiently continued, "The enemy did not know it was there or they might have destroyed it. They could have been distracted, ready to run like 'tails up' deer. They left many other things on the ground in their haste to avoid being discovered.

"The spirits and I say it was meant to be, and we are passing this bundle on to you. I have added more power to it, and the spirits have agreed. As with our traditions…you will find something each from the plant, animal, and rock worlds. These will all help to protect and heal your spirit. Now that you are a brave, there are also extra arrowheads, a flint for fires, and your father's own sacred spearhead to replace the one the Water Spirit has claimed for a distant other.

"Your father's pipe and tobacco are here, and as a new brave, you will use his pipe and we will smoke the tobacco leaf together. Today and forever with this pipe, he will still be able to touch upon your heart."

Little Turtle watched as Gray Tongues showed him how to fill his father's pipe, light it, and draw the smoke deeper into his lungs. Little Turtle grew dizzy as he did so, not like the first time in the council meeting when his smoke was never fully inhaled. Despite the new effect, he was able to pay attention to Gray Tongues as he explained the ways of the pipe. He told Little Turtle this was to become the living breath of the Great Spirit and the way of peace and freedom and help with all future decisions.

Gray Tongues then continued, "The council elders and braves believe you spoke with a true heart of the visits by the great Crane Spirit, and their help will make you a great warrior and leader of men one day. We have had many good scouts looking for this band of Iroquois strangers since the council ended, and you know we have made a war upon them. Once we find them, we will return our justice to them. Soon we will pick a new chief, but there is still much discussion."

Gray Tongues took a long draw upon his own pipe and after a prolonged exhale continued, "You…Little Turtle, will be a warrior with us as we seek to find them. It will be your first warpath. We do not make war with all the Iroquois. They are a large and powerful group of tribes who live a long path away. We would need a great many warriors to fight them, and much pain, death, and sadness would come if that happened. But the band that disgraced our chief must be punished. The elders, warriors, and spirits have all agreed."

Another long pause came with the addition of a few small pieces of nearby wood to the fire as Gray Tongues concluded, "Once we find them, if they are still nearby, you will be our truthful eyes of justice for the spirits. You will need to point to them as the ones…but only if true.

We do not make war with all strangers—only those who raid our territory, our people, and harvest our beaver without counsel."

Little Turtle looked at Gray Tongues in awe as he spoke all these words. Little Turtle was beginning to realize the Water Spirit was still his wise friend, as he must have known his father's bundle would eventually be passed on. Now he had heard straight from Gray Tongues what his first warpath was to be, and it would include words derived from his truthful eyes.

Little Turtle's prayers had been answered in his quest to be able to actively help his tribe with hunts and battles, no matter whether it be looking for the wandering buffalo or a perceived enemy.

With his last words, Gray Tongues signed that he was finished, and extinguished his pipe while motioning for Little Turtle to do the same with his. And, as the light of the small fire was growing dim and the wise words had grown still, he passed the new medicine bundle across the glowing embers to Little Turtle's outstretched arms with these parting words:

"You must keep this bundle and its strong objects as a secret only known to you and the spirits. You alone…will add one more secret ingredient to make this bundle completely your own and ensure good medicine will follow you in all that you do."

Gray Tongues finished his private session with, "The Crane Spirit spoke of the soft strength of the white pine, and so it must be part of your bundle…be it a longleaf, sap buds, or bark. It will be your guide in this life and in war to always stand tall. With it, you will not fear the darkest winters of your life. Always keep your new bundle wrapped around your shoulder and behind your back, so it is closest to your heart. It will help you to wear your feather upright and proud. And remember…our grandfathers' teachings passed down through the ages…as a warrior, you will learn from the animals, the land, and the river. You must respect all things of Mother Earth as if they were from your own heart. All men and all the spirits of the earth are equals. According to the spirits, we are all connected. As a warrior, you must continue to seek wisdom in these things…and learn from even the dullest, for they all are our teachers."

When Little Turtle got up to leave the shaman's hut, it was with a true warrior's heart—glad and full—for the benefit of his tribe. Not only were the elders proud to have learned of Little Turtle's heroic efforts, but also, he was told the spirits had looked fondly upon him on this celebratory night. Gray Tongues may have caught a momentary glimpse of a future heir in this young steadfast brave when he heard Little Turtle's words in the council with the elders. As he did, he reminded Little Turtle of the power of his father's bundle.

"It will guide you to better days. You will have to trust its power in your heart."

As the two villagers parted, a wolf's haunting howl came across the distant woods, silencing a chorus of active crickets nearby. The call was another signal, to anyone within earshot, that could have easily been interpreted as a grim reminder of the troubling stories as foretold by Father LaFleur and many others. But tonight, instead of taking the howl as an ominous warning, Little

Turtle in his euphoria, clutching his well-earned treasures, heard the howl much differently.

He stopped to hear more. Tonight, the wolf's distant howl was coming from another leader, speaking in a language he understood. The effect generated a strange new magic. The distant insight of the howl echoed Gray Tongues' inspiring words from within: *We are one,* but the wolf's message also helped Little Turtle realize his long-standing tribal calling was still calling—stronger than ever before.

Adding to the moment, his father's image and strong words also returned: *Act like a leader and you will become one.* The combination of the shaman's encouragement, the meaningful howl, and his father's enveloping image claimed Little Turtle's heart. The impact convinced him he was ready for whatever the spirits needed. His nerves tingled as his mind calmed, and he became focused upon his village. With a newfound determination, he gathered himself and headed homeward, reassured, and comforted with a warm cloak of courage. He was ready.

Chapter 14

A Truthful Eye

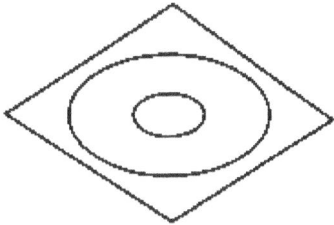

With Gray Tongue's private counseling reveal, and the prospect of an important warpath to begin, Little Turtle's night passed long and slow, offering little time for his many physical wounds to heal. Sleep was evasive and his pain abundant, but by morning, Little Turtle's story had created strong tensions and rabid calls for revenge throughout the village. The topic of the Iroquois attack continued to pass back and forth long into the day. Without question, one of the groups of the Iroquois Federation was responsible for the surprise attack and the death of their honored chief. The discussions included many possible remedies. All day long, runners and scouts came and went. Later, another council fire was lit, but no enemy was found, nor was a new chief decided upon.

Little Turtle, despite his lack of sleep, emotionally he had grown a fraction stronger. Besides hoping to track down the responsible Iroquois, he was also eager to know who the tribe's choice for his father's replacement would be. Everyone knew there were several qualified braves to choose from, and the continuing oral stories for and against were many. Even though this choice was in its second council fire in the making, all the elders knew that, in the end, a strong chief would eventually appear from that important decision-making hut. For Little Turtle, despite the wait and uncertainty experienced by all, he believed his father's power and influence would be hard to replace.

During this period of indecisiveness, Little Turtle's concern for Many Winds returned. He wanted to know who was tending his father's ponies, especially his favorite. He hobbled about and checked the familiar grazing areas. The herd was found, but Many Winds was not among them. He checked with his brothers. They had no knowledge. Finally, he went to his mother for help.

She was returning from the river with a basket of herbal and medicinal plants she planned to use to help accelerate the healing of Little Turtle's more-serious wounds.

"Where can Many Winds be? I must see him."

"He is being taken to your father's resting place. There, he is to be sacrificed to help carry your father's spirit deeper into the promised lands. Gray Tongues and another are walking him to the site in preparation of Many Winds joining up with your father and the spirits."

"Where is that?"

"It is to be near the sacred burial grounds."

What she told him Little Turtle knew to be true. This was a common burial practice, usually done in secret, but he wondered if it had to be Many Winds. He had to find Gray Tongues before another hidden cicada sounded its unique chirp from high above.

Despite Little Turtle's weakened physical condition, he made his way to the large council hut close by and checked there first, thinking Gray Tongues might be consulting the spirits beforehand. No one was there.

Next, he made his way to the shaman's small hut. Nothing. However, it was at that site he spotted fresh pony and human tracks intermingled. He took it as a true sign and followed, hoping they hadn't reached the burial grounds. After more long and labored strides down the trail, he spied them: Gray Tongues, a young helper, and Many Winds. The pony was already tethered with multiple ropes and waiting for a war club's fatal strike to the head.

Little Turtle was mortified by the sight of the group, complete with a stacked burial pyre, waiting only for Gray Tongues' final signal and a flint's spark to send flames spiraling upward to carry the pony's spirit into the afterlife. Little Turtle reacted in the only way he knew how and let out a blood-curdling scream. Startled, both Gray Tongues and his helper turned and appeared apprehensive with the abrupt interruption. It was as if Little Turtle was alerting them of an intruder's attack. However, they quickly realized this was not so.

Little Turtle was unabashed and forceful as he moved closer to say, "You must stop! Big Turtle said I shall ride this horse when I became a warrior, but not before. My father wanted Many Winds to carry me into a battle, to help defend the tribe in my strongest way as he would.

This sacrifice will mean my father's spirit will never rest. Some other pony, strong but not so proud, not so young, can be carried on to the afterlife. My father said I was a part of him, and he was a part of me. I know this to be true, with his darkened blood still heavy in my heart."

Little Turtle held up his new medicine bundle. "Gray Tongues, you gave me his bundle. With your knowledge, you must know that these words are strong as the winter's winds."

It was a bold move on Little Turtle's part, with spoken words that carried far beyond the reach of the open meadow and well into the canopy of the trees, quieting even the cicadas. The shaman stood and stared at Little Turtle. He saw something, but said nothing. A tense silence prevailed between them until Gray Tongues finally replied, "You have a strong heart and the will of a hungry bear." And again, he paused with greater effect, until he instructed his helper, "Release the pony to this young warrior…bring me another strong enough to carry a mighty spirit."

Little Turtle was astonished, but relieved. His unconstrained passion had carried through. Gray Tongues' helper dropped his weapon and untied the pony. Without a word, he handed the last of the restraining ropes over to Little Turtle. No other words were spoken or needed. It was a respectful understanding, a truce, between the young warrior and an ancient shaman. With a grateful nod, Little Turtle and the sacrificial pony turned and hobbled back to the village.

Little Turtle kept Many Winds away from the rest of the herd, and decided to keep him in a quiet place near his father's vacant hut. Little Turtle stayed nearby under his watchful eye. There would be no horse stealing or mistakes. Little Turtle had decided this to be so.

Later that day, he gathered his few items and his makeshift buffalo robe bed and moved into his father's empty hut. All his father's items had either been given away or were destroyed. All that remained were memories. A few days later when he felt he might be well enough to ride, he approached Many Winds with steadfast intentions. The pony flinched, raised his tail, and pawed the ground, signaling he was not ready. Many Winds could be forceful, too. This pony reflex lasted for several more days, but Little Turtle was patient. He used no force. He knew there had to be an agreement.

After the series of rejections, Little Turtle returned Many Winds to the meadow to rejoin his father's herd where he again he was closely watched by himself and his brothers. Little Turtle believed Many Winds needed more time, and decided not to press him any further.

One early sunny morning, a scout came running on foot fast and hard into the village. There was much yelping and chatter afterward. The scout's words traveled fast throughout the tribe, and it wasn't long before Little Turtle's clan found the basis of all the commotion. The scout had found the warm remains of a small fire, fresh beaver entrails, and hacked bones associated with rapid skinning and consumption. Trappers of unknown origin were again within the tribal hunting grounds along the river.

    The fire looked to have been another source of a brief signal because the charred evidence was not from a long-burning campfire, full of charred wood and ashes—one that would unerringly point to the white man. Instead, this was a telltale spot from a small grass fire. Once a brief fire such as this was set and then quickly covered, the fire smoldered and created a large volume of smoke when the fire was re-exposed to air. This type of fire's sole purpose was to be seen from a great distance for communication. It was clear no Miami villager had created such a signal.

    It was decided a larger band of braves and scouts would return to the site and look for more evidence the mysterious hunters or trappers may have left behind. Where did they come from, or where might they be headed? All were certain that no Miami hunters had been previously in the area the scout had described.

    Upon a return to the site, by the eyes of many more scouts, and a more thorough review, it was judged from the remains of the fire, and the number of footprints found, that these were the remnants of a small group on the move. However, was it a small group of rogue French-speaking travelers who occasionally frequented the river, or another stray group of peaceful hunters from a neighboring tribe like the Potawatomi, Erie, or the Menominee? Or, more pointedly, could it be another hostile group like the Iroquois? Better yet, could it be the same enemy group they were looking for, still boldly lingering in the area?

    It didn't take much longer to discover the scant but

revealing impression of canoe bows upon the firm, damp sand near the shore, along with a few clear moccasin footprints. They were considered not of the white man, who typically used a distinctively thicker sole for steps taken on surfaces not found among natural forest floors.

    Little Turtle's tribe, and those tribes living around the entire Great Lakes area and even extending far into the eastern woodlands, all used a leather sole meant to feel the soft earth of leaves and grass, such as were typical of these forest and savannah floors. However, even with the soft soles, there were subtle differences between what Little Turtle's tribe wore and what was worn by other groups within the Great Lakes area. The tribes of the Miami and those neighboring them all wore a moccasin style that had wide fringed flaps around the outside of the shoe that at times could be a visible pair of lines in the loose or dry sand outside of the moccasin imprint.

    The fresh prints found by Little Turtle's party, however, were different. They did not display the familiar flap lines, because they must have been shorter. Instead, these prints clearly showed a small tag at the end of the heel, marking these prints as those belonging to one of only two tribes—both of which were from the Iroquois Federation.

Miami   Iroquois

    Those two tribes were the Senecas and the Oneidas.

One of these groups had ventured far from home, and judging from the visible evidence, may have been secretly moving around the region as recently as only a few hours ago. The scouts, recognizing this minute sign in the prints, quickly returned to the village to consult with the tribe on how they would react to the new information that another Iroquois group had returned. It was decided a larger force would need to be assembled and return to the site and spread out along the river. They also agreed they would focus on the larger known beaver huts and dams up and down the waterfront, as the animal carcasses found at the site proved the group's interest was still focused on mature beaver.

Sentries would be posted in those areas and all available canoes brought along. There would be no ponies. Complete silence would be necessary. If this group was the Seneca, the task of finding these people would be difficult. They were known to be crafty hunters and easily alerted to intrusions. For Little Turtle, if these were the same ones who had attacked his group and held him captive, it was hard to understand why they would still be moving around in this area after the murderous attack. It must have been that the harvest was going exceedingly well, and a trading site had been set up that was not a great distance away. There could have been other reasons. It was all an ongoing mystery.

    Later in the day, Little Turtle became aware that his fellow braves were planning to wait until just before dark and move under the last remaining daylight to be shielded from any of their random noise by the regular chorus of the evening crickets and frogs. They were hoping for an additional coup with the element of surprise.

    This plan carried a great risk, however, because it was believed by his tribe that a warrior killed during the dead of night might dwell (suspended in eternity) in a lower level of the afterlife. To skirt around that belief, the light of the night's current moon was a sign the time was right.

    The plan was good medicine. Whoever this still unknown group turned out to be, they would be easier to find with the aid of a moon on the rise, and a lasting revenge for those lost would justify the effort. If these travelers were so foolish as to be spotted, undetected, and remain near the shore, they would be even more unsuspecting of an early nighttime encounter. They too, more than likely, shared the same belief about death and darkness.

Many scouts—the tribe's expert "sign" hunters—accompanied by a designated group of braves went out that night in their canoes and patrolled the waterway, but there was no success. However, the second night was a different story, plus the moon was brighter. Another brief small fire was spotted out in the distance in the late afternoon before the rising moon was high off the horizon and the dusk had yet to find the sky. The scouts who spotted the smoke carefully memorized the configuration of the shoreline landmarks near the approximate location. The most prominent of these was a known cluster of three permanent beaver huts and several young birch trees recently felled by the animals, destined for their summer food supply. The Iroquois must have thought this site offered a great potential for many more pelts from the industrious and unsuspecting beaver.

    The scouts and the others made their way back to the village believing they were undetected, and alerted the most available braves and important elders with news of the latest sighting. The news created much chatter and excitement. Gray Tongues was one of those present. He would need to seek the war spirits' approval for the surprise attack and any other associated actions before anything more was undertaken.

    Gray Tongues briefly conferred with the elders, and then began meditating alone in the great central hut with the spirits. Meanwhile, the elder braves, who were the most knowledgeable of war matters and had already agreed to the plan, began enlisting a larger group of forty to fifty experienced fighters to approach the unsuspecting suspicious camp on foot. Another group of twenty more were selected to approach the camp area from the water and quietly ensure the alien trappers could not escape with their watercraft.

In the meantime, Little Turtle had been retrieved and made ready to be a part of the group that would advance by land. The scouts who had found the source of the smoke relayed the precise location to all the parties who were making ready for the raid. The only unknowns were the number of violators involved and who exactly these people were. The only fear was there could be many more others in support of the group still lurking elsewhere. It was obvious these people had been bold enough to communicate with another group situated at an unknown distance away.

By this time, many of the younger and more aggressive braves in the village were calling for much blood and a thoroughly torturous revenge, while the council elders were encouraging restraint. From a practical sense, these young advocates could not be a part of the nighttime strike. The Miami was primarily a peaceful tribe—unless provoked. The tribe was already enduring harsh times brought on by the encroaching white man, and any unnecessary feuds with neighboring tribes were not welcome.

The younger braves were reminded of the tribe's several moves resulting from warfare, starting from as far away as the territory referred to as "Indiana." However, they were assured if it were proved this band had caused the sudden death of their honored leader, their deaths in turn would have to be certain and sadistically long. The young braves understood the consequence.

Conversely, if it were shown that this group had been nothing more than a group of trappers carelessly trespassing, having nothing to do with the ambush, they could be spared. It was up to the circumstance and the amount of resistance displayed during the encounter.

Additionally, if more support were needed to handle a much greater force than what the scouts had discovered or anticipated, the young braves would fill in as reinforcements. That was the plan, and for the honor of the tribe, the elders made sure it was understood.

While the plan was mostly unpopular with the restless young braves, Little Turtle's participation in his first war party made the decision even more so. However, here again, the elders' judgment was an important one and firm. The decision for Little Turtle's participation should have been obvious to all, as it was well known he was the lone witness of the notorious Iroquois attack. A mistaken identification could become an opportunity for fierce retaliation for the error and could provoke an extended warpath. In that respect, the results had to be right.

Despite the young braves' reactions, it would be Little Turtle's duty alone, with his truthful eye, to make the identification. If it were found this group was to be in any way involved as the cove attackers and Little Turtle's captors, it would be his opportunity to see firsthand how the injustice of the loss of a great chief would be carried out. Little Turtle was more than grateful to be able to help on any level in anticipation of an exciting raid to avenge his slain father. He became confident and eager to do his duty.

Once Gray Tongues emerged from the central hut and signaled the spirits were in agreement, those who were to advance on foot separated into smaller bands of fifteen to twenty experienced braves and left the village, using established deer trails heading toward the river. Initially there were a few torches, but only held by those who were in the lead. They had to move slowly, as the moon did not provide that much light in the forest, and any noise had to be avoided. These braves knew the land and trails during the daylight, guided by the distinctive landmarks they could see, such as a simple decaying log or an ordinary clump of rocks. However, traveling at night was not preferred. With the moon not affording an easy glide through these woods, the group was uncomfortable and edgy. And there could not be any breaking out on one's own way by veering off the trail—at least not yet.

The moon became generous with its light pouring directly overhead when they stopped and made their weapons—knives, clubs, and hatchets—ready in hand and in mouth after the torches were doused. Arrows would be of no use in the subdued darkness. If a fight were necessary, this battle would be a hand-to-hand encounter.

The braves traveling by the river were given ample time to reach the site of the encampment before those on foot. If the intruders were there, the use of their canoes for an escape would not be possible. Meanwhile, those on foot would eventually fan out and surround the camp, making the only choice for the intruders to either surrender or stand and fight.

The Miami warriors moved in slowly and diligently, without a sound. The paddlers did the same in the water. The planned wide noose was tightening. All stood in silence with their hatches and clubs raised and ready for the leader of this raid, Yellow Dog, to give a sign to move in. He was an established and well-respected warrior, with much proven courage and battle knowledge.

Confident of a surprise, Yellow Dog moved in a slow tiptoe like manner and slightly ahead of the others. He stepped ever so lightly toward the area of the known fire ashes' location. He wanted to see his prey firsthand and would be the first to spring the trap, once sighted. Closer and cautiously, he moved with knife drawn. The others around him followed suit behind him toward the camp.

Yellow Dog readied himself to sound the battle cry, with the others hardly breathing, ready for the encounter.

But, alas, his signal never came. Yellow Dog discovered the camp deserted and gave a short whoop of distress as he searched around the fire's remains of tiny dots of charred embers still emitting random whiffs of smoke just a few feet away.

The others moved in and discovered the same situation. It was clear the hunting band had slipped away only moments beforehand, unnoticed. Yellow Dog was angry with this revelation and signaled for his band to be alert and check along the shore. The water group was also alerted to the first group's embarrassing and shameful predicament. This was bad medicine.

The intruders hadn't tried to use their canoes. They must have realized that their primary escape was sealed off, and made a run for it by land, well before Yellow Dog and his group were the wiser. Judging by the small number of canoes discovered, sunken and abandoned, the unknown enemy was another small group—ranging no more than six to ten individuals. They had to have realized they would be no match for a battle, and chose the forest for their rapid retreat.

In hindsight, this group was savvy enough to keep a sentry on careful watch, and once suspecting the bad medicine of being sighted by water, he had alerted the others, and all went into hiding to wait out a senseless confrontation. Such a group, used to traveling long distances in other tribal territories, would rarely resort to building a fire; but if one was necessary, they certainly would not bed down near it.

Everyone in Yellow Dog's party knew this group could be anywhere. Regardless, even if the hunted had a head start and were still within the vicinity, the Miami braves were confident. They all knew they'd hunt them down. That's because even though the moonlight varied and the abundant landmarks were difficult to see, Yellow Dog's band still had the greatest advantage. This was their territory, and they knew it well.

Little Turtle was excited by the thrill of the chase. He watched his leader closely as he instructed his band of warriors to look for any signs that would show the direction or directions their prey took. The moonlight was a help but, for that moment, it wasn't strong. A discovery would take patience and strong eyes. Yellow Dog signaled for the water band to search up and down the waterway for any swimmers. There could be no crossing on foot because this part of the river was too deep.

After a brief period of random searching, one grass bedding was found, as the blades in the small patch were still bent downward. Pelts and random food waste were also found scattered about, with no real effort to hide the evidence of their harvested furs. The appearance indicated this was to be their overnight site. Because they left in a hurry; nothing was hidden.

It was clear the renegade trappers hadn't been gone long. Yellow Dog shouted to those on land to find a sign of their trail's direction. He was sure the race was about to begin.

Thankfully many of Little Turtle's wounds had healed, and so far, he was able to stay close to Yellow Dog's every move. He hoped that would continue while they waited for the inevitable evidence of the suspects' trail to be discovered.

If a race was to begin, those to be pursued would soon find the Miami braves to be equally aggressive. It was chaotic and exciting. Many of the warriors lived for moments like these—the thrill of a beginning hunt—whether it be for man or beast. Little Turtle was particularly excited to join any war party. His excitement was rampant, typical of many of the young braves left behind in the village. The difference was, he had discovered he had an apprentice's mind, and he was watching and "listening hard" to all that he could.

Shortly, one of the warriors called out with a yelp. A sign had been found. One of the suspected hunters' lost arrows had betrayed him. In his haste, a tree limb had slapped his quiver and bounced the arrow out undetected as he moved in a crouched position through the tight terrain. A quick examination of the arrow showed a fletching of an unfamiliar bird feather pattern on the shaft. This had to be the elusive trail at least one within the group had fled upon. The fact that the arrow had not yet been claimed by the ground and remained precariously cradled between a single widespread branch said that Little Turtle's band was not far behind those fleeing.

The trackers knew this trail and moved quickly, making sure their quarry had not deviated from this path and might have stopped to hide. It was doubtful they would stop and fight just yet. It was too early in the chase. All the while, Little Turtle envisioned a hungry coyote stalking a jackrabbit trying to escape its death, to no avail. That vision spiked repeatedly in his head and kept him energized as he stayed close behind Yellow

Dog's strident steps.

Yelping and victory screams soon told what was happening with those in the front of the group. The hunted had been sighted, cut off, and met. Like the younger braves who were calling for blood, pain, and torture of the perceived enemy, Little Turtle found himself lost in his own excitement.

But not Yellow Dog. He was confident the yelping meant the enemy was still alive and now in hand. The group of handpicked braves on this assault had been chosen specifically for their seasoned reactions in the hard and unpredictable ways of war, and it had paid off. If torture was to be the result of this capture, it would be seen by the whole group, not a select few. That meant the unidentified intruders would have to remain alive—at least for a little while longer.

By the time Little Turtle and Yellow Dog reached the tightened circle of fifty or so triumphant warriors, two of the hunted already lay on the ground, severely bloodied with labored breathing, but alive. As expected, they had resisted at first.

There were at least four or five others, also bloodied, but defiantly standing strong. There was no mistaking the commotion; they were being held from further resistance by their sweating and excited captors. All had stopped struggling and were bravely ready to face what they believed to be the inevitable. With courageous faces, the enemy showed an inner will to try to endure whatever amount of pain that was likely to come their way.

The enemy's brave posture was a common act of defiance, and it was the same with the Miami, to try and deny their torturers any satisfaction from the pain being inflicted upon them for as long as humanly possible. It was an attempt to resist the torment without displaying any visual acknowledgment of the horrors they might be enduring, both for the honor of their tribe and the Great Spirit above. However, for the successful captors, the torture was a game meant to overcome that defiance. Overcoming the defiance in the quickest way possible was also the Miami way.

    When Little Turtle arrived, he at once recognized that this was the same general type of group that he had seen before at the sacred cove attack. These looked to be matching members of the Iroquois that Big Turtle had recognized, readily known by the distinctive headgear worn by all tribal males. All these captives were still adorned in that way within the tight circle of Yellow Dog's war party.

    Yellow Dog also knew of this group of Iroquois. They were called the Seneca. He knew their traits from war stories told by the tribal elders on various occasions and from Father LaFleur directly. These natives were known to have passed through these distant western waters before in their continuous quest to supply the white man's desire for more furs.

    Similar stories were being told by random traders and trappers relating to other serious encounters. All the stories included the Seneca's skills as a formidable foe in their earlier skirmishes, with many never caught.

    To further expand their trapping territory, it was primarily the Seneca who traveled extensively using the available river highways, namely the Allegheny, Genesee, and Tioga, and traveling by land on what was known by many tribal peoples as the Great Forbidden and Warrior paths.

    The Seneca, besides being bold and aggressive travelers, always wore their distinctive tribal headgear on their wide-ranging travels. Little Turtle had not known this beforehand, but these hunters with their tight-fitting skullcaps made from a combination of woven soft deerskin leather strands and dyed corn husks intertwined the mix with their natural hair, usually included one lone upright feather in the back. Because of the effort to make them, they were always worn. Aggressive in expansion, bold in warfare, and flamboyant in dress, tribal traits such as these made them a unique and fearsome group, who could easily make their presence known or not known, depending on their desire.

    For the current victorious captors, this small group of Seneca was a great prize. Vengeance would be well deserved, whether or not this group had taken part in the atrocity of the killing of their Miami chief. Death on this occasion was a real expectation. Whether it would be quick or slow was another matter.

    Yellow Dog motioned for silence and brought an excited Little Turtle through the circle of proud warriors gathered around the Seneca braves. Once the two stepped forward, the braves who weren't directly restraining the captives moved back, giving Little Turtle more room to test his truthful eye. He thought of the new medicine bundle secured around his neck and resting behind his back. It brought about the strength of the pine as he felt his father's spirit and power embrace him. He felt no fear. Fate was in his hands, and his heart was pounding strong.

This decisive moment belonged to Little Turtle. If he said nothing, the innocent might be spared many torturous actions and be quickly killed, as they were now proven fur thieves. Little Turtle knew repeated theft of any kind was always dealt with harshly, even for those within his own tribe. If this group were known as the ones responsible for the chief's death, the end for them would come unmercifully slow, all during the night.

Anticipation of Little Turtle's final judgment had reached its ultimate climax, with all eyes fixed upon him. Other than the heavy breathing by all present, the woods were quiet. Little Turtle stood alone, deep inside the circle of anticipation, within just an arm's reach of those being held. Carefully he studied each of the men captured.

Little Turtle had already believed he recognized their head dressings. And then, his truthful eye recognized without fail one of the braves—the leader of his captors. This one was the same one who had come over to him and slapped him backhanded while he was bound and standing on the shore. And it was he who had first held up a fresh Miami scalp with a blood-curdling scream, as they paddled away from the scene of the ambush. Little Turtle had seen him up close on those two occasions, and once again as part of the group when he was initially captured and carried off. The others looked equally familiar as he judged each—one by one.

The haunting memory of the two sentries also came

to mind as Little Turtle bravely took a step closer to his enemy to clear the darkness of all those horrific memories. He was not afraid, even though was sure he was again within the reach of these same marauders. With justice in his heart, he nodded his head, then let out a victory scream of his own at the top of his lungs. All the others in the group responded with corresponding unabated victory whoops.

    The captives' fate was sealed. They were henceforth doomed, and Miami justice would be carried out after they were returned to the village. The much predicted and most unimaginable torture devised would inevitably follow. It would be reserved for all in the village to see as public revenge forevermore. But Yellow Dog was angry. He wanted his own revenge for the Seneca spoiling his surprise attack and adding bad medicine by their initial escape. Yellow Dog had lost a valuable war honor coup. Therefore, there would be no opportunities for any future surprises or possible escapes on this dramatic night.

    Without hesitation, he ordered death for these invaders where they were standing for stealing their clansmen's spirits and stepped forward to the leader, who was held fast and closest to him. As a last act, the enemy leader spat into Yellow Dog's face. Unperturbed, Yellow Dog drew out his hunting knife. Little Turtle was taken aback, astonished at the sight of what he began to see and hear. Even though he did not take part in the process, he was torn between the horror at what he was compelled to witness and the desire for payback for his fallen father. His tribe had to come first.

    In the end, the reckoning finished in a grisly manner

that lasted several hours and consisted of many other torments used to intensify the brutality. It was clear the Seneca weren't the only group who could be experts at delivering unspeakable amounts of anguish.

Little Turtle saw firsthand how the aftermath of torture became a grueling contest between the two tribes: the victors inflicting as much pain as possible on their enemy, while keeping them barely alive while the captors tried to withstand the tormenting for as long as they could. It wouldn't last. Despite their attempt to resist the inevitable, it wasn't long before all the Seneca were dispatched to the Great Unknown in the most dishonored ways.

The war party's savagery ended with the gathering of the enemy's severed heads to be brought back to the village for a tribal display of justice well served. Little Turtle now vividly understood what his elders meant in their stories of the sorrowful ways of war. The lingering effect of battle always traveled both ways and was never forgotten, including the terrifying enemy's faces they encountered, and the sorrowful mourning of any comrades lost.

Nonetheless, once the long torture had ended, the warriors all screamed, yelped, and whooped in a death dance around what remained of the headless corpses spread out on the bloodied ground. For the aggrieved, this revenge had become an exciting cause for celebration. Despite Little Turtle's first revulsion at the horrific images that had seared deep within his memory, he had become battle hardened without ever taking part in the display that lay before him, other than using his truthful eye. This ugly, bloody confrontation had made him understand the visual meaning of "war."

   The warriors left the battered and desecrated enemy corpses where they fell for the nighttime flesh-eaters that would eventually roam into the area once the victors left. As they all retreated toward their village with joyful hearts and a continuous chorus of chanting, Little Turtle was happy to have helped the tribe find justice for his ambushed tribesmen, and thereby help supply the good medicine needed to allow their departed spirits to be at rest in the afterlife. Little Turtle gave thanks to the Great Spirit as they moved through the thoroughly darkened woods, as the moon had partially slipped behind the clouds. The muted moonlight, however, did not match their hearts, nor Little Turtle's. *Make me wise so that I may understand the things you have taught my people…*

   As the group moved homeward, Little Turtle had time to also give thanks to the Water Spirit for proving to be generous and for guiding him back to his village safely without any more contact with those same hostile invaders. He knew that with the punishment of these treacherous Seneca, his lost stone had held a much greater purpose, one that was not meant for him alone. He wondered if the Water Spirit would support fresh eyes to find it, and whether it would offer the same power and courage to the finder as he had been given. Only the Water Spirit would know.

   The elusive mystery of the stone and the many spirits that governed his life wasn't always clear, including the stone's future recovery. He was grateful the stone had buoyed his own good medicine when he needed it the most, and hoped it would do the same for the next brave one day. The Water Spirit would surely decide when it was ready for that to happen. His trust now lay in his father's stone resting safely in his new medicine bundle. *Will it continue to serve me during the rest of my days treading upon our great Mother Earth or be claimed by another spirit?* With no answer, Little Turtle's heart was left to wonder.

Chapter 15

Destiny's Answer

Eventually the war party all returned safely back to the village with stories to tell for those who came out to greet them during the night. Over the next few hours, the village would be clustered with the curious, eager to find out all the details of what had happened and observe the fresh spoils of war. Later, when the sun was higher, there would be another bonfire, fueling new tribal celebrations. A subsequent council fire hosting the elders would be sure to follow. Little Turtle thought the elders might now have a clearer idea for a new chief, Yellow Dog, as they honored the other warriors who had helped in the tribe's victory.

As the villagers were getting ready in earnest for the bonfire burning, with visions of dancing and chanting, there were some who suspected this victory could become the beginning of another long stretch of violence. The bad medicine brought about with the Seneca smoke signals remained a mystery. It was becoming a common question: Who were the smoke blooms for?

So, despite the upcoming moments of glee and good medicine, even Little Turtle was wise enough to suspect the tribe's good feelings might be short-lived. Especially so for the village scouts, who would be sent out to find more information. For these reasons, the celebration was different. This time the good feelings would be measured.

Starting with Little Turtle's vision quest, his horrific capture, and now becoming an experienced young warrior, he had come to see his world in a much different light. Even while he thought the results of this evening's bloodshed could easily provoke more incidents like those from the Seneca, especially if they somehow discovered the remains of his tribe's retributions, he knew he had to be, and would be, ready.

According to Little Turtle's father, long ago the Miami territory was once a place that extended beyond the "dark wood" far into the prairie's edges and was traditionally a safe homeland. But skirmishes like what had happened between the Miami and Seneca were becoming more frequent, ever since the white man first stepped upon their territory. Their sacred earth was becoming more infringed upon, even stolen or parceled away by the many foreigners bringing the inevitable conflicts before their tribal eyes, pushing them little by little ever northward. Big Turtle had said, "These new visitors all want something." Little Turtle thought: *Those Seneca warriors were acting the same.*

So, despite the growing festive chants, the promise of a brighter tomorrow for Little Turtle and his clan would never be assured unless something changed. The subtle communal fears of another crisis involving a bloody retaliation were not likely to be diminished by this celebration for long. The cherished days of the abundant buffalo, once roaming freely near Little Turtle's neighboring prairie lands, and the numbers of the silky beaver busy working and feeding carefree in the ever-present river, were already falling.

As Little Turtle mingled with the others, he found himself reflecting upon his personal lesson of war's brutality. It reminded him how the elders who had once likened their tribe's ancestral memories, once ripe and plump, at times were referring to their old stories of glory as though they had become a withered fruit, infused with sadness. The old ways full of good medicine were fading. Little Turtle didn't want his future memories to be the same.

For Little Turtle, Gray Tongues, and all the Miami people, the initial sounds of the rhythmic drumbeats and the soon-to-be-accompanying victorious fireside chants, echoing within the village like so many times before, had so far been unable to muffle the sharp calls of much larger voices advancing throughout the land. Those same menacing voices associated with reckless greed, behind-the-back betrayals, and the inevitable deadly conflicts were believed to continue, unless someone, or the revered spirits, could somehow intervene. A strong leader needed to be found.

Despite the night's victory and more hard lessons

sure to come, Little Turtle had already been torn away from his boyhood ways. After playing a key role in serving justice to a condemned enemy and internally recounting his experience, he realized one thing overall. He had not lost his longing to do more than he had ever done before. Somehow the increasing encroachments on his tribe had to stop.

As he reflected, he felt a stronger longing emerging. In fact, he was still following a mysterious calling that had started as a child: to be better tomorrow than today. Becoming a brave was only his first step. Even the wolf's eventful howl, heard as he emerged from Gray Tongue's hut with his father's modified bundle, could have been heard as a voice for greater days.

It made Little Turtle realize his deep longing was always a wish to walk in his father's footsteps— to be strong, faithful, and dedicated to serving his tribe. Once again, his father's memorable words energized his inner will: *You are a part of me…and I am of you.* With a firm resolve, Little Turtle promised himself*: I will make it so.*

Little Turtle's thoughts then drifted to his father's gifted horse, Many Winds. *Where is he? I must find him!* It was midmorning already, and the sun was competing with the glow of a new fire. Without any hesitation, Little Turtle left the village gathering and headed straight were he guessed the pony might be.

He checked his father's herd. Many Winds was not there. Instead, he found the pony tethered outside his father's hut out of harm's way. *Thank you, my brothers!*

Relieved, he approached the pony with caution.

Today would be the day. Little Turtle was a tested brave now. It was time to test another. He cautiously untied Many Winds. But, instead of the little stallion bolting away, he waited. As Little Turtle's heart swelled, trying to quell an inner storm of its own, he reached out his hand and touched the pony's soft muzzle. Many Winds flinched at the touch, but stood his ground.

Undeterred, Little Turtle paused and watched Many Winds' eye and ear positions. He waited. Many Winds, in turn, studied Little Turtle's eyes and open hands and sniffed them both. Little Turtle leaned forward and sniffed Many Winds' muzzle. It was then that there seemed to be a communication, an understanding. Little Turtle backed away and Many Winds responded by stepping forward. Little Turtle reached out when the pony was close enough. He touched him again as both hearts seemed to thunder in unison. This time the horse understood the genuine intention of no harm.

Encouraged, Little Turtle stepped closer and began whispering in the pony's cocked ear. Many Winds listened to Little Turtle's words, spoken so soft, they floated. The understanding continued as more gentle caressing and muzzle strokes followed. Many Winds' rich spirit of remembrances of a strong rider, still absent, may have stirred. He neighed in response. For a mustang stallion, that sound was enough. With lightning flashes of daring encouragement and without any fear emitting from either the young warrior or the beast, Little Turtle instinctively knew they both were ready.

He jumped—stomach first—onto Many Winds' back. The pony didn't buck or resist. He held strong. He had carried a much heavier weight only days before. Once Little Turtle moved his leg over and was straddled upright, he touched his heels against Many Winds' sides, and they were off.

    In a matter of minutes, they were seen racing around the village bonded as one, in the same manner as Little Turtle's father had done with the pony so many times before. Was it Many Winds' yearning to stretch his legs in rhythm with his new rider? Or was it a rekindling of a familiar scent emanating from Little Turtle's new medicine bundle? Could it have been the great chief's spirit lending a helping hand with the tender muzzle strokes? Many Winds could not say, but it easily could be seen the horse and his rider had connected. They had found their sacred place.

    Gray Tongues happened to see the incident from start to finish and understood all that the event implied. The ancient one nodded in approval as he watched Little Turtle complete his rite of passage right before his weary eyes. It was as though he could see the spirit of Big Turtle riding along. Despite the loss of their great chief, Little Turtle imagined a stronger place within the tribe's future. With strong warriors like Yellow Dog, Little Turtle felt he could race along a similar path.

    And so it was that Little Turtle was not only able to answer his original longing, but also find a new courage burning in his soul, one to match his father's and his ancestors before him. His new bundle firmly hugging his back had brought a new freedom. All his fears were gone.

    Little Turtle hoped Gray Tongues and the tribal spirits

above would clearly see a new hope—one that the Seneca, and those like them, could never take away.

For Little Turtle, racing on Many Winds with no hands, his dark hair flowing, arms outstretched to the sky, the day had suddenly become brighter. There was a new shining, one not coming from the morning sun or a great ritual fire. It was like a golden thread weaving a focus, a new beginning. It came with the excitement of dashing through the wind unencumbered, and the many village hearts beating as one, taking notice of Little Turtle's celebration as a newborn brave.

And so, a new promise was stringing itself together. The sacred Crane Spirit's words had rung true. If courage could be faithfully wrapped around a true and steady heart, fear cannot last. Sometimes it takes the darkness of a turbulent storm to make the sun shine even brighter, when it finally comes. With Gray Tongues' approving nod and Many Winds' ironclad faith, Little Turtle had survived an enemy's evil hand and found his long-sought-after destiny. His calling was being answered and his daring ride had become sweet and eventful, forging his own dedicated path to greatness, never to be forgotten.

It was good medicine.

June 2001

Chapter 16

A Different Journey Begins

It was an offer, a grand opportunity extended to young Ben by his father to go on a late summer wilderness fishing trip to the Manistee National Forest. It would be for eight days. Better yet, it was to be just the two of them. As far as Ben was concerned, this was his big chance to reconnect with his dad, Dr. Fred Nelson. It had been a long wait for something like this to happen, and completely unexpected, but a satisfying break, nonetheless. It helped Ben believe his long-lost good times with Fred would eventually return. And even though he hadn't any previous experience with this kind of a remote backwoods adventure, he knew it was something he'd have to try in hopes of ever salvaging a fading relationship.

The fact was, over the past few years, Ben's dad had

become too busy for any meaningful time with his youngest son, or for that matter, hardly anyone else. Somehow, over the past few years Ben and his dad had grown distant. So, this offer was a genuine source of secret delight. It felt like he had miraculously been dealt a winning hand from a worn-out deck of cards.

Additionally, Ben was excited about this possibility to not only spend some quality time with his family hero, just like the old times, but to catch a mess of fish and learn about the natural world would be an extra bonus. His fond memories of them together had held strong over the years and hope for more was envisioned. However, once the trip was underway, with two long and uneventful days already logged into their trip, Ben's high hopes for this rare chance to "partner up" again seemed to be headed in a different direction.

It was on their third morning together when Ben, only a few minutes out of his one-man tent, began to feel an undertow of disappointment. Sitting in silence directly across from his dad, stiff, shivering, and situated as close as possible to a charging campfire, not only did Ben feel physically dragged out, but he also was already wondering what this new day would bring.

Staring into the darting flames, while his dad fidgeted with one of his fancy kitchen camp gadgets, it wasn't long before Ben's thoughts pulled inward. He found himself mentally asking: *When is this trip going to get better? I know Dad is right about how nice it is out here, but when are the continuous nature lectures and facts going to stop? Why can't we just fish a little more and talk about other things like we used to?*

Before Ben's self-questioning and doubts could continue, Fred refocused his attention on his son and opened the morning conversation first.

"So, Ben, what do you think? Lots of work, huh?"

Still mired in reticent thought, Ben tried to recover by faking an expanded yawn and casually rubbing any remaining sleep from his eyes. Without answering what he considered one of his dad's usual rhetorical questions, he instead pulled his long-sleeved sweatshirt further down over his exposed hands. The morning air felt cold and gave Ben a little more time to try to abandon his early morning mood as he inched closer to the fire.

Hearing no response, Fred continued, "I just love it out here, don't you?"

After another moment of silence from Ben, Fred added, "It's been two days, and you ought to have a feeling about this kind of remoteness by now. This is the true wilderness. It is the kind of landscape the pioneer explorers, Lewis and Clark, saw on their way to the Pacific mapping the country. Isn't it beautiful out here?"

Ben glanced at the moving water. He thoughtfully agreed, but still gave no immediate response. Instead, he leaned closer to the fire's heat. Undeterred, Fred tried another tactic. "Can you believe how quiet it is out here?"

Even though Ben was only a few minutes away from leaving his warm, comfortable sleeping bag, complete with its soft foam padding and pint-sized pillow, he couldn't help but appreciate the scenery all around him as he shifted his eyes from side to side.

Sure enough, the river still looked clear and welcoming with its remaining morning mist floating softly upwards into a clear blue sky. The nearby trees looked stately, erect, glistening with green, and sharply contrasting between the overhead morning sky and the large granite gray rocks that dotted the river's shoreline. While he could clearly smell the strong mix of wood smoke and fresh pine scent, he heard no birds calling, no machines working. The silence was complete, and Ben could at least agree with that.

Without much further thought, Ben half-heartedly responded, "Well, I think it's pretty nice," as he returned his stare into the campfire flames flickering upward. "I'd say it's plenty quiet out here…that's for sure."

Ben did not want to stifle his dad's growing enthusiasm with a wrong answer, but to be honest, he wasn't sure this place was all that great as his dad had originally made it out to be. Yeah, it looked beautiful, but the mornings were shivering cold, the afternoons muggy, and the flying bugs were always around. Plus, it was hard paddling long distances against the shifting winds in an eighteen-foot canoe, loaded down with a week's worth of camping gear and food. Sure, he had paddled many times before, but only for short distances at various family outings, and that was long ago. And, despite regularly wearing a brand-new pair of paddling gloves, the newfound blisters on his inner hands were proof of his current efforts.

Beyond his growing blisters, he found the whole wilderness experience was rather peculiar. So far, he had seen nothing but trees and water, and a reduced number of people and their usual associated noises. The sudden absence of his high school friends, girls in general, and competitive sports during his summer break was bad enough. Judging from these past two days spent roughing it in the wilds, Ben was beginning to believe this remote and overly strenuous camping experience might not be the setting for the kind of opportunity he had envisioned.

Worse yet, they hadn't done much fishing. That was supposed to be the main purpose of the trip and another reason Ben had been interested in the first place. Besides, it was way too early for heavy thoughts or his dad's pointed questions. For now, he was more interested in staying warm and keeping to himself. Maybe, getting some food started with a nice warm cup of hot chocolate to hold and something solid to eat would be even better.

Remaining respectful and feeling compelled to continue with his dad's topic, Ben managed to sidestep his darkened mood and asked, "How come we haven't seen many people around here, anyway?" He was used to those earlier times when the family took their regular campouts. There were always lots of campers at those places. At the family lakeside campgrounds, they even had all the extra amenities, especially for young kids. This area had none of that.

Before Fred could answer, Ben said, "I mean, we've only passed a few groups of people camping along the shore and not that many boaters. I thought people like these woods and everything."

Fred was more than ready to reveal more of his long-winded, camp-life knowledge as an unmeasured response now that he had gotten his son's attention.

"Well, there's a few simple reasons for this. The first is, this is a designated wilderness area…a national forest. Out here, it's understandable not to see many people. Even though it's not as large as other parks, they still want to keep this area as natural and unspoiled as possible. They do that by limiting the number of people that can enter the area. It's like issuing out your school's hall passes. You know what I mean?"

Ben shrugged and said, "I guess so."

"Only a small number of campers or boaters are allowed on the river system at any given time, so those like us can appreciate the area as it was long ago. Besides, the fewer the people, the less negative environmental impact. Right?"

Before Ben could respond, Fred added, barely taking another breath, "Secondly, it's rough out here—no electricity, running water, soda machines, game rooms or showers and bathrooms. That will limit a lot of people all by itself. You hear what I'm saying?"

Fred's passion for nature was reappearing in earnest with his attempt to impress his son.

"Finally, there are a limited number of entry points for public access. Where we entered a couple of days ago was about in the middle of the Pine River area."

Fred stood up and stretched—the rock he was sitting on was becoming hard—and he gestured toward the river.

"Since we'll be spending most of our time further down through these woods, going eastward toward the headwaters, I wouldn't expect to see many paddlers or boaters. That's because where we are and where we're headed is more challenging for the inexperienced. As you can see—pointing to the river's shoreline—the current here is a bit faster than I expected, and I'm sorry to say there may be a few more required portages around the white-water rapids or other unpassable obstructions. You know…like the ones we've already seen around here. Then again, maybe it's as simple as the weather being hot and humid. Anyway, the good news is, there won't be big motorboats anywhere around these parts, and I expect the fishing pressure will be low where we'll eventually end up."

Ben acknowledged the information by checking the river flow and answering with a nod, signaling he was at least conscious and still listening.

"Besides," continued Fred, "I thought you'd like a challenge. You're a budding sports guy, right?"

Fred grinned and returned to his sitting rock, stretched out his legs, and waited. Ben didn't respond.

Fred ignored Ben's empty stare and went on, "Just enjoying the peaceful scenery is fine, but camping like this takes a certain amount of work and difficult challenges. Most people don't care for that. However, I've been reassured the fishing will be great where we are headed. We might even have it all to ourselves."

The subject of fishing roused Ben enough to comment, "I suppose those are good points, and I get it, but it's still a little strange from what I'm used to."

"Well, don't worry about the quiet. You've got me here. You can ask me all the questions you'd like, and it won't be quiet for long."

Fred got a kick out of his self-deprecating comment

while Ben agreed by cracking a faint smile. That smile, forced or not, encouraged Fred to continue unabated.

"Actually, Ben...there really are serious anglers around here, plenty of them, many of whom will stay awhile like us. Some even fish when no others will, even when the weather is good and lousy. Others are just day trippers. Some have small, silent motors, others rely on paddles like us. I suppose there are many anglers in the side tributaries that flow into the main water we are riding on. You see...fishing is personal around here, with most of them looking for their own quiet spaces. You know what I mean?"

Taking silence as an answer, Fred continued, "Speaking of personal...I want to remind you to always keep that whistle on you. I see you still have it around your neck, and thank you for that. It's part of our safety team while we are here. One tweet means 'Where are you?' Two tweets mean 'Stop what you are doing and come on in.' Three long ones mean 'Help!' There will be no exceptions. Got it?"

"All right, I got it. You know, Dad...you've told me a couple of times before." Ben held the whistle up as visual proof.

Startled, Fred paused to invite a longer response from his son about safety in the woods, but when none came, he paused to add a few more short sticks to the fire, readily staged nearby, and emphasized, "No matter where we go, don't worry, we won't be completely alone. Trust me. Help is nearby. And remember, in the meantime, we're all trying to get "the big one." The guys up here are just like you and me. And if that's not enough, just wait until later, when the sun gets higher. You won't be lonely at all. You'll hear plenty of mosquitoes and see a bunch of those tiny gnats again. You might even have to take a few swats at those overly friendly black flies right after we get rolling. Those things you can count on."

Fred smiled, hoping an additional dose of early morning humor would improve Ben's demure, and glanced to see if his lighthearted joke had worked. Seeing Ben force a smile, the wannabe humorist continued his mostly one-sided conversation.

"And you know what? Ben, listen to me…" Ben looked up. "If you are lucky, you'll get to see an eagle or a beaver or two today. Just think of that. You might even hear coyotes yipping back and forth to each other later tonight, too. What do you think of those apples?"
At this point, Ben was beginning to think his father was acting like an unconvincing attorney trying to win his first big case in front of a skeptical "one-man" jury.

Even without a response, Fred kept going, "Just imagine, Ben, those are sights and sounds most kids back home will never experience. Not ever…unless they come from a television or a movie. Who knows, you might see a black bear or hear a wolf howl, if they are still around here. Well…I'm not sure about that, but I think I'd be disappointed if you don't at least hear a chorus of peeping tree frogs or the fluttering of whippoorwills tonight before you go to sleep. You certainly would have heard them last night if you hadn't been "sawing the logs" so darned early. I could hear you all the way over here."

Fred gave his son a big toothy grin. "You must have

been tired from all that paddling and exploring we did yesterday. Correct?"

Ben, admittedly still tired, ignored the snoring tease and instead responded with, "Bears?" He glanced into the heavily shaded woods and asked himself: *Oh boy... what am I going to do now?*

With the look on Ben's face and his alarmed response, Fred changed the subject.

"Oh...and one more thing. Don't ever forget about the people who live in this area. And I mean it." Fred's tone had returned to serious. "They take a great deal of pride in preserving this area for people like us to enjoy, and you should appreciate that. I know I sure do. Hopefully, many generations to come will be able to enjoy what we have been able to see so far. You know what I mean?"

"Yeah, sure. I get it. I was just wondering," Ben responded, nodding in agreement, while he was still thinking: *Bears? Wolves? Why didn't this come up when we were home?*

With the length and variety of the fireside conversation, Ben was more than ready to change the subject to things that weren't so boring or alarming. Fred's explanations were clear enough and made sense, but they didn't really address Ben's apprehension about what was "just around the bend" for the rest of the trip. Not only that, but Fred's answers didn't do anything to stop Ben from reflecting on his emerging doubts about the past couple of days, roughing it and moving deeper into the forest's untamed wilds. He was already exhausted, worried about all the strange nighttime sounds, and thanks to Fred's flippant comments, a whole host of brand-new camping anxieties was about to emerge.

So, there Ben was, close to seventeen, out in the middle of "nowheresville," and forced to depend on his dad for not only his safety but also his daily comfort, meals, and sole companionship—if he didn't consider the bugs. Except for the meals, Ben was beginning to feel uneasy with everything else. Even Fred's attempt at old-fogy humor hadn't come close to helping with that.

Another quiet spell ensued as they both stopped talking, and instead, watched the fire's dancing flames. It not only allowed Ben to close his eyes for a few more minutes, but also allowed a little more time for a reflection or two about Fred.

The fact was, the older Ben got, the more he considered his dad, Dr. Fred Nelson, an odd duck. He was a doctor, but not medicine; he was an associate professor at the University of Michigan. On top of that, he was one of those people who liked to work all the time at the expense of the family. Yet, he somehow always found the time for camping in one way or another, even if it wasn't that often anymore.

At first, it was family weekend campground getaways throughout the summer. They were fun for all until Fred's work made them infrequent. Then, it was the annual extended wilderness camping adventures with a close friend or associate. Those were the ones Fred usually bragged about upon his return but, they too, became infrequent. Then, they mysteriously stopped all together.

It was bewildering because Ben still could remember

Fred's enthusiastic recounts of his stories of long winding trails and casually paddling throughout this majestic network of waterways close to where they were now. Those stories, whether exaggerated or not, sounded colorful and exciting.

On those extended trips, Fred had said he ventured to this area mainly because it was only a three-hour drive from where they lived in upscale Ann Arbor, not far from the university. To Fred, it was wild and challenging enough, and for a time, seemed to be the one special interest he still allowed himself outside his home or work environment.

Then, unexpectedly, came the random celebratory camp trips with one of the kids. They were always at the same park, but spontaneous, and always exclusive. With no exceptions, it was a trip for two. They had become special with a specific purpose. It could be celebrating a graduation, a major achievement, or a birthday. The problem was no one ever knew when their turn was coming or what the reason would eventually be.

In the beginning, it had started with his oldest son's high school graduation and cascaded downward to his three daughters, becoming a rite of passage for each one of them. Not only did those four trips help Fred stay in tune with nature, but they also had become a celebratory ritual. It was a serious experience with a dynamic duo, Dad and Mother Nature herself as the guides. The problem was, while these trips were unique, they ended up being a once in a lifetime event.

However, these camping trips invariably did entail a certain degree of bonding opportunities and were aimed to help each of Fred's kids connect with the elusive meaning of life, while they were challenged by nature, based on their individual physical abilities and general interests. To Dr. Nelson's way of thinking, these trips made up for and recaptured (in one great big swath) volumes of lost quality family time he had previously sacrificed because he was always working, always teaching, always striving to get ahead.

Those extra-special extended trips deep into the wilderness not only helped renew Fred's own essential sense of living, but also helped shore up his distorted role as a regular family guy. While these special adventures were intended to positively influence each of the kids through the grandeur of nature, they also cemented his self-absorbed idea that he still was a supportive parent whenever his work wasn't blocking the way. It released whatever guilt he may have had from being more devoted to his career.

With those individual treks, Fred invariably felt he had achieved his hidden intentions with the four children who had previously ventured with him. He even tried to make the trips extra memorable by faithfully documenting the daily experiences in his camp journal and taking a multitude of pictures along the way.

After the adventure was over, as time allowed, he eventually transcribed his camp notes and merged the corresponding photos into an engraved leather-bound hardcopy journal of the entire journey as a token of their achievement. It was like receiving a hardbound diploma for having successfully completed a comprehensive nature course with the family's learned professor leading the way.

So, when Fred abruptly told Ben he was planning one more trip; Ben was truly surprised. This time it was to be a quiet sojourn into a more remote part of the Manistee Park; it was to be in the Pine River basin. More mysterious was that the basin was a part of the park where Fred admitted he had never camped before. Notwithstanding, remembering those previous stories helped Ben remain curious enough to want to experience his father's renewed enthusiasm for himself.

This new occasion was to celebrate Ben's upcoming seventeenth birthday, later in the month. To Ben's surprise, without any real camping experience, let alone for eight whole days in the wilds, he couldn't think of anything better.

Finally, it was Ben's turn to experience nature's abundant and subtle teachings, while spending some premium alone time with Dad. His opportunity had arrived. For Ben, Fred's choice didn't matter, even though it was still a part of the same general destination his dad knew well, but on a lessor river he had never visited. In a sense, there were two new explorers in this region.

Once into the adventure Ben found the reality of this trip to be an unusual enterprise, already filled with several minuses. The morning's discussion was a prime example. Ben had hardly been out of his tent, doing his best to wake up and keep warm, while his dad was already perky and chatty, blitzing him with all kinds of nature facts and information. Right from the trip's start, there didn't seem to be much interest in what was happening in Ben's world at school, at home, or anywhere else. Instead, for the last two days, Ben felt like he had been verbally hit with a series of environmental pop quizzes he had never considered preparing for. Not only was his dad already pouring out a steady variety of area information, he also was throwing out random jokes to make them sound even better.

While his dad's enthusiasm was a partially welcomed shock from his dad's usual "I'm all exhausted" demeanor, why couldn't he just talk normal? Why such a conflicting persona? Back home, he was always missing dinners, social events, or general family time, or not talking at all. Here, he was "all in" as long as it pertained to the wilderness. Ben suspected the conflicting reasons were work related. His mom usually confirmed them in one way or another. To Ben, the glumness usually meant something distant was on his father's mind that required a certain level of intense concentration that had no end.

So, on the one hand, while Ben had been optimistic about spending his fishing trip with his dad, after two long days, he was becoming uneasy about being in such an unfamiliar place with a father, in recent times, he hardly knew. Worse yet, deep down, he was beginning to suspect he might not ever. He had only agreed to come along on this trip because he secretly hung on to the idea it might improve their relationship, and perhaps he would have a chance to find out what was driving him so much at the expense of everything else. So far, his hopes for an answer were in doubt.

Being true to himself, Ben still felt obligated to suck it

up and stride on. After all, this trip was his turn, and it still could be quite grand. It was still early. Even his mother thought it would be good for Ben, and he trusted her opinion. Besides, his brother and sisters had experienced something like this with no apparent ill effects. Undercutting it all, this adventure's end could still ultimately bring his dad's interests back homeward and into Ben's inner circle. He wanted that.

    Besides being uncomfortable with his dad's continual absences, Ben was a sentimental kid. He missed the attention and the memories he had with Fred when he was much younger. There were many times with his dad that were not only good, but also gratifying. Most of those occasions were when it was just him and his dad. Occasionally, his brother Tom, ten years his senior, would be included before he left home for college.

    Almost all of Ben's most cherished times involved sports. He and his dad had always kept track of the Detroit Lions and Tigers in one way or another, and especially, the beloved Wolverines. So much so, Ben usually couldn't wait for the new school year to start in early September. It meant the upcoming fall Saturday afternoons would be spent with the three of them at the university stadium, "The Big House" as it was called, and watch the Wolverines play their Big 10 home games. Fred knew some of the football team's coaching assistants, so tickets with good seats were easy to get. Fred was a savvy sports guy, too.

    To Ben, the Ohio State games were the absolute best because they usually determined the conference "champ." To a certain extent, all the games were exciting because they all included exceptionally rabid cheering crowds, marching bands, and jumbo hotdogs cradled in their matching buns. And special for Ben, his dad always made sure his "dawgs" (as they called them) featured an extra topping of ketchup, just the way Ben loved them. Side orders of warm roasted peanuts, with some favorite sodas or a couple cups of steaming hot chocolate were the usual. Those sounds and tastes were magical to a young kid like Ben.

Combine all that with the exhilarating look of the perfectly manicured green grass down below the stands, complete with its contrasting white striped yard lines, painted perfectly straight. Of course, to experience the thrill of the start of the game watching the whole team charge out to the field with their fierce looking blue and yellow striped Wolverine helmets, ready to start butting heads with their opponents, was exciting beyond words. Even at a young age, images like those were magical. Even better, most of those times Michigan won.

Best of all was to see Fred shed his lecture hall coat and tie, acting ordinary in his worn-out blue jeans and favorite ballcap, yelling and jumping up and down after a great play like everybody else. It made for a thrilling afternoon.

Not only that, but there were the subtle things they often did together. Their early Sunday quiet morning excursions before church taken to the bakery to bring back at least a dozen donuts, or some other goodies to satisfy the family's sweet tooth, was one. Usually, it was under the pretense to also pick up one of the city's big

Sunday newspapers (with its extended sports section coverage of the game's highlights) outside the local drugstore next door. Ben could still hear the laughter inside the car when his dad would invariably manage to smear powdered sugar or gooey jelly somewhere on his face and hands as he tried to sneak a bite and drive.

Of course, the newspaper sports coverage was extensive and included many column recaps of all the games his dad followed. After church, the discussions between them, highlighting those big game "stats" over more donuts were always a bonus. Those were good times.

Many more memories still lingered. Sadly, those types of meaningful occasions, and many more that meant the world to Ben, began to taper off when he was around the age of 12 or 13 years old, about the same time his parents were starting to become what was known as "empty nesters." One by one, his siblings graduated from high school and moved on, leaving Ben the only one at home to entertain himself or help his mother, with Fred rarely home.

To try and rekindle the bond that he and Fred once shared, Ben first joined the Boy Scouts. But the father-son camp outs or weekend field trips never materialized. As a result, that solo Boy Scout effort was quickly abandoned. As soon as he could, he then turned to sports, taking on football and baseball, but they didn't rekindle that much. Come game time, his family hero wasn't there to watch. In fact, he had disappeared. Something had happened between then and now.

To make matters worse, Ben had always envied the

way his older brother had spent lots of time with Fred by the time he graduated. Tom even kept his father's camp journal from their one-time wilderness trip together on display in a front and center fashion on his sporting awards shelf in the bedroom he and Tom shared. It was like a special leather trophy he posted prominently as a tangible memento signifying a great accomplishment. It was another remembrance of the good old family days they all had enjoyed together.

Ben's compelling evidence of old photos and mementos, still distributed throughout his room, had become daily reminders that even though he was still only sixteen, he was already on his own and alone. In a way, not only had he felt like he had been in an unresolved competition with his brother from a long time ago, but perhaps, he suspected, he was now competing with something much more complicated. Ben hoped this trip might help him put a finger on it.

Not that Ben was destined to be a hopeless loner or wasn't up to a good challenge. He had spent an enormous amount of time and energy at home and school trying to be a multi-sport athlete. Despite his efforts, they helped create other areas of disappointments, especially with his grades and girls. And, being stuck on the varsity's second team as a sub didn't help either, but he put in the work. Overall, he treated his sports drive as an accomplishment. It filled his void at home.

Not accepting his stature on the team, Ben proved he was a serious competitor and worked hard to improve.

He more than made up for his average size and speed, and slender build, with his bulldog determination by never quitting. However, as far as this fishing trip was concerned, he wasn't quite convinced he was ready to become a great nature lover. Being mired in this type of foreboding territory, especially with its eerie quiet surroundings, disappointed him. Being alone in his tent at night time was scary enough, but now, the notion a hungry bear could be wandering around, right outside his tent, was even worse.

    Setting all his early morning doubts and youthful memories aside, Ben resigned himself to making the best of the situation while he hoped for a little more fishing time. Staring at the fire, he asked, "So, Dad, what do you think we'll be doing today? More paddling?"
    Fred, happy to hear Ben's sudden interest in the upcoming travel plan, responded, "Well...let's look at the river map. It's in the big canoe pack, you know, next to my tent. Do you mind getting it while I get breakfast started?" Ben looked up as Fred pointed to the collection of camp gear between their two tents.
    Ben got up and quickly fished the map out of the canoe pack.
    The map was easy to find, because his dad kept it readily accessible, just inside and atop the main canoe pack. Plus, the map was noticeable in its bright, purple-edged case. The front side was a clear flat windowed plastic, twelve by fourteen inches, a handy waterproof package that was readable as they paddled along the river.

Fred, as the camp leader and the self-designated navigator on the water, always fastened the map package with adjustable straps to the canoe's thwart, a crossbar directly in front of him in the stern, where he sat and paddled. When it wasn't on the thwart, he kept it on the inside top of the canoe pack. He had spoken on many occasions about the importance of the map. "There is nothing…I mean nothing…worse than being lost in the deep woods, especially in unfamiliar terrain. This map is our ticket to a guided tour throughout this park."

Ben could see the logic in that statement. Therefore, as far as they both were concerned, the map would always be an accountable item. And, as far as Ben was involved, the map hopefully would guide them not only to a productive fishing region, but also safely back home as a renewed team.

Chapter 17

The Challenge

Ben and his father studied the map for a moment, then Fred pointed and revealed, "See how far we have traveled since the start of the trip? I would say we just passed Big Beaver Creek. Our campsite here is not too far from Sprouge Creek. Once we get to the East Branch of the Pine, we'll slow it down because that's where we'll be spending most of our time, on the Diamond Lake and Rose Lake outlets. See what I mean?"

"Yeah, I do. I'll be looking forward to that," Ben said.

"You know, if we hadn't had to portage through those low spots back in the river yesterday, plus the lift-overs around those awful tree windfalls, we could have done even better, maybe made it all the way to the Rose Lake outlet. Who knows? I'll admit, those weren't much fun."

Ben nodded in agreement.

"I suppose the lack of rain the past couple of summers hasn't helped." Fred continued, "If we can get a reasonable start this morning, and it looks like we will, we should be able to make ten more miles and finally get in some serious fishing time. Then the rest of the trip will be gravy—all fishing time."

Fred pointed skyward. "The only problem I can see right now is those high wispy-looking cirrus clouds creeping up out there. They generally mean we could get wet weather...probably in no more than a day or two. I hope the wind continues out of the west a little longer and helps push us further along."

"Yeah, I suppose that back breeze did make the paddling a little easier," Ben said, not mentioning his blisters.

"I'll say one thing, Ben, for a semi-rookie paddler, you have caught on again pretty well to the canoe. Your ability to maintain a constant rhythm to stay in sync with me has been impressive. Up in the bow, you really are the power of the canoe. With me in the stern, I am the directional operator. I do appreciate your energy. Just remember, no sudden jerky moves from one side to another, and don't stand up to clap when I catch the big trophy of the trip later," Fred said as he displayed a big grin.

"Don't worry. I'll just bow down on my knees, instead, to honor the great fisherman king."

Ben's remark was a lighthearted response to his dad's tease, and he added a light smile. Ben's mood appeared to be coming around. It looked as if his usually dead-serious dad was doing the same. However, Ben wasn't entirely sure it would last for very long.

Back at home, it was Karen, his devoted mother, that Ben turned to for schoolwork help and general parental guidance. Even though she worked as a full-time registered nurse, she was reliable and always managed to find the time for him and his siblings or reveal a rationale for Fred's behavior.

Now that the older kids were out of the house with jobs of their own or away attending college, it was Ben, not Fred, who helped his mom with the yard work and household chores. She had always ended up as the family captain, anyway, and over the years had become his personal confidante. She had even helped him learn to drive and had taken him to the Motor Vehicle Department for his road test. That one was especially big in Ben's mind.

He and his mom had grown close, while his dad moved in and out of the family circle. Even though Ben understood most of his dad's excuses for his continual job-related duties, there were times when he could see the strain on his mom's face and in her choice of words when the subject of his father arose. He had grown to resent that part of his parents' relationship and his dad's career.

Brushing that all aside, it was unusual to see his dad totally interested and focused solely on him for a change and in charge of this adventure, beginning with the original at-home plan, and being out here roughing it with him on the waterway. Ben was finding the relaxing morning fire and an engaged dad a surprising, but welcome, plus.

Recalling when he and his dad were together planning the trip at the kitchen table, Ben pictured the camping adventure to be entirely different and much easier. Most of the time, he believed this trip was all talk and might not even happen at all. The stories of the persistent bugs, the peculiar animal sounds at night, and traveling light (moving along with just their clothing and essential equipment) couldn't be all that bad. They might even have been exaggerated.

For some reason, Fred had a tough time committing to things with only Ben left living at home. Ben figured the camping idea was just a subject they had talked about lightly and would never really happen. It was an exciting challenge to think about initially, but now reality had arrived. The open river was flowing only a few yards away. In fact, the woods and nature's secrets, which Ben largely knew nothing about, were draped all around him. According to Fred, none of it was to be taken lightly, good or bad. Ben was right in the middle of something big, mysterious, and overwhelming. He secretly hoped that not only would these striking new hardships lighten up soon, but also that his dad really knew what the heck he was doing, because Ben didn't.

Ben could easily understand the warning to stay alert, and he did his best to go along with his dad's wishes, but along with feeling like a stranger in a strange land, he still wasn't comfortable with his new paddling duty assigned to the bow of the canoe. He had forgotten what little bit he knew about the energy his paddling role would require. Although his dad's genuine compliment helped change that particularly big minus to a small plus, it didn't reduce his swelling blisters.

If all of that wasn't enough, tenting it all alone with Mother Nature's wild range of nocturnal creatures moving during the dead of night was another hardship that Ben hadn't come to grips with yet. Sleeping in separate one-man tents—by far Ben's biggest concern—had been reasoned by Fred because of camping equipment space and weight concerns. A single large tent would be too heavy, too crowded, or too cumbersome. Even though those reasons made sense to Ben before the trip, the reality of it was different. The crickets, cicadas, bullfrogs, mosquitoes, and other creepy miscellaneous river sounds were relentless and played with Ben's imagination more than he ever thought they could. Now, he had to consider bears and wolves.

Right from the beginning, his hope for an early sleep the first night was postponed by rustling leaves and imaginary four-footed steps just outside his tent entrance, which started almost immediately after he nestled his head on his little camp pillow. They only increased his concerns when he turned off his tent light. It wasn't long before the light was back on and kept that way.

Two days later, sitting around the pleasant early-morning fire gave Ben a little more time to discount his early negativity about the trip. But he knew he was stuck, and his fearful thoughts of future nocturnal animals ready to attack lingered. *If this keeps up, I'm going to have to say something.*

The hanging thought prompted him to consider revisiting his dad's earlier comments about the black bears and howling wolves, and the need to hang up the food pack at night in a tall tree. That one statement finally took precedence and triggered Ben to interrupt his dad from his ongoing map calculations.

"Say, Dad, a few minutes ago, you said I might even see a black bear or hear howling wolves out here. Was that for real?"

Startled, Fred looked up. "Well, I suppose it's possible, but I wouldn't worry about it. I haven't experienced either one out here. They're both naturally shy. I'm sure there are bears in the area, but I certainly doubt there are wolves left anywhere around here. Further northward there could be a chance, but I don't know for sure. However, coyote yelping at night is a real possibility."

Not satisfied with his dad's response, Ben prodded, "What about the food pack? And you hanging it up at night? I didn't really think about it before, other than it might be a new camping thing. Is it really for bears, or not? I thought it was for less-threatening guys like raccoons and opossums. You know what I mean?"

Fred, anticipating Ben's real concern, answered, "Now Ben, take it easy. There may be a few bears around, but I've never personally seen one up here. You need to relax. Bears are shy creatures, trust me. However, stumbling upon a mother and her cubs could certainly be a big deal. Or, if one should happen to find an easy bounty carelessly forgotten to be stashed away at night, that might also be a different story. You wouldn't want to be anywhere near a bear with a pack full of camp food.

"All we're doing out here is trying to be prepared and making sure that finding our camp food is not easy for them—or any other rascal, for that matter. I have heard of campers having their whole food supply ransacked and ruined because they weren't cautious enough. Even raccoons can do that. That's all we're doing. In any case, we won't be personally attacked by any varmints—day or night. We'll be fine. If it will make you feel better, I did bring a can of bear spray with me, and you can keep it close by in your tent if you want. Sound good?"

Surprised, Ben said, "Gee, I guess so."

Getting frustrated with Ben's reemerging sour mood, Fred wrapped up his comments with, "Okay, I know we haven't fished that much yet, but we are going to be anglers on this trip once we get further up the river, if that's what's bothering you. As far as the animals are concerned, we'll be fine camping close to the water. We're not going to cross through the forest, and we're not going to be attacked or eaten."

Finally, trying to avoid an argument, Fred resorted to a little more of a lighthearted twist, "Besides"—he smiled and pointed in Ben's direction— "you know what they say: It's all about being prepared and not feeding 'daaa Bears.' We're Michigan people. So, we both are going to continue to be Lions, Tigers, and Wolverine fans around here. Right?"

Fred's response countering Ben's concerns regarding the nighttime wild animals was one that a country or farm boy might typically shrug off as the way of the land, or at least appreciate as a stab at lightening up the moment with a little offhand sports humor. But for Ben, a kid only two days removed from a comfortable home in suburbia and fresh from an unfamiliar anxiety episode, Fred's answer symbolized a learning curve that needed to be grappled with. Ben took the humor with a slight nod but a straight face.

Fred noted Ben's demeanor and changed his tone to a stern challenge. "Okay, Ben…let's say you're back home on the football field in one of your conference's big games, and the coach signals in the next play. Your team needs to get a crucial first down, which is a good eight yards to go, to keep the winning drive alive with time running out. The quarterback looks at you and calls the play the coach signaled. It's a run off-tackle and you're to be the ball carrier. You glance at the defense. The two biggest guys on the other team have already moved to the gap you must get through. Are you going to just half-ass it because you don't want to get hurt? Or are you going to bust through that line with all you've got?"

Anticipating a defensive response, Fred added, "Now, hold on…you don't have to answer that. Those are rhetorical questions and we both know the answers. The point I'm trying to make is: Try and relax a bit about being attacked by a bear or any other wild animal. Out here, it's no different than that big play and the game on the line. We are in a major forest and we're in the "big game" in the world of camping. It's how real camping and living was done here only a few generations ago. And thanks to the people around here with a vision, they have saved a good part of it for us. Whether it's bears or huge linemen, they come with the territory. This is your opportunity to overcome adversity—whether big or small—and shine. And I mean…really shine. Your team is depending on you to get mentally into the game and stay there."

Ben thoughtfully studied his dad's forceful point. After a minute to affirm all that was said and realizing he really didn't want to take a chance of wrecking his camping vacation or the hope of reclaiming a long-lost comradery, he conceded with a slow grin and added, "Okay, Dad. I get it. We really are Lion and Tiger fans, and especially Wolverine ones at that, aren't we?"

Ben's retort was a good tension reliever, and it gave him a moment to grasp the importance of being on the same team. He hoped his father would be willing to join up as well. One thing for sure: the odd mix of this current father–son adjustment, combined with the trip's physical challenges, had Ben thinking a brand-new ballgame was underway. Only this one was taking place on a much bigger playing field and with its own set of rules.

Chapter 18

The Find

While the first overnighter had been rough on Ben's confidence, thankfully, last night's tenting was much easier. It seemed it had been but an instant and he was out—exhausted again—affording a day like today to have the opportunity to be a little better. As the fire continued to burn, Ben was able to envision the next few days doing nothing but fishing. He was slowly becoming more positive. All he had to do now was bask in the morning's sunshine, accept whatever the next few nights had to bring, and imagine what kind of fish might be swimming by. He was ready to shine.

"Say, Dad, what's for breakfast, and how soon before that packet of hot chocolate over there will be drinkable?"

"In just a few more minutes, the water will be hot enough. We aren't going to really cook much this morning, just heat up our drinks. The rest of the menu will be an assortment of breakfast bars, sliced cheese and sausage, and trail mix. I don't want to spend too much time cooking or cleaning up. The sooner we get upriver, the sooner we will be fishing. Okay?"

"Sure, sounds great. I'll admit it; I'm definitely hungry."

Once the morning's breakfast was laid out and ready, all was quiet again. Ben finally had his hands cupped around his warm cup of hot chocolate and Fred was savoring his steaming, slightly sweetened instant black coffee, while he admired the surroundings as sources of future snapshots. Ben eagerly consumed his breakfast portions, finished his last gulp of hot chocolate, and wiped the sticky stuff off his face with the back of his hand. Fred, completely relaxed, reviewed the river map once again while he slowly sipped his coffee. That left Ben without much more to do or contemplate. Full, but bored, he interrupted Fred's ongoing river review.

"Hey, Dad, what do we have planned for supper tonight? I know I'll be starving by then, too."

Fred looked up and laughed. "Really…starving?" They both got a nice chuckle, and camp life for Ben became a bit better now that the anxiety concerns and hunger pains had quieted down.

"Listen, Ben, we really should get moving and be on our way. I'll take down the tents and get things organized. Why don't you take the water bottles and the purifier and pump us our drinking water for the day? When you get done, we'll load up the canoe. Sound good?"

Since Ben's mood was still inching upward, and he had pumped their drinking water several times already, he said, "Sure. I'll do that."

Ben knew there wouldn't be any problem cleaning up after such a Spartan meal, and surmised taking down the tents, putting out the fire, and getting the camp equipment organized wouldn't be, either. He didn't really know for sure. What he did know was organization and being in control were important to Fred, so the camping "I'll do it myself" arrangement wasn't a surprise.

Fred had a history to make sure he knew where his things were. Wasting time at home looking for items when they were needed was one of his major pet peeves. He had been clear before they left home about how they would need to stay organized. It was Fred's way, and out here, it would remain the same.

With that in mind, Ben easily spotted the pump and grabbed a couple of quart-sized water bottles nearby, secured his wide brimmed hat, and put it on, hoping to ward away any potential deer flies. With his hat secure, he hastily headed down to the water's edge.

The morning air was a lot cooler away from the fire, as the emerging goose bumps on his arms mounted. The chill made him determined to pump quickly and get back to the fire for a few more minutes before the flames had to be dowsed.

Down at the shore, Ben spotted a large flat-topped boulder a few feet further into the water, which looked to be a suitable place for the anticipated pumping action. From the shore he managed to jump to the exposed rock without slipping or getting wet while maintaining his balance. Stooping over, he extended the pump's drawing hose deeper into the water in between the rock he was perched upon, and a large, ancient branch submerged nearby. The trick was to pump the water through the rubber tubing and into the filter without sucking any bottom sediment into the hand pump. The deeper the water, the easier the process.

Ben had no trouble filling the first bottle, and set it aside. The pump had a good draw. He was amazed how pure the water always looked after it flowed through the charcoal filter, no matter how bad the water looked before. As he was filling the second bottle, however, a strange image suspended barely above the river bottom, caught his eye. It looked like a bright white rock with an interesting shape.

That's strange. What can it be? The longer he eyed the object, the more curious he became. Once the second bottle was full and secured along with the other bottle, he took an extra minute to check out the mystery rock.

He stretched toward it, but it was just a bit beyond his reach. Even straining as far as he could, it was no use. If he were to retrieve it, he'd have to get into the water. It meant his tennis shoes and socks would have to come off. *Hmmm, is it worth the trouble? I hate icy water. Well, is this my vacation or not?* Looking over his shoulder, he saw his dad was still busy packing things up. *What the heck?* He rolled up his pant legs, pushed up both of his sweatshirt sleeves up to his elbows, and removed his shoes and socks. He stepped in. *Oh…it's cold all right!* He bent over and reached in. He was still a bit short of it. The water's reflection had falsely made it look closer than it really was.

He stretched out again, about as far as he could

without getting the bottom part of his pants wet, and finally was able to touch it. *Aha!* Surprisingly, it felt like it was wedged tight into a semi solid portion of an age-old branch. Equally surprising, despite the slimy feel of the wood, whatever the object was, it felt sharp to the touch. Determined, he braved the cold a bit longer, got a better grip on himself (and his curiosity), and reached in again. *I can do this.*

His second attempt wasn't so bad. He got a little wetter, and despite the water's reflections and distortions, he dislodged it. *Victory! Only now, I'm freezing.* The extensive goose bumps on his forearms proved it, but he took the time to check it out. He was right, it was a stone. *Wow, this could be a keeper. It's unusual, all right.* Ben deduced it was a large arrowhead. *Dad will surely know all about this. I can't believe it!*

Ben was excited about his good fortune, and now that his feet were numb, he forgot about how cold the water was or how long his water-pumping excursion had turned out to be. At that same moment, his dad's call brought back to him the idea that getting further down the river was still the main mission for the day.

"Hey, Ben, come on! What's taking you so long? Is there a problem out there? Did you fall in?"

"No, Dad. I'm done! I just found something interesting down here you might be able to help me out with!" Ben shouted back.

"Okay…but hurry up. You want to get in some fishing today, right?"

"Be right there!"

Ben grabbed the two bottles and pump, his dry shoes

and socks, and wallowed dripping wet back up to camp. Thankful the fire was still burning, he sat down on the closest log, pulled down his sleeves, and propped up his sandy feet toward the fire and said, "Check this out."

Fred stopped filling one of the canvas canoe packs with the tightly rolled-up tents and walked over to the fire ring. "Okay, what have you got here? I hope it was worth it, because you're good and wet and that water can't be much more than forty degrees out there."

Once Fred spotted the stone, he took it from Ben's extended reach and turned it over several times, then handed it back to Ben.

"That's quite a find. It's impressive, because what you have here appears to be a ceremonial arrowhead or a special spearhead," Fred said with an air of authority. "I say that because even though this looks like an extra-large arrowhead, because of its elongated size, pointed shoulders and rock type, I'm certain it was special to whoever owned it long ago."

"Really?" Ben said with surprised delight.

"Really. I can say that without hesitation, because of the stone's shape and color. I know you have seen all the arrowheads and the other stone-tipped hunting weapons I have in and around my office. Most of those are made from a common rock material called chert. You know, the ones that look like they were made from gravel? As a rock, chert can be found almost anywhere. It's strong enough, but is also brittle, so it can be chipped or flaked when struck by another ordinary rock. Stop me if you know this already."

Ben shook his head no.

Fred was delighted to be back in his element, and drawing on his expertise, said, "Well, this is done by striking it at an angle with a good bit of force to make the object into the shape one would want to tie to the end of a wooden shaft. The chert arrowhead could be large or small, depending on the purpose. One, with more rounded shoulders, indicated ordinary hunting purposes, and could be easily reused when removed. Pointed shoulders, such as this, were the opposite.

"Of course, the larger the object, the more a precision type technique is required. Once the desired shape has been hammered out, a sharp cutting edge is created by what is called pressure flaking. The maker would use a softer object like a bone, a hard-pointed piece of wood, or an antler, and press hard to break off tiny pieces or flakes off the edge. As you can see and feel for yourself, what you're holding is still sharp."

Nodding in agreement, Ben added, "That's amazing."

"What makes this so special and unique is the arrowhead material is quartz. It's a much harder form of rock, and therefore harder to work with. Most regular arrowheads were quickly made, and the diverse colors in chert weren't as important to the hunter as its easiness to chip it into shape and move on."

Fred gestured at the stone and said, "Secondly, this is nearly pure white. I'm surprised no one has seen it before this because it does stand out. We don't see too many of these and don't have many at the university lab. Anyway, whoever made this piece was skilled indeed, because of the size of this stone."

"It really got my attention, because I found it stuck in

the side of a large piece of wood...a big tree branch on the river bottom," Ben added.

Fred brushed off the interruption and continued.

"It looks to be about a good three inches and, as I said, because of the unique hardness of the rock, plus the shape, it was more time consuming to make compared to an ordinary hunting arrowhead. Whoever made this one had to be quite sure of what he wanted it to be. It could have even been traded for a nice return or reserved for higher importance."

After another pause and mentally checking to see if Ben was still listening, Fred continued, "I would say this artifact could have been meant for a chief or one of his relations, or even a shaman, who had a great deal of influence in his day."

"Okay, Dad. Slow down. A shaman is some kind of a healer, right?" Ben asked.

Ben's curiosity encouraged Fred. "Yes, you are right. A shaman is like a medicine man, except a shaman could also communicate with the unseen world, namely, the vast spiritual world. Shamans had a great deal of power and authority. For example, they were usually responsible for calling upon the spirits for rain, hunting successes, guidance for warpath issues, or curing the sick. Most shamans were considered odd in a peculiar way, but they were respected, simply because at one point in their lives, they had been able to visually show many others they were specially allied with the spirits by exhibiting a rare quality...like an extraordinarily brave experience in battle or having performed a proven feat of unexplainable magic."

"That sounds interesting."

"Another thing that you may not know, our state of Michigan was home to several different tribes. Items like this one would have been valuable to another person and might have been traded for other highly prized items like fur pelts, steel knives, special tools, horses, or even wives."

"Really?"

"Yes indeed. A shaman had to have a certain supply of these valuable stones, either derived from more trade or provided by a skilled tribal member who had access to special stone materials known to influence the tribe's spirits."

"And this is considered an artifact, right?" Ben asked.

"Absolutely. An artifact is simply a handmade tool crafted by a human. It's an archaeological term used to describe primitive prehistoric workmanship consisting of implements of wood, bone, clay, shell, stone, and metal that was created to either cope with or help conquer the natural world. Most of the artifacts that remain from early man, and our Native Americans, are the stone, bone items, and remnants of pottery. Of those, the stone arrowheads are the most common, but the one you have found here, Ben, is certainly special."

"Why?" Ben, still listening, inadvertently encouraged Fred to add more depth.

"Because it was sure to have been created with great meaning. If it were eventually passed on to a warrior, which is entirely possible, the possession of one of these items would certainly help him erase the fear of entering the horrors of battle—including death. It also helped him overcome any other bad medicine or pitfalls associated with daily life, knowing they had a connection with the spirits. It helped provide supernatural courage to face whatever the warriors were to be confronted with.

"We archaeologists don't commonly find these whenever we are conducting our prehistoric field digs throughout the country, but there are plenty preserved in museums. Ones like this were not to be used for hunting and possibly lost with a wounded animal getting away. I would just say we should put that in a special place, so it doesn't get damaged or lost to history. I will say, you may have already won the souvenir lottery of the trip."

"Wow. You really think so?"

"Yeah. I really think so. Now, let's finish packing up and head out."

Now understanding the significance of his find, Ben was more than ready to go. The day was continuing to improve.

Fred himself wasn't so sure it was a good idea to just tell Ben to put it in a safe place, so on second thought he suggested, "Why don't we wrap it up and put it in my waterproof camera case until we get home?"

Ben looked at the stone again and said, "How about if I just put it in one of the zip-top pockets in my life vest for just a bit? I'd like to hold on to it for a little longer for good luck when we go fishing. Then we can put it in the camera case after I catch 'the big one.' Okay?"

"All right, Ben. You're going to need all the luck you can get to catch a bigger fish than me today," Fred teased. "Now dry off your feet and let's get going."

Ben returned a smile, got up, and with bare feet went

over to the canoe, grabbed his life vest, and carefully placed the special artifact in his top left pocket. He then zipped it all the way shut.

Not long thereafter, Ben sat down on a nearby log, brushed the sand off his icy cold feet, and put his shoes and socks back on, while Fred dowsed the campfire completely. The sun had already burned off what remained of the cool morning mist, and the day was starting to warm up. As they were ready to shove off, Fred paused and got a little emotional with an afterthought about the artifact that Ben had just found.

"You know, Ben…a unique piece like what you found is what got me interested in archaeology in the first place. It's the history and the mystery of these prehistoric man-made objects, these representatives from an age long past, where there is no written record, which is so intriguing. It's fascinating to me that you had in your hands an object that was of immense value to someone long ago. That person lived a life we will never know. We can only surmise a few clues of what that person did based on the artifact itself. Where it was found and the circumstances surrounding it are examples of prehistory's abundant mysteries that must be pieced together to understand people's lives and the reasons why they did what they did.

"We know one thing for sure: These people survived despite many unknown hardships, but the good news is, we are learning more. They had only their wits to survive harsh winters, disease, the continual quest for food, and the underlying fear of enemies along the way, while trying to raise a family without the aid of a car, electricity, or a phone. It's hard to fathom."

Fred gave Ben a wink and bravely continued with a piece of his youth. "I guess…I got interested in those things when I was just a kid about your age working in my parent's vegetable garden, hoeing weeds for my weekly allowance. I hit what I thought was a rock, but upon a further glance, I noticed the object was flat and reddish. Curious, and a bit bored or plain tired, I picked it up to check it out. It turned out to be a piece of Native American pottery.

"We archaeologists call pottery pieces 'sherds.' Anyway, it had the maker's fingernail impressions on it as a basic form of decoration. I can't explain it, but I wondered about the person who did that. In a way, for that moment, I was connected to that certain person who lived a long time ago. Even then…whoever that was… was trying to make their life just a little bit better, even in a tiny way. It was a small snapshot of a life that occurred in the same vicinity as my parent's house. I think if I had a time machine, I'd still like to meet that person. The problem is we don't, but I hope what I'm doing at the university has gotten us a bit closer to learning more about our unwritten human history, and the people who struggled and endured in it. We wouldn't be here if they hadn't."

Ben didn't say anything while his father paused to reflect on all that had been said. He felt a bit awkward to hear a new story from his father's childhood, and appreciated what he had heard. It gave him a better perspective of his new find, a better understanding of his dad's intense passion for his teaching profession, and just a bit more to think about.

It wasn't long thereafter before Ben was persuading himself that sometime today might be a good time to bring up his concerns about all the alone time that he and his mom had been experiencing. He was planning to bring it up at some point anyway, and with the way the day was shaping up with his dad's sentimental reflections about his teenage past, Ben was beginning to think that bringing up the subject sooner than later might actually be possible. However, knowing how his father could easily overreact and just blow him off, he had to find a way to do it without ruining the beginning of the day's travels, or even the rest of the trip. He had an opening, but his dad already looked anxious to be moving along, so Ben cautiously decided to postpone the idea, at least for now. It was obvious that this wasn't the time, but at least, he had found an approach to "tackle" his ultimate plan.

Without any further comments from Ben, Fred temporarily regained the moment and hopped into the waiting canoe as he said with a sense of accomplishment and change of tone, "I put plenty of water on the fire to make sure it's dead out, everything is set, and now, it's off we go. Our departure this morning is making for a good start for today's travel plan. Hopefully, we'll find a nice place to camp this afternoon and get busy with fishing. Sound good?"

"You bet," Ben said. His enthusiastic response seemed to be reflecting his hopeful attitude for more answers as they both began to push the canoe away from the shore with their wooden paddles. "The sooner the better, I would say."

As they carefully shoved off, before paddling deeper into the river's midsection, Fred gave the canoe a couple soft pats on the outside of the craft. Ben noticed. Besides his dad's expert knowledge about Ben's recent river find and his dad's fondness for long-winded descriptions, one more thing was becoming abundantly clear. Besides camping, Fred loved his canoe. To Ben, it was like his father's personal lifeboat used to carry him far away from the rigors of civilization whenever he could break away. Fred often insisted he would be the one to carry the canoe over his shoulders for any obstacle carryovers. It was light enough, and it helped save hiking time when paddling the canoe became a hazard.

The canoe was special, and he had it a long time. When he bought it, it was the best Fred could afford. Despite the expense, it was constructed of a strong, lightweight Kevlar material with shoulder crossbars for one-man carries. Fred reminded everyone, purchasing this boat was well worth it, mainly because ordinary canoes made of wood or fiberglass were much heavier and harder to maneuver. When it came to camping, this was his baby.

Even for shorter portages of only a few yards, Ben and his father shared the canoe-carrying duties—one at each end paying attention not to bump or scrape it on anything. However, more times than not, when the walking trail was too narrow or rough, it was Fred, not Ben, who carefully carried the canoe over his head. Even though his son appeared to be physically strong enough, Ben posed no argument. He could see the duty satisfied

Fred's protective care of his prized possession.

   Unfortunately for Ben, it meant he had to carry the bulk of the rest of the gear, unless the walk-around was an extended one. Then, they would make a return trip hike together. The process worked out okay for the most part. At least, that's the way they had rolled for days one and two with the canoe. It would also explain why Ben might have been so unusually tired and sore in the beginning lugging the rest of the gear.

   In the past, Fred always took the canoe on all the shorter family campouts, and at times bragged about the way it performed. He even referred to the craft as "Ole Yeller" for no other reason than the Kevlar material happened to be yellow. Ben had thought more than once his dad treated the boat like an added family member, never to be left behind, even during those simpler outings. His mother never knew exactly why there was all the fuss over it, but the quirk was another part of Fred's camping style that he kept to himself, and everyone tolerated.

   On this extended trip, Ben figured part of Fred's attitude about the canoe was obvious. To ensure that their only means of transportation was carefully paid attention to, and not risking accidentally damaging it, made a tremendous amount of sense. That part he clearly understood, including the unique portaging routines.

   However, Ben could also see there was something a little more about the canoe. It was like Ole Yeller was an old friend; one Fred respected and valued. Unfortunately for Ben, judging from Fred's lively reaction to the stone's discovery and his unusual childhood revelation, it dawned on Ben that it might behoove him to treat the stone and its intriguing history in the same way.

As the "three" of them moved along, Ben was gratified to see a mild current in this section of the river allowed the paddling to be much easier despite the weight of their cargo. The relative ease of the paddling afforded them both more of an opportunity to see the tranquil beauty on the shore, and to entertain idle thoughts in the quietness all around them. Other than the rhythmic sound of the two paddles dipping in and out of the slow-moving water, the quietness prevailed.

For Fred, the paddling time meant he was no longer obsessed with work or even that the roof back home needed repair. Now that they were well into the third day of the trip and most of the preplanning was proving to be successful, Ben could see his dad was finally beginning to relax.

Ben was too. And when Fred suddenly said, "Stop. Don't move. Look over there to your left." Pointing in the direction of the shore, Ben saw a doe watching the two of them slowly float by without paddling. It not only increased the mutual good feelings, but it also made for a great photo opportunity, which Fred promptly got.

"You don't see that every day, Buddy Boy," Fred said in an I told you so manner. "See how grand this river is?"

Ben turned, gave a thumbs up signal, and said, "Don't forget to put that in the journal."

After the photo's excitement passed, Ben got bored again, but instead of thinking about the girl he had his eye on back at school or the possibility of getting a part time summer job, he began thinking about the river, reliving the moment he found the artifact, and digesting what his dad had explained to him about the stone and what it may have represented to its previous owner. Key words like "artifacts," "a special courage," "Indian shamans," and "fingernail impressions" stuck out in his mind. Even how it could have become wedged in a branch in the first place was puzzling enough.

No doubt, the scenery was peaceful, and the deer's presence exciting, but with his father's words, Ben's imagination began to shift into wondering who could have had this special arrowhead, now zipped tightly into his upper pocket. The history of where it came from, how it got there, and who may have used it before was easy to think about in the middle of nowhere with nothing to do but paddle and watch nature's objects pass by. Even thoughts of his upcoming football camp, and, more importantly, a serious talk with his dad, took a temporary back seat.

After about an hour further downriver, Fred interrupted Ben's train of thought and said, "Hey, Ben, let's head to the shore for a few minutes. That extra cup of coffee went through me faster than expected. I'm going to have to make a quick trip into the woods for a few minutes, if you know what I mean."

"Sure. Any particular spot?"

"Let's get a bit closer and stop where there are as few rocks as possible. No sense in scraping up the bottom of Ole Yeller if we don't have to. We'll just head over to that area directly ahead and see what that looks like."

"Okay," Ben said, looking to see where Fred was pointing.

In no time, they found a landing area with a nice open

sandy spot. Upon reaching it, Fred promptly hopped out and said, "If you don't have to go, too, help yourself to an assortment of trail bags while I'm gone. They're at the top of the food pack."

"Okay. Thanks. I think I'll stay here, but I could use a little extra snack."

"I'll be right back."

Ben plucked out a large zip-locked baggie containing the same delicious mix they had for breakfast. As his dad moved out of sight, Ben had an additional idea. After thinking about the arrowhead for so long, he just had to see it one more time. He unzipped his life vest pocket and carefully took it out. With one hand in the trail mix bag nestled between his legs and the other clutching the stone, he once again wondered how it had gotten lost in the river in the first place.

Staring at it as he did, a different thought stirred. *What if Dad's words about the power of this stone are overblown? Then again, I suppose it must have been important to someone back in those times. Maybe, its presence will help me talk to Dad in the way I need to. I hope so.*

Chapter 19

A Fisherman's Luck

Fred wasn't gone long. Ben took one last look at the spearhead and put it back into his life vest before he thought his father would spot him. Too late, Fred smiled at the sight of his son's curiosity with the stone. It prompted the thought that Ben might have a future as a fellow archaeologist. The notion brought no further discussion as Fred reentered the craft. Once it was steady, together they pointed the bow back on course and got back into the rhythm of paddling in unison.

    As they moved along, they found the scenery still beautiful, including a rare sighting of a bald eagle sitting on a branch in a tall pine tree near the edge of the woods. The continuing paddling effort included two short pit stops to rest and devour more trail mix and a stack of peanut butter crackers. Both found it pleasant to be able to stop along the shore for a little while to soak up the sun's warmth and appreciate the surroundings they were in.

After their most recent stop, Fred suggested, "You know, Ben, it's close to midafternoon. We should be thinking about finding a decent place to camp within the next hour or so, and then we can get in some fishing time after setting the camp up. What do you say?"

Ben jumped at that suggestion and responded, "You were reading my mind."

"Well, keep your eyes peeled. You are in the front and the real eyes of this ship. I'm just the navigator, and according to our map, we have already met our distance goal for the day. The sooner we find a spot and get squared away, the sooner we can get some serious fishing action started."

"That sounds great for sure," said Ben with a smile. "I can't wait to test my new lure I bought the other day."

"Really? Just remember our time will be limited to sundown, because it won't be long after the sun sets that the mosquitoes will take over this place, and they will be looking for both of us. So, if you are going to get the big one, you shouldn't play around with one lure too long. Don't be afraid to switch things up a bit. That's what I do."

"Sure, Dad." Ben nodded in skeptical agreement.

Ben was a bit amused by his dad's last comment. He couldn't remember the last time his dad ever went fishing. However, now wasn't the time to mention that, even though Ben was always up for a good challenge with or without an experienced opponent.

"If the next campsite looks halfway decent, we will definitely take it," Fred said. "It doesn't have to be fancy.

This will be just an overnighter, anyway. Tomorrow will be a different story, because we should be in some real unspoiled fishing country, and we can slow down and relax with a solid couple days before we have to move on."

Ben was already distracted with his lure setup image and did not respond.

"Ready to hit it?" Fred said a bit louder as an attention-getter.

"Gotcha. Like you said, the sooner the better," Ben replied while he fantasized a battle reeling in his future trophy for his bedroom wall.

Without any more comments, they put away their remaining snacks, pushed Ole Yeller from the shore, and continued their journey in rhythmical fashion.

Ben was still incredulous over the fact they had only seen a few other groups of people the whole morning. Maybe they were already in their favorite hideaways down some quiet side creek, he mused. Here, all he could hear were the continual buzzing of darting flies hovering around him, an occasional sound of a distant songbird deep in the woods, or a random cawing from a solitary crow high above the shoreline.

And then, there were the endless trees and the multicolored dragonflies skimming and hovering just inches above the water's surface. The emerald-like reflections of the sun against the water's ripples, plus the light splashing sounds of their paddle strokes dipping in and out of the water, intensified the uninhabited remoteness of the trip. To Ben, the long periods of time spent in solitude was difficult getting used to. It made him uncomfortable.

The more they traveled upstream, the more his newfound aversion to isolation was becoming apparent to him. It probably was why he gravitated toward sports as his father drifted deeper into his work.

As Ben grew older, he found relief in a life of baseball and football competition and the tests of endurance, strength, persistence, and team fellowship. Even though this outing had most of those elements, and despite his father sitting only a few feet behind him, the overall silence fed the feeling. Ben hoped that fishing would offer the prospect of being able to forget about not having the camaraderie and interactions of his friends back home. The anticipation of seeing who would catch the biggest fish also helped.

Fred, for his part, was the complete opposite. Ben could see his father loved the isolation amid the scenery. He figured that this nature thing was more of a relief for his dad, a primal soul-cleansing, a concept like Ben had stumbled across in a textbook at school. Even when they had spotted the bald eagle earlier in the day, Fred had to stop paddling, point it out, and reach for his trusty camera. To Fred, this was a big deal. For Ben, it was nice, but another delay before reaching an immediate goal: real, earnest fishing time. During these long travel times, the teammate's objectives were at direct odds.

Beyond pointing out wildlife, the two didn't talk much when they were paddling. The steady stroking rhythms were hypnotic-like. Other than the personal preferences, for now there were no other worries. Ben trusted his dad's navigational skills and had faith in the course they were taking. Even though it was a flowing river, there were many other choices to take as they paddled along, involving forks, outlets, and tributaries derived from the river's watershed. Occasionally, Fred liked to deviate and change course, taking the added time to explore such side branches along the way before turning back and continuing the main journey. That part of the excursion Ben liked, because the constant paddling could get monotonous. Plus, it meant less power paddling against the steady current and the warm prevailing wind. It was more rest time for Ben, while his dad discovered more photo opportunities.

"Say, what time is it getting to be?" Ben asked.

Without looking, Fred said, "It's around three o'clock." It was about that same time they came upon an accessible area just after passing a wide fork in the river. It looked like a possible overnight camping site. Fred pulled his paddle into the canoe and said, "Okay, let's check this place out. What do you say?"

"Sure." Ben turned back to his dad and gave an appreciative glance.

They stirred the canoe shoreward and disembarked. Once on the river bank, Fred said, "Let's pull in Ole Yeller and scout this place out. It looks like it has some potential. We'll just leave the camp gear onboard for now."

Ben straddled the bow and helped lift and pull the boat a little further onto more solid ground. Fred grabbed the map from its flat plastic container and pointed to a spot on the river.

"Here's where we are. That's Sprouge Creek. We are right here near the fork. Can you see that?"

"Sure."

"We are further along than I expected, and if we can find a decent amount of dry wood and a level spot to pitch our tents, we should take this one now, so you can get some quality fishing time in. What do you say?"

Ben was agreeable because the site looked fine enough to him. Besides, the sooner he was fishing, the better this trip would finally become.

"Sounds like a plan," Ben replied, still trying to be cool about the whole thing. Football players were a tough lot and seldom showed real emotions except for the final glorious victory or after a punishing defeat. In that respect, Ben continued to practice his newfound sport demeanor.

Fred caught the mixed signal Ben projected and, pointing skyward, added, "Not only that, but the way the sky is starting to cloud up, even if you didn't have fishing on your mind, it wouldn't be a bad idea to get our things set up earlier in case the weather changes. Out here with no weather alerts, we'll just have to be prepared."

Ben checked the sky and frowned, knowing his dad was right. He was still hoping he'd have a good amount of time to fish once the camp was set.

Fred saw Ben's frown and said, "Okay, Ben, I'll tell you what. Let's take this site for sure and offload the canoe. If you'll just pump us more drinking water—enough for tonight and tomorrow—I'll do the rest."

"What do you mean?"

"Just pump enough water for both our bottles and a little extra for our cooking container for tonight's dinner and tomorrow's breakfast. I'll set up the tents like I usually do and get the site and equipment organized. Later, I'll gather up some firewood, and if the weather holds up, I'll put on a nice campfire like we had this morning. You go ahead and get started with the fishing operation until I get our supper ready. I'll go fishing with you after we eat, and I get things cleaned up. Sound good?"

"Sure. Sounds like a good deal. Just take your time getting things done, if you know what I mean," Ben said, trying not to grin. He had found pumping water was easy enough and wouldn't take more than ten minutes, max. He might even find another interesting artifact.

"Where do you want all this gear?" Ben asked.

"Let's put it over by that big boulder over there. It'll be easier to get to in case something unexpected comes up tonight."

"No problem. Let's do it." Ben's excitement was beginning to grow. There was no game face this time.

As soon as the equipment was secured by the designated boulder, Ben grabbed the water filter pump and bottles out of the food pack and headed back to the river's edge to fulfill his part of the bargain.

Fred made a more complete campsite survey and mental notes about good tent placement sites, the amount of available wood nearby, and a secluded spot for a makeshift privy. Walking around, he saw plenty of dry wood lying here and there. This amount would certainly be a blessing for an extended campfire later tonight. All else looked great with a pleasant view of the river passing by. So, without any more delay, he began setting up the tents and the rest of the gear. The site was all his to organize.

When Ben was finished with his water-pumping duty, he went back to the camp area and exchanged the water bottles for his fishing pole and small tackle box, then quickly returned to the water's edge. The tackle box held the ordinary basics: weights, leaders, and a long stringer; but more importantly, it included his personal assortment of lures and other artificial bait. Not sure what fish were in this section of the river, he grabbed a bobber and decided a scented plastic worm with a double hook on the end would be first.
 While he was setting his line up, the sun was still shining, but a slow cloud and wind buildup had begun. When he had everything ready, Ben couldn't resist putting on his polarized sunglasses for the full angler effect. His anticipation of his dad taking a photo with his big fish with a cool, casual sportsman's look was too much to resist.
 A stroll further along the shore led him to a nice, comfortable old log, where he sat down and attached his surefire bait to its leader. Next, he adjusted the bobber just a little better and made his first cast. The "worm" landed just where he wanted in a good spot and let the current keep the line taut. If a fish dared to take the slightest nibble, he'd know right away. Finally, he was content. He had reached his camping ideal for the day.
 The water's flow against some fallen branches, and

an occasional croak of a bullfrog hidden in the nearby tall sedge grass, became music to his ears. All he needed was for that bobber, only about thirty feet away, to drop below the surface and the day would be even sweeter.

Time passed and the bobber did go down on occasion, but yielded nothing. He switched bait; a spinner held against the current and no bobber for a while. Nothing. He tried a diver with the same result. *What the heck? Where's all the fish?*

"How's it going over there, Ben?" Fred called, interrupting Ben's momentary frustration.

"Not too great right now, but I did get a few nibbles a while ago."

Fred headed over to where Ben was fishing, curious about what was happening by the river. Mostly, he wanted to make sure his son's mood was still decent, but he also hoped the fishing was better than it sounded.

Once he reached the shore and sized up Ben's frustration, he asked, "What's up?"

Ben shrugged and said, "They aren't biting much. I'm using a diver right now, but I've tried a bunch of other options. Not much is happening. I did get a few bites with my plastic worm, but it stopped, so I'm experimenting."

"Okay, but remember it's midafternoon. A little later, the fish might be more active. The sun is still high right now, though it looks like things could be changing based on those distant clouds. That could get things started. I've heard there are supposed to be trout, walleyes, and smallmouth bass in this area, so it's only a matter of time before we get some action. I'll tell you what: I'll start dinner a bit earlier, and after we get done with that, we'll take Ole Yeller out, anchor it, and fish from the water toward the shore. I even brought a little surprise for you to check out during our dinner."

"What's that?"

"A little fishing handbook I picked up before we left. It's supposed to be a good guidebook for the fish in these parts and how to catch them. I'm going to keep things rolling back at the camp and give you a little more time. Sound good?"

"Sure. Absolutely. I didn't know you had a fishing book," Ben responded with a look of surprise.

"Well, what have I always told you?" Fred said with a pause for effect. "Always be prepared. So, when it comes to fishing, I've got you covered, Buddy Boy. Besides, I've never fished on this river before."

Ben had to crack a smile, and gave a short chuckle. *Maybe things won't be so bad after all.* It was even better knowing that his overly fact-based dad was still coming around. His subtle admission of a lack of knowledge when it came to fishing around here helped.

But, not surprisingly, Fred wasn't done and said, "Who knows? Catching a regular batch of fish from here on out could even be our Plan B for our overall food plan in case something happens to our food pack. Right, Benny?"

"Right." Ben nodded in agreement, realizing his dad was on a good roll. The idea prompted him to visualize his fish string full of their daily legal limit all battered up and sizzling away, while enjoying the after effects of the rich pan-fried smell filling the air all around him, that is, until his dad interrupted.

"You know what else I always say? It's usually good to pick up a little something extra from those who know. You get what I mean?" Fred wrapped up with, hinting that he was still a bit of an expert when it came to collecting the appropriate book knowledge of the day.

Even though the off-the-cuff book reveal was a surprise to Ben, he liked it and suspected his dad would have something more to rely upon other than pure guesswork when it came to their fishing. Ben knew his dad liked books. He filled his home office with them, and not just those about anthropology. Natural science and history were also his favorites, but Ben knew a few interesting camping and photography items were sprinkled in there, too.

So, having at least one fishing book on this trip as a good security blanket was reassuring, especially on a subject Ben suspected his dad still didn't know much about. However, he could recall one of Fred's favorite sayings to his kids whenever there was doubt about how to start a project they weren't familiar with; he'd remind them with his standard, "You know, any task that has been printed and bound, can always be interpreted and done." At least, Ben thought, his dad was consistent in that regard with the casual reveal and having the last word.

Other subjects that related to this trip, however, like general camping and nature, were a different story. Fred seemed to be already well read and tested from his previous woodland experience, and in that regard, he could travel light.

"Gosh...it's almost four o'clock, Ben," said Fred, glancing at his watch. "I'm going to get dinner started, so we can eat and check out the fishing book and see what it recommends. Then, we'll get our gear, launch the canoe, and fish until the sun starts to go down. At that point, we'll have to head back, otherwise, the mosquitoes will eat us alive. But for now, we should be able to log some extra fishing time together."

Fred continued, "Keep in mind, we'll have to be back in time to put away all our equipment, especially the food pack. Judging from the way these clouds are moving in, I think a change in the weather with the wet stuff will be in our future. Even if it rains soon, we'll wait it out and go back out after it passes. As I said before, the fishing can be especially active after a storm."

Ben nodded as Fred raised his hand to signal goodbye. Ben thought the idea of an earlier mealtime sounded appealing. He was getting hungry, and the prospect of a better fishing opportunity with Ole Yeller involved sounded even more inviting.

When they parted, Fred went straight to the food pack. He got out his tiny portable cook stove and set it up for a small pot of water he'd need to reconstitute the quick meal of dehydrated camp food he had planned for dinner. However, before Fred's cooking process began, Ben abruptly returned to camp. He had gotten to thinking about that shaman's stone since all the fish in the river were ignoring him and he was fighting the corresponding boredom. He decided it was time to take a break and make sure his dad didn't need any help. If not, he'd get that stone out of his life vest and take it back down to the river with him. It might bring him a little luck.

"How's it going, Dad? Do you need me to do anything?"

"Not really, but it won't be dinner time right away. I'm going to deviate a little bit and get busy getting camp prepped for some possible rain, but I will start cooking shortly. I'll give you a holler when the food is set. We're having spaghetti and meatballs, some sliced cheese, and, as a little treat, a blueberry dessert I thought would be worth a try. What do you think?"

"Sounds great. Since I'll have more time, I'll go back down there and give it a few more shots until you're ready. I just wanted to see if you needed some help with anything."

"Thanks, Ben. I appreciate it, but go ahead, and good luck. I'll give you a shout when I'm all done."

Ben nodded and went over to his tent, checked out his vest, and secured the artifact. He stared at it for a moment and again pondered: *I wonder what stories it could tell if only I had that time machine Dad had spoken of. Then, I could see not only how the spearhead was made, but also, for what purpose it had been intended or how it was lost. Better yet, how many hunts or battles has this stone seen? Maybe it could add a string of fish to its stories.*

Ben's mini fantasy didn't last more than a minute or two, and before he knew it, he had the artifact secured in his pants pocket and was back to the river armed with some new power and renewed hope. Once he got his fishing gear reset and made his first cast, he got a bite.

It was a good one with a long-fought struggle to bring

the fish in. When he got it close to the shore, he could see the fish was some kind of small trout. Despite its size, it brought his excitement to a new level. Once it was reeled in and the hook removed, Ben wasted no more time and ran back to camp to show his dad his prize.

Fred was equally excited and reminded his son that he should release the thing, as it was obviously too small to keep. But first, Fred insisted on taking a photo.

"Hold it up, Ben. I'm going to have to document your first fish for the journal."

"What kind of fish is this one?"

"Looks to me like a brownie."

"How do you know?"

"Well, these guys have a reddish-brown color and a long narrow head. We can double check with the book later, but I'm pretty sure."

"Okay, Dad. Thanks. It'll be the first of many."

"Okay, then. Let me get a few more photos, and then you can go release the guy. I will have our dinner ready in about five minutes. Don't hang out down there too long, unless you're not hungry anymore," Fred said with a laugh.

"Okay. Will do!"

Spirits were high despite the fact the weather was surely changing and dinner was going to be on hold a little more. That's because Fred had deviated from his setup plan to secretly check out the new fishing book to verify his identification, and still later, a little more time refortifying the tents and securing Ole Yeller against a series of alarming wind gusts.

Overall, Fred was able to ease his mind with the extra

camp security compared to putting together a quick freeze-dried meal. All that's required is the time to bring the water to a boil, mix, and wait for the packets to cool down. However, the rising wind and now the distant oncoming thunder had become an overriding matter.

Once Ben was back down to the river, he carefully let the fish go. Then he thought: *I've got to try as many casts as possible while I can before Dad calls.* It was a good decision. It wasn't much longer after only a few more casts, he started getting bites. Something out there was interested. Just when time had become forgotten, he got the dinner call.

"Ben, the rain is coming! Dinner will be ready before too long."

It was at that same moment; he got a real strike. Ben had the good-sized bite he had hoped for, but a great battle ensued. The problem was this fish, not only was it a serious-sized fish, but it was beginning to sprinkle. Ben was focused. He was going to win this battle, even though his clothes were starting to get wet.

This fish was a fighter. It ran the line out fast and furious. Ben pulled against the taut line and then reeled in the slack as the fish turned and came his way. *This must be a big guy.* It took off again and leaped out of the water, straining against the line. Ben could readily see it was a big one, all right. *Wow! I think it's a bass!*

Just as the fight was getting intense, with several more back-and-forth swings, the line snapped. It was over. Ben sagged in disappointment. He reeled the loose line in. To make matters worse, he was getting soaked from the steady sprinkling rain. And, what had started as a few distant thunderclaps were beginning to be a little more frequent.

At that same moment, Fred called, "Ben! Ben! Come on up! Food's ready!"

"Coming, Dad! I'll be right there," Ben dejectedly responded.

He picked up his little tackle box and headed back to camp, excited and upset at the same time. *If only it wasn't starting to rain,* he thought. *But as soon as it stops, I'm coming back. I'll be reeling them in, for sure.* With dejection written all over his face, he couldn't wait to tell his dad the big story, which would surely prove at least his luck had begun to change.

When Ben returned, he found Fred had already set up a tarp over the empty fire hearth and was setting up the cheese slices and utensils. The bags of hydrated spaghetti and meatballs were staged and still steaming. The dinner's array, plus a fancy blueberry cobbler dessert, were all laid out and looked inviting enough. Ben, spotting the meal in its entirety, remembered he was good and hungry, but at the same time couldn't wait to tell his dad the exciting news down at the river.

Ben was also impressed with the tarp mounted on extended foldable, heavy-duty, collapsible nylon poles and anchored rope lines, which created the illusion they came out of nowhere.

"Dad, when did you do all this? It's nice to be out of the rain. That's for sure. But you won't believe what just happened down there."

"What's that?" Fred reached for his pouch of hot spaghetti.

"As soon as I went back to the river and released the trout, I started getting a series of bites. Then, suddenly, I got another big bite with my very next cast. It was a huge bass! I don't know for sure, but I think that's what it was because I saw it. We'll know for sure when I see the book."

"Interesting. That sounds exciting…here, take some of this cheese. Your mom said it's one of your favorites; it's Colby. Come on and dig in," Fred said proudly of his menu's display. "You ought to start eating while you tell me this bass story. We've got to get a move on because it's starting to look like a good storm is heading our way, and we may have to head for our tents soon. So, let's eat, and say…where is that fish?"

Ben sat down on a dry boulder, one of many that were situated in a tight circle around the empty fire ring, and grabbed a spoon and his spaghetti pouch. Even though he was practically starving, all he could see was the image of that huge fish when it leaped out of the water.

"Dad, this was a big one. I really do believe it was a bass. I don't know what kind, but…I lost him. The line broke and he took my lure and sinker. If you'd been able to take a picture of me holding that big guy up, that would have been super. The guys back home wouldn't have believed it, that's for sure!" Ben's excitement made him oblivious to the increasing force of the rain.

Ben continued, "He really put up a big fight. I must have played him wrong and tried to reel him in too quick,"

Fred listened while he was also sizing up what needed to be done after the meal, while the rain pattered harder against the tarp roof. The approaching thunderstorm was beginning to concern him.

"Ben, I'm happy for you. At least you are finally getting some good fishing action and time is on our side, because after today, at the next site we pick, we are going to do a lot more fishing. We will be as far as we intend to go by then, and we can relax. But for now, once we get done eating, we'll have to get into our tents until this storm passes us by.

"I already hung up the food pack, covered everything, and tied up the canoe. All we have to do is wait this thing out. Hopefully, the rain will stop shortly, and we'll go out again with Ole Yeller and get a bit more fishing before it gets dark. That big hulking prize is still out there, and there's surely a lot more like him for you to test out their fighting will."

"That's a good idea," Ben responded. After a short pause, he continued, "This dinner is sure hitting the spot, too. I didn't know I could ever be this hungry out here. Thanks a lot."

Camping was certainly getting better despite the rain. The food was satisfying, and the fish stories were starting to be told. If only the rain would stop, this camping spot would be ideal. Unfortunately, with the lightning flashing more often against the darkening clouds in the distance, and the wind beginning to swirl along the water's open surface, Mother Nature was starting to paint an alternate scenario.

Trying to keep a hopeful and positive light on the situation, Ben again commented on the dinner, "You know, I really can't believe this kind of spaghetti tastes so good."

"That's the thing. Out here in the wild back country, food always tastes better and we're hungrier. The good news is there's more where that came from. Besides, you won't get hungry soon with the size of these portions. I can assure you that."

"That sounds good. I sure appreciate it."

Then, it was quiet between the two campers sitting under the tarp, savoring the meal. All they could hear was the steady downbeat of large raindrops crashing against the leaves and branches all around them and a steady stream of water beginning to cascade off the tarp edges. Despite Ben's disappointment, the sweet earthy scent of the fresh rain and wet pine bark helped soothe his mood.

Fred broke the silence first and said, "Ben, I know I said it already, but once we get done with our meal, we should retreat to our tents for a while and wait for this rain thing to clear out. It looks like it may not stop anytime soon, and with the lightning, we'll be better off in our tents. I'll take the tarp down later. I don't want to fold it up all wet.

"As I said before, I have us ready for the rain. I even added an extra tarp on top of each of our tents, just in case. Just so you know, all our gear is taken care of and protected. Hopefully, everything will stay dry. That's why I bring extra tarps. We can't afford to have anything happen to any of it, especially Ole Yeller. He's our lifeline back home. Otherwise, it could be a long hike back to civilization. You know what I mean?" Fred finished with a wry smile.

"Sounds great. Thanks for doing all that. I appreciate it." Ben grinned and added, "I don't want to sound like a broken record, but do you think we'll still be able to get into the river later?"

"Sure, if it's not too late and the mosquitoes aren't too bad. I'd like nothing more than being able to snap a couple more shots of you with a big one out here," Fred replied as they were finishing up the blueberry cobbler. Ben liked the idea and nodded in full agreement.

When the two had nearly finished their meal, Fred's demeanor turned more serious as he mentally noted Ben's wet clothes. It prompted him to express another thought for Ben to ponder besides fishing.

"I want you to know, this experience out here mingling with nature should end up being a rewarding one for you. In a selfish way, it already has been for me. And, despite the rain and the occasional bouts with the bugs, I hope you are enjoying the many sights and sounds that nature has to offer. At the same time, and I believe you may know this already…but I want to be clear, for those who don't keep their wits about them, nature can turn on you just as easily. She can be harsh. Basically, it's all about being in harmony with your surroundings."

Ben looked puzzled, "What do you mean?"

"Well, take this rain, for example. We could be miserable, all wet, cold, and hungry and all our equipment soaking wet. I'm not meaning this to be interpreted as picking on you in any way, because at one time or another, I've said the same thing to all the kids on these extended trips. But, while you were busy fishing, rather than interrupt you and rob you of your fishing time,

I did the storm prep. That's why being organized is so important. It wasn't a big deal. However, if you were alone, you'd have to be aware of your camping priorities."

Ben nodded confirming he was still listening while thinking: *I'll never be out here camping alone, organized or not. That's for sure.*

Fred continued, "I know our fishing time has been limited, and I don't want to pause that part of your enjoyment any more than necessary. But in the future, you're going to have to pay closer attention to the elements out here. What if I wasn't around and all your things got soaked or ruined? You might be sleeping under the canoe for the night and fishing in earnest for your next dinner. Worse yet, you might be wondering where Ole Yeller drifted to. You know what I mean?"

Ben had no response to the comment other than a slight nod and reaffirming his previous thought. *I will never be out here by myself with or without the elements, whatever the heck that is.* Fred's tone had dampened Ben's enthusiasm, but he didn't let it upset him.

Encouraged that Ben was still paying attention, Fred went on and said, "It's like baseball. Out at your position somewhere in the field, I'm sure you are always thinking…what if? More to the point, what if the ball is hit to me on the next pitch? What's my play with the ball? Granted, this is our first rainstorm of the trip, but we both need to be thinking of outcomes. You know what I'm saying? It boils down to, if we don't take care of our equipment, our equipment won't take care of us. Right?"

Ben didn't like where this topic seemed to be going. "Yeah…sure."

"Even though I don't believe this to be the case yet, I feel it should be said as a reminder not to become overconfident out here, and always stay alert as best you can. Nature can be truly exhilarating. She can teach us a form of harmony, a connection many are not aware of, and may never fully appreciate for that matter. And, as you have seen, there aren't many people out here or with the resources to help us out of a jam. For the most part, we are roughing it. I want you to remember that. Thankfully, I see you're still wearing your whistle. I appreciate that."

Ben rolled his eyes and lightly gave the whistle a token practice blow. His response clearly indicated he had heard enough, and it apparently showed.

"Right. So, enough of that. Another one of my class lectures is over for now, but stand by for a pop quiz a bit later, Buddy Boy. Now, let's hit our tents. You can always read your sports magazine or get out your cards and play some solitaire. I'm going to catch up writing in my camp journal.

"As far as the rain is concerned, we are set. If you want, we can always talk on our walkie-talkies, if you need something or just want to chat. I will rinse and lock up these food packets and utensils. And don't take offense from what I just said. I just want to keep your guard up to keep this trip pleasant and in perspective, especially in bad weather."

"Sure, Dad…no problem," Ben said.

Hoping to change the subject, as he scraped the last morsel of dessert from its container, Ben recovered with, "This pudding, or whatever it is, was really good. We should get Mom to pick some more of this up at the store for home, someday." Ben finished with a little smile.

"Glad you liked it. I'm sure I'll have to be the one to get that stuff. It won't be in a typical grocery store, that's for sure. By the way…it's a cobbler," Fred responded with a returning smile. "Now, make a run for it and get out of your wet clothes. We'll just have to hope the storm passes before too long and stay dry."

"Okay, Dad."

Ben stood and stretched and patted his belly as a sign all was well again. Then he turned and grabbed his fishing gear and made a dash for his nearby tent. Once he was safely inside, to make sure there were no hard feelings, he stuck out his head and shouted, "Thanks again! I'll be ready to fish as soon as the rain stops…for sure!"

"No problem!" Fred shouted back over the increasing sound of the rain with a thumbs-up signal.

Inside his tent, Ben dried his head and face with one of his smelly T-shirts, peeled off his wet canoe pants and shirt, flipped off his shoes and socks, and crawled into his inviting down-filled sleeping bag. Once completely settled in on his camp pillow, alone with his thoughts, he tried to forget the last lecture, reached down for his sprawled-out pants and pulled his spearhead out of his pocket. Fearing it might have gotten damaged when he forgot it was still in his pocket, he couldn't help but recheck it over. Fortunately, a quick examination proved it was the same pristine condition as before, and he did not have to face his dad with any bad news.

Relieved, Ben held it close, and as he did, he

marveled at his sudden change of luck after having this mysterious artifact in his possession. Even though suddenly catching some good fishing action was more than likely a coincidence, it sure helped improve his standing in the casting department. *If I keep the stone long enough, will it help my chances in football camp later this summer and help make me a first-string starter? Maybe, MaryBeth will notice me for once.* He had been hoping he'd be able to muster up the courage to ask her to hang out with him sometime. *Can it help me with that?*

He turned the stone over many times looking for a hidden clue. *Come to think of it, except for the lecture, Dad has been friendlier ever since I found it. I wonder if it really helps with courage, as Dad implied, or is it just a lucky charm?* Despite not seeing anything beyond what he had already seen with it before, the intrigue continued. *Maybe this thing will help make this fishing trip really work out the way I'm hoping for…and not just for the biggest fish.*

With no answers to be had for his thoughts and questions for the immediate future, Ben's mind turned to a much simpler fare, namely his rod and reel. *If only the rain would hurry up and stop.* However, it was clear the bad weather would last for a while. The thunder was growing louder, not softer. The earlier rainfall was also growing stronger with each passing minute. Ben's hope for a late-afternoon or early-evening fishing prospect was beginning to grow dimmer with each booming thunderclap. With reality starting to take hold, he carefully returned the stone to its pocket hideaway.

Chapter 20

A Stormy Night

Little did either Ben or his dad know that a serious storm was approaching, but now it was a moot point; they were already hunkered down. After an hour of continuous rain, thunder, and lightning, Fred radioed over.

"I'm sorry, Ben, but it looks like we'll have to pack in the fishing idea for the night and remain in our tents. It's going to be dark soon and there's no point in trying to fight this weather. Tomorrow, I'll make sure we get up early enough to log in the promised fishing right after a quick, no-cook breakfast."

"Okay, Dad. I understand." Ben replied with a raised voice, trying to drown out the pattering of the driving rain. "We'll get going early tomorrow for sure. Just wake me up."

"Will do. The fish will still be out there, hungrier than ever. Good night and don't let the bed bugs bite," replied

Fred, trying to lighten the mood.

"That's for sure…good night," said Ben, not entirely enjoying the humor.

It was obvious that they were in the middle of a prolonged storm, and Ben prepared to bed down. Even though it was still light outside, it was already after eight o'clock. And though Ben didn't admit it to his dad, all the paddling and other physical outdoor activities they had done today had tired him out again, both physically and mentally. Despite the fishing cancellation, he was more than ready for some quality sleep.

Ben turned off his radio and made sure his flashlight was nearby. As he slipped deeper into his cozy down sleeping bag, he hoped his one-man lodging would keep him warm and dry throughout the night. The steady downpour not only provided a white noise, but it also meant there shouldn't be any nighttime roving animals outside his tent.

The combination of sheer exhaustion and shedding his fears allowed Ben to fall fast asleep. He remained so until he was startled awake by a flash and a tremendous thunderclap. *Whew! That one sounded close.* The flash had lit up the entire sky, including inside his tent. It was followed by a rolling and crackling thunder that felt as though the sky was being ripped wide open.

The rain was coming down in earnest, given an extra driving force by the wind. So far, the tent seemed to be doing its job keeping the moisture out, but for how much longer? Despite the nylon roof repelling the heavy rain, Ben was getting nervous, and considered calling his dad on the radio. Being only semiconscious, he instead decided to try and go back to sleep. Besides, what could he say that wouldn't make him sound like a rank rookie Scout? A trembling tenderfoot, as it were.

However, a prolonged sleep was to be denied as the crashing thunder claps persisted. It was getting well past the time to resettle in, but try as he might, another huge crack of thunder and its associated flash lit up the sky— including his tent and his wits.

At times, the explosions sounded directly over the campsite. Other times, the thunder sounded like a Fourth of July bomb had gone off. The tent would shake and move back and forth as the winds swirled through the trees. Even the entrance flaps shook and vibrated as though they were being systematically ripped away. Judging from the sounds of the pouring rain, it must have been coming down in torrential sheets, causing a lot of branch movement and general outside commotion. Ben hoped his tent wouldn't collapse, and began to fear that the inside would start to flood.

The good news was everything was holding up, and Ben was grateful for his dad's efforts fortifying his tent with extra tarps. One was stretched and anchored outside, over the tent roof and fly; another was under the tent directly on the ground; and a third was inside the tent, insulating the sleeping bag and its thick camp pad from the ground. Fred had explained his chief reason for the extra barriers many times before on earlier family outings. Ben remembered his words: *Other than being lost, being out in the woods and trying to sleep in a soaked and cold sleeping bag is not much fun, either.* So, even though Ben had thought the extra work a bit much when he was younger, tonight's heavy storm helped him to see the value of his dad's effort and the wisdom of his words.

The thunder and lightning gradually diminished as the heaviest part of the storm moved away. However, the rain kept coming down. Its steady patter on the tent's protective tarps recreated a white noise that helped Ben drift back to sleep. His strongly held secret not to admit how physical the trip had become had finally taken its toll. That is until he was startled awake with wet feet. *What is this? How can this be?*

Ben immediately reached for his pocket-sized flashlight kept near his pillow. Once he was able to survey the back end of his tent with the light, he noticed the rear screened window, directly opposite the tent entrance, was not zipped completely closed at the bottom. The rain must have been splattering up from puddles that had accumulated right outside the tent.

*Oh boy...*was all an exasperated Ben could muster. In his after-dinner haste to run and get out of the rain and dive into his tent, he had forgotten to check all its windows. At least, the two side ones were closed. Consequently, the splashing and wind-blown rain had been pooling inside the tent floor, and the portions of his comfortable bag that had moved off his sleeping pad were busy soaking up the excess water. Not only that, but the bottom of his personal backpack next to that same window looked soaked, too. The sight helped Ben remember his dad's words—*Nature can be harsh*—and mentally agree as he sat up and zipped the window completely shut. *How could I have been so forgetful?*

Equipment priorities…man oh man!

Ben did the best he could to move and dry off the bag and his soaked pack with an extra T-shirt, and tried to wipe up the large puddle of water at the foot of his tent floor with a few more. He knew his efforts wouldn't be much help until the morning, provided the rain had stopped, and he could then hang his wet things out to dry.

For now, Ben's concern about the thunderstorm and his wet conditions succeeded in changing his mellow nighttime disposition into a bewildered disbelief about this watery catastrophe. Surely his dad was awake through this crazy weather, too. *Maybe I should radio over to him and see if he has a little more camping wisdom on how to deal with this.* Hopeful, he set his light down and reached for his walkie-talkie. He turned it on.

"Dad."

There was no response.

Again, Ben called over with a louder emphasis, "Hey, Dad!"

Still there was no reply.

Okay…that's odd. Surely his father couldn't have slept through all the storm's noise, either. He called over once again, even louder yet. Still nothing.

Fortunately, this set of radios had an attention-seeking beeper feature, so he pressed on it. Even though he could hear it beeping in the distance inside his dad's tent, verifying that the radio worked over there, he still received no response. This was truly odd, but he rationalized that his dad was out of his tent checking on the covered equipment and the condition of his prized canoe. *I suppose that's not out of the question. Take care of the equipment and it will take care of you,* Ben remembered him saying again.

To find the underlying cause of the mystery, he grabbed his flashlight and unzipped his tent just enough to briefly poke his light out the entrance flap to see what on earth his dad was doing in the rain-soaked night. Even though the rain had slowed up, he couldn't see clearly enough. So, he took his dad's advice and blew his whistle once. He waited a couple seconds. Nothing returned. He blew it again. Once.

Becoming concerned, he extended himself further out of the tent with his light. This time he noticed a dreadful sight where his dad's tent was situated, no more than twenty feet away. He thought he could make out multiple pieces of a medium-sized tree branch straddled across the tent's roof. He could not believe his eyes. He checked again. His jaw dropped and exclaimed out loud, "Holy cow! This can't be real."

With all the rolling thunderclaps, he hadn't heard any branches breaking or anything else hitting the ground. If it indeed was a branch, it had to have happened when he was briefly asleep. Nevertheless, his slumbered eyes were bulging with mortified shock.

"Oh no! I don't believe it!"

Despite the miserable conditions, he immediately grabbed and put on a nearby tee shirt and reached for his hat, but he didn't immediately see his pants anywhere. His undershorts would have to be good enough. Flustered, he loosely clipped his light to his hat brim, and with hands free, and thinking of nothing else, he began his barefooted and bare legged slosh over to his dad's tent. He hoped a semi-flattened tent was all wrong—a distortion of sorts. *I have to find out.*

Even with the darkness and the weakness of the beam from his little camp light, Ben could readily see by the shape of the tent's outline that something was still inside—hopefully, just a couple lumps from packs or a pile of clothes. In the back of Ben's mind, though, he knew he was looking at a potentially dreadful crisis. *Is this the makings of a horrible night? I hope to God I'm wrong.*

His answer came quickly as he approached the front of the tent. The downed branch and its remnants looked bigger, and they were clearly strewn all over and around the tent. The large, jagged end of it had just missed the entrance door, but the connecting smaller branches had reached up and over the top like a dark spider web. It looked intimidating and ominous.

As Ben was about to bend closer, a gust of cold wind caught the brim of his hat and tossed both it and his clip-on flashlight into a nearby puddle. The light went out before he could retrieve it. *What the heck?* Fortunately, even though it was behind him, it was within his reach. He turned and grabbed the hat and at once tried the light. Even with forceful shaking, it stayed out. *For God's sake. This can't be!* For Ben, his inner darkness had become matched by his surroundings. A complete darkness had taken over.

All the while, as he tried to adjust to the sudden depth of the darkness, Ben was frantically calling, "Dad!" to no response, holding out hope that his dad might still be out checking the state of his equipment and the tarps. *Why didn't he answer my whistle?*

Undeterred, he removed the dead light from the brim of his hat and snuggly returned the sopping hat back upon his head, so it would at least keep the rain out of his eyes. Then he tried to rub the light dry and shook it several more times in hopes of making it work, but to no avail. Giving up, he awkwardly bent down and reached for where he thought the tent fabric might be, but he stepped on a large piece of the wooden debris and stumbled a step backwards. *Wow. What next?*

With a quick reflex, he regained his balance while managing not to drop the deadened light again. Amid the darkness, he remembered what the scene looked like before the light went out. He bent down to the ground and felt for an extended branch. Hoping it would lead him to the tent, he resorted to using the limb as a guide. Moving in a hand over hand motion along the crumpled branch, the effort worked. He made his way to the tent and to the portion he hoped was the front of the tent. Reaching out, he felt a zippered seam. It was a good start.

Positioned at the entrance, and with no pockets, he placed the light tight under his armpit and encountered another portion of the fallen branch. It felt like the big broken end, but discovered it was way too heavy to push. Frustrated, he tried lifting it away, but he was only partially successful. *At least, I got it to move.* Not giving up on his light, he stopped and tried shaking it again. It still would not work.

The continual darkness was maddening. It only made

his clumsy attempts to get past the wooden barrier nearly impossible, without being able to visualize the results of his struggles.

Ben took a long breath. He simply had to keep trying to unravel his father's fate. With all his might, he tugged on the branch until he thought it would clear the door. Not forgetful of the value of his little flashlight, he kept it tucked tightly under his arm, as he battled the branch's size and weight. Struggling mightily and repeatedly to clear away the obstruction, while mindful of not letting the light get wet again, the rain added to his personal drama by coming down harder.

Undeterred, Ben was finally able to slide the branch sufficiently enough through the mud to clear an opening and return to the tent's entrance flaps and zipper. *Thank God. That took forever.* With out hesitation, he tried unzipping the crumpled nylon and inner screen combo. To his dismay, the opening was positioned at such an odd angle—pinched, more than likely—it could not be moved freely.

"Dad!" Ben pressed his face against the tent's fabric and fumbled to straighten out the zipper enough to pry it open. However, just looking at the tent's shadowy outline more closely as he struggled to get in, he felt the tent contents and realized, *Dad's here.*

Ben had feared the worst, but was also anchored in denial. *No…this must be something else…probably his pack. Dad's going to show up from around a dark corner in his rain gear, wondering what's happening.* Ben was beginning to lose any semblance of rational thinking, and everything he did was occurring in slow motion. What was lying inside the tent was already unthinkable. Ben was feeling a heavy stinging pain of dread, while feeling he was being smothered from a lack of oxygen. There was already an uncontrollable trembling in his hands, but now, reality was beginning to creep much deeper into his uncertain mind.

Using all his strength, which was considerable thanks to his football weight-lifting training, and not dropping his camp light, he tried the zipper again and got it to move. It was just enough. Not wanting to risk dropping the light, Ben instinctively placed it in between his teeth, so he could get both of his hands inside the zippered seams and muster all the remaining strength he had. He ripped it completely apart with one great adrenaline-induced pull. Without his light, he blindly reached in and felt the side of his father's wet and sticky head. He screamed, "No! No! This isn't happening!" His worst fears had been confirmed.

Discovering his father lying still, but not being able to make out the extent of the injuries because of the thick cloak of darkness, he feared his dad was crushed and already dead. Desperate, he tried the light one more time. Nothing. He shook it a good one and tried it again. This time it worked, but only weakly flickering. It had barely come to life. If only his dad would, too.

Thanks to the spotty lighting, he could see his dad was faced away from him to the right. One of the smaller shattered branches had broken off, and its pointed end had punctured completely through the tent roof and was still resting across his dad's head and shoulder. Ben carefully grabbed it, turned, and gave the injurious object an angry toss into the rain. Another pole like piece was still impaled into the tent floor like a crude spear. He tried removing it as well, but it wouldn't budge. Not wanting to waste time, he gave up on it.

Ben then turned his attention to sizing up his dad's condition. He was taken aback by the blood splattered on his father's face and the tent floor. He also could make out a good amount of fresh blood pooled along his dad's back side and neck area not covered up by the sleeping bag.

Ben finally froze. Aside from minor football injuries, he had never been this close to a serious accident. The sight and smell of the blood made him feel woozy.

So much so, he coiled back and struggled to keep himself from fainting. However, despite his own condition and unadulterated shock, he knew he had to continue to see for himself how bad the situation really was. He silently chanted: *keep it together, keep it together.*

He managed to collect himself, took a deep breath, and moved in closer to check his dad's head. Although he hadn't tried detecting a pulse, his dad felt warm to the touch. All this time he was trying to wake him up by repeating, "Dad! Dad!" and giving him a slight shake.

What should I do? What should I do? This can't be happening. I've got to think.

Ben's mind was racing while he tried to be rational, but his dizziness had increased. He had always become revolted by the sight of someone else's blood. His dad's was no exception. Even under normal times, he could barely stand to see his own.

Welling tears were another obstacle. *I simply have to*

think straight and quick. What would Mom do? She's always had a good answer for my aches and pains. If only she was here.

After a brief pause, he forced himself to lean further into the tent and check the source of the blood he could readily see. Once he had an idea from where most of it was originating—the forehead, nose, and a large gash on the side of the head—he set his light down and ripped off his wet T-shirt to wipe the blood and the sticky debris away. It was a terrible sight. This was his dad. *This is my family. Is he gone?* His dread consumed him.

I've got to do something more! Ben took a closer look. Judging from his dad's position, he had been sitting up; and from the large gash above his left ear, he must have taken a grazing blow against the side of his head as he fell away from the branch's striking force. This might explain the wound's severity and his resulting unconsciousness.

To get a closer look, he removed his hat and moved in as much as the outside branches would allow. The weakened flashlight revealed another deep gash on the front of his dad's forehead, and it appeared to be the source of the blood pooling under the neck area. His damaged reading glasses lying nearby amplified the significance of the blow.

When his light flickered once more, Ben feared his flashlight's power could be near its end. It prompted him to look for his dad's. It wasn't nearby as he hoped it would be, and the downed obstacles were limiting his efforts to continue. *Nothing could be worse than all this. I just hope this light stays on!*

Ben refocused and deduced that another portion of a branch piece, still outside the tent, must be responsible for not allowing more access inside the tent. Despite being on the verge of passing out from the horrific scene before him, thanks to his first aid training from his Boy Scout days, he managed to take some basic medical action.

First, he took his bloodied shirt, wrung it out outside the tent as best he could, and rinsed it out with fresh water from another large puddle right outside the entrance. Then he wiped his dad's forehead as gently as he could. He repeated the process many times, each time lightly pressing on the head wounds to help stop the bleeding.

With the fresh blood partially cleared away and the rain continuing nonstop, Ben could see his father's head and eye sockets were already black and blue. His nose was crooked and swollen, much larger than its normal size.

Ben continued pressing, wringing, and soaking up more water with his shirt as gently as he could. This was all the first aid he could muster without retching. While the sight of his dad's oozing blood was gradually making him physically sicker, at the same time, trying to get rid of it helped keep him going.

Glancing up, Ben noticed a portion of his dad's backpack at the rear of the tent. It appeared to be pressed under another sizable piece of the branch and looked inaccessible. *There must be something like a camper's first-aid kit in it that I can use, or better yet, lying nearby.*

Ben scanned all that he could see, the tent floor and along the walls. No kit was visible. *Is there one in here at all?* The trouble was he couldn't remember exactly what his dad had said about a kit or where he kept it. Whether he said anything or not, Ben hoped getting at his dad's personal pack would provide an answer. Otherwise, he'd have no choice but to venture back out into the weather to check out the big canoe pack staged with all the other equipment. That could take a while.

Struggling to stay calm, he knew he'd have to secure his dad's pack first. To do that, he'd have to move the rest of the branch off it—no matter what. Once he felt the bleeding had sufficiently slowed, maybe stopped, he backed out of the entrance and moved to the rear of the tent. There, he placed his struggling light between his teeth once again and approached the branch. There was more than one. There was a mix of large and small pieces. Despite the amount, he was able to lift the largest piece straight up and completely off the tent. After making sure it was clear of his father inside, he tossed it away from the scene. It was heavy and broke into smaller pieces as it hit the ground. The whole thing must have been thoroughly rotten.

That left only a few more straddled around his father's feet and the pack itself. Ben disposed of those, too, even though the combination of those were about as heavy (more solid) as the larger one. Once again, weight lifting at school was paying off.

Ben then tried reentering the collapsed tent, but it was more damaged and flatter than before. Thanks to the weight of the large pockets of surface water that had collected, and a change of the tension from the removed branches, the entrance was now completely inaccessible. It forced him to go back to the previously broken branch pieces and find a couple relatively straight ones to prop up the tent. Of those pieces, he found two. They were each about three feet long, and he used them, as best he could, to replace the crushed tent poles and prop up the roof from the inside. They weren't the best solution, but they worked as he had hoped and kept the roof up, stable, and the inside accessible once again.

With this modest success, Ben was able to get deeper into the tent and keep the slick tent material off himself and his dad. This was important. He still needed to finish his assessment and figure out what else he could do. It was grim business, but he was determined now more than ever. *Is he hurt anywhere else? How bad is he overall? Is he still breathing?* Despite Ben feeling like his skin was crawling from what he saw lying before him and becoming wild eyed with howling panic, he found a baffling presence of mind to sort out what to do next.

First, he held his father's wrist to try and find a pulse. After a long pause, he thought he felt one. He double-checked to be sure. *Yes! Thank God!* Now that there was solid hope, he could still react if he were in time. He also noticed his dad's weatherproof watch and decided to take it off and put it on. *I'm going to need this.* He checked the time. It was close to one o'clock in the morning, and it would be a long time before sunrise, typically around six. He was quite sure no one would be traveling around here until at least then.

Next, with his light still weakly strobing on and off, he decided to check his dad for any other more serious injuries. After he placed the flashlight back into his mouth, he carefully unzipped his dad's sleeping bag and opened it up. To Ben's dismay, he discovered his dad's lower bare legs were also bleeding. Portions were black and blue. While he couldn't tell if anything was broken, there were plenty of visible cuts and bruises. He wiped them off with the same shirt as before.

When Ben was finished, he reached for the crushed backpack and pulled it closer. He thrust his flashlight into it. Rummaging through its contents, and to his great disappointment, he discovered most of his dad's personal camp clothes were all that was in there. However, he also discovered his dad's knee-length hooded raincoat, which had been partially covered under the pack, was now exposed. It was a welcome sight. He had been working nonstop in just his undershorts and was thoroughly miserable and shivering. Without further hesitation, he managed to put it on without leaving the tent. His dad was taller than Ben, but it fit okay, and most importantly, it felt warm.

Next, he checked the bag's side compartments, but only a few miscellaneous camping items were there— no first-aid kit, large or small. *What the heck?* Shifting the pack into a better position, he spotted another small flashlight and a Swiss Army knife with a variety of blades. Both had been partially covered by the sleeping bag. *What luck!* Ben set the knife aside and instead tested his dad's little light. It worked much better—*thank God!* He put his failing flashlight and the new found knife into his raincoat pocket.

Through the process, Ben was becoming more distraught with alternating waves of ineptness and dread. All he could do was react and hope someone would pass by and get him some help. He wasn't sure if there was anything else he could do or had forgotten to do. As it was, he was acting on rapid sporadic impulses and a well of pure adrenaline.

Searching around the tent floor and in the bag further, he didn't find anything more of value than his father's extra clothes, which Ben used to line all around his father's injured areas to help soak up any more blood and rainwater. Finally, he rezipped the sleeping bag to help keep him as warm as possible.

However, rainwater was still dripping into the tent from a small hole in the ripped roof. Somehow, he had to stop the incoming water. Satisfied he was finished comforting his dad as much as possible, Ben grabbed his camp hat, and went back outside and moved the top tarps into a better position to prevent any more rain from getting inside the tent.

By this time, Ben was emotionally and physically exhausted. Despite the shock of the whole matter, Ben was beginning to realize that if he were to save his dad, he'd have to do more than sit and watch him—only to wait for untold hours for help. The bottom line was clear: *I must find help…and fast.* From what he could tell, his dad had at least two major injuries besides the obvious cuts and bruises. But he was still alive. That fact made him realize time was of the essence. Urgency and surges of panic were fueling his reasoning to leave the site and find help on his own.

I must get back on the river, and in reverse course, to see if I can spot another set of campers close by. Ben looked at his dad's watch. It was half past one. Time was moving along, but Ben knew it still would be many more hours before dawn. *Is the river the answer? Should I really leave?* He made a frown.

With a better light source, Ben also knew he'd have to check the condition of the canoe to see if the river was the answer. Ben rushed as best he could through the streams of water and slick mud over to Ole Yeller to make sure it was okay. A quick examination told him it was. *Thank God, it's still here and appears to be okay.* However, the light also exposed the force of the blowing wind against the forest undergrowth, tossing loose leaves all around him, and pushing long rows of rippled waves rushing to the shore. Being alone in the dark was bad enough, but this sight had a definite hellish feel to it as the cruel wind pressed itself against his raincoat.

Trying not to think of himself, his dread of leaving, or facing his nighttime fears, Ben turned his back against the wind. He took an extended deep breath and did his best to continue moving. He headed for the canoe packs. They were nearby and still tucked under their protective tarps. Unbelievably, they felt dry enough.

As he began his search for more essentials for the possibility of a desperate trip to find help, he thought of his mom, his sisters, and brother. *What can I tell them if I can't at least tell them I tried to find someone to save Dad? What would they think, if instead, I just sat here?* He again thought of his father's last lecture with his familiar clichés: *"Nature can be harsh," "Be prepared," and "Plan B." Well, this was an accident, for God's sake. Surely there's something in one of these packs that would make sense for me to use and help me figure this out.*

The first-aid kit and the map were already known items he'd surely need, but was there something else that his dad had spoken of that he'd brought along specifically for emergencies? *The whistle was one*—but Ben still had his around his neck. *How about a bigger light? What about the bear spray?* At least, he had a decent flashlight, the whistle, his dad's camp knife, and a spare light with its weak batteries with him. Certainly, not having one of those new mobile phone packs at camp was awful, but he wondered if they would even work out here. *We have one in the car at home. I suppose Dad knew it would be of no use here in the wilderness.* He dropped the thought.

His search through the large packs was quick, but maddening. None of the extra things he was looking for was on top or readily evident. There was no compass, no matches, no survival stuff that he and his dad talked about at home, that he could readily see. *Are they in some special place...somewhere separate?*

However, Ben's search wasn't completely in vain. He did manage to find a small box-sized first-aid kit, the map, and a small bottle of mosquito spray, but no bear spray or a much bigger light. He rationalized that dad's emergency things must have shifted to the bottom, or surely must be stashed somewhere else. Ben was at a loss where that somewhere might be.

Nonetheless, he thought: *I have all that I need for a short trip to another campsite. All I need to do is check the bleeding, get back to my tent and fetch a dry shirt, my canoe pants, and my tennis shoes. I already know Dad's raincoat will do.*

As the minutes flew by, the more wild-eyed Ben was becoming. *I can't waste any more time!* Uncertainty dogged him with more questions. *What's the best course I should take to find someone quicker, and what extra items should I bring along that I brought?* Ben knew what he had so far wasn't much, but he was fairly certain he wouldn't have to travel far before he'd find help. *At least, I have a more reliable light. This rain is bad enough. One thing for sure, I'm not going to attach this one to my hat.* He took a deep breath. Satisfied he had all that he considered sensible from the big travel packs, he returned to his dad's tent.

Nothing had changed. His dad was still unconscious. Ben didn't spot anything more essential he might need, either. He then verified his dad was still alive with one more pulse check and rechecked the bleeding. His dad was still a mess with fresh blood. He grabbed the first-aid kit he had found and opened it. To his dismay, there wasn't much in it to address all his dad's more serious wounds. However, he re-wiped off what he could around his father's head and face and applied some gooey ointment that looked like it might help.

Despite his unwavering aversion to the sickening sight of blood, thankfully, there was less. Frantically, he tried to tape the gashes with pieces of the available gauze to help increase the clotting. As he did, he prayed his dad would open his eyes or move a bit. He racked and stabbed his mind for any last-minute clues wondering: *What if I was hurt like this? What would Dad do? Am I forgetting something obvious?* He only drew a blank.

Frustrated, Ben began administering as many of the varying types of bandages he found in the kit. When he was finished, he began to feel better that he could satisfy his urge to go out and look for help. *Surely, that's what Dad would do. I just need to figure out if I should walk the shoreline or really take the canoe?* Ben knew he'd have to leave one way or the other, and without any solid facts or even where he was, rationalized that Ole Yeller would be quicker with less obstructions.

To leave, though, was hard. He wanted to get help, but at the same time, he didn't want to abandon his dad. Ben was numb with stress over his fear of not getting help soon enough and doubting whether he'd even find the right way in the dead of night. His confidence was lagging far behind his will to help.

However, with the impact of the bloody scene sinking in deeper, he abruptly cast all his doubts and fears aside, and finally firmed his decision to leave and get help.

Even his worst fears of being alone in the dark took a back seat. His rescue attempt was not only for his dad's sake, but he felt his whole family was depending on him. Leaving was simply what he had to do. *I've got to do something more than this. I've got to find help…now.*

Before Ben began to back out of the tent, with every nerve in his body standing on end, shaking and bewildered, he knew he had to say something before he left.

Looking at his foreboding difficulty in the eye, he remembered his dad's inspiring words earlier in the day: *no matter how big or small the adversity, it's time to shine…really shine.*

Still on his knees and only inches from his dad's ear, instead of a silent solemn goodbye, in the hope his father could somehow hear his words, he managed to eke out something positive, something reassuring.

"Don't worry, Dad…I'll be back…as soon as I can. I won't rest…until I get you out of here. I promise."

Afterwards, draped with emotion, Ben drew a long, deep breath. Realizing he may never see his dad alive again, he stalled and wiped his eyes. Then, miraculously, he pulled himself away and readied himself for what he passionately believed would be a quick return with help in hand.

Chapter 21

At the Water's Edge

As Ben backed further away from his dad's gravitational pull, he wondered how he'd gotten into this predicament without ever anticipating the harshness of nature. With that in mind, he made sure he had both of his camp flashlights, his dad's Swiss Army knife, and the silver whistle. He even gave it a blast, assuring that it worked. It was an ear-piercingly shrill and certainly loud enough, but not loud enough to rouse his dad.

    With a firm resolve, he made his way back to his own upright tent. There he grabbed his pack and went through it. All the packed clothes inside were soaked. Looking for anything else that might help him when he moved his wet sleeping bag aside, he spotted his nylon canoe pants underneath. Despite their wetness, he put them back on over his underwear as fast as he could. He checked his pockets. His large red handkerchief and the shaman's stone were still there. He kept them both. *What else? What about the mosquitoes? They haven't been a problem yet, but what about later?* He had found a pocket-sized plastic bottle of spray in the canoe pack earlier, but it had felt light. *I thought I had more around here. I must have left mine outside somewhere by the river when I was fishing. I'll have to remember to use what I have sparingly, not like I did yesterday with those awful biting black flies.*

There was no luck finding any additional spray, but he noticed his tennis shoes. *I almost forgot all about them!* Even though he had thought about them earlier, with his being wrapped up in his continuing adversity, he suddenly realized he had been in his bare feet all this time. He wiped the mud off as best he could with the edge of his tent's entrance flap, slipped on the shoes without ever bothering with his socks, and tied them tight.

While hoping he had all that he'd need for a short trip, deep in the back of his mind, he still wasn't sure. Ignoring those fragments of doubts, he seized his dripping wet pack and headed back to the canoe equipment packs. Wiping the rain from his eyes, he thrust his dad's flashlight into each to see if there was something he should bring, one last time. *Is there something I haven't thought of yet?* From the looks of it, all he saw was mostly the standard camping equipment and assorted cooking items. There wasn't any bear spray to be seen, but he did spot a flare gun container his dad had not referred to. *What the heck is this?* It looked important, so he grabbed it. He had never used a flare gun before.

Hoping he'd figure it out, it was coming.

Worried about wasting any more essential time, he gave up his search and sloshed his way back to Ole Yeller, turned it upright, and threw in two of the three paddles lying nearby, the map, and his personal backpack. Just as he was about to untie the canoe from its tree-based anchor, he had a sudden mental flash. *What if someone comes by while I'm gone looking for help? How can I alert them?* It might be a long shot, but he decided to scurry back and make a sign to get someone's attention.

With the flashlight and thanks to the strong wind, he found several straight pieces that were about two-to three-feet in length scattered around the camp rather quickly. With them he created a makeshift H-E-L-P sign and placed it at the water's edge. He was satisfied that the branches were large enough that anyone floating by would readily be able to see the word.

Next, he hurried over to the canoe and took one of his brightest T-shirts out of his backpack and tied it to a long pole and stuck it upright deep into the sand to create a more attention-getting flag above his crude H-E-L-P sign. To be doubly sure, he braced the base with rocks and added his red handkerchief a little lower on the pole. *I can't take any chances on someone not seeing this sign.*

He took a deep breath. He was ready. *It's now or never.* With dread and hope pitted in a slugfest, he was locked in with his decision to leave. *It's time to roll.*

It was true. There could be no more delays. The turbulent river was to be his watery ride, and its wayward current was waiting.

Determined, Ben turned his attention back to the canoe, and this time, untied it and dragged it to the water. With the rain continuing to come down and sporadic thunder sounding off in the distance, it was hard to tell which way the current was flowing. He knew the downstream direction was the one with the current, and would be the return course home. The floating debris from the storm lent a clue of the current's strength and direction. The other way meant he'd be traveling further upstream, facing a harder time paddling and moving deeper into the unexplored boonies.

It was simple enough. Convinced downstream was best, he shoved off, soaked with a combination of nervous sweat and the chilly rain. *I'll find someone soon enough. All I have to do is get there.*

Even though he was moving with the current, he soon discovered that paddling a two-position canoe as a solo paddler was much harder to control than he thought. The swirling wind and strong current were even more challenging.

With the ongoing difficulty managing the bouncing canoe derived from waves driven by the forceful wind, Ben discovered the only sensible course was to stay tight to the shoreline. For the most part, this portion of the shore seemed to be much smoother, with only enough depth to allow the canoe to float. In that way, he used the river bottom and his paddle to help steady the boat and push it in the direction he felt he needed to be going as a counteraction to the wind.

However, the good flashlight was proving to be no real help. He simply couldn't hold it and push at the same time to see where he was, and there was no way he was going to risk losing it attached to his hat or getting soaked from the rain. His ultimate pattern came to be checking what was up a few yards ahead, putting the light in his raincoat, then pushing a bit more and periodically rechecking again. It was slow and awkward, but steady.

All the while, the downpour was constant enough to prevent Ben from seeing the opposite side of the river. So, even if campers were over there, he would never know it. That notion alone was stressing him more than he realized, conceding he was searching for help on only one side of the river.

With his erratic flashlight observations, occasionally he got the canoe suck in the sand or hung up on an extended, low-lying branch. To make matters worse, Ben was reminded there were groups of submerged rocks when encountering hard scrapes on the canoe's bottom. Deeper depths only allowed the wind to easily grab the canoe bow and attempt to twirl it backwards. He had to make sure he stayed in the shallows, but as his improvised paddling methods proved, over and over, this was not so easy.

Many times, Ben needed to forcefully push the canoe forward much harder to make any progress because he had run aground. All these conditions tested his self-imposed calls for urgency and sense of purpose. *I could have walked quicker than this.* Ben was finding it difficult just trying to remain calm and stay on course the further he moved downstream. However, he knew he couldn't give in to his mounting frustrations and try to go back to the camp. He had already mentally crossed that line.

The good news for Ben was that the overhanging tree canopy gave him a measured amount of relief from the pelting rain. It let him size up where he needed to go to get further down the stream with a better view of the shoreline straight ahead with his light. This was important, as he knew of the little side inlets that flowed into the river like the ones he and his dad had explored and enjoyed along the way earlier in the day. As far as he knew, those smaller tributaries wouldn't supply much of a chance of finding a campsite on one of those side courses, anyway.

As he moved along, Ben's assurance that he was even on the main flow of the river began to fade because the current was diminishing to the point of being almost nonexistent. He soon found that without any visual landmarks, which correlated with the ones on his dad's map, the effort to get his bearings was futile. He decided the aid of the map was a total waste of time. His paper compass's value had disappeared.

Without the map, he'd now have to take his share of chances. To help move along a bit quicker, he'd occasionally try to venture a little more from the shore, whenever he suspected the wind gusts had died down. The urge to paddle in deeper water and gain more ground was great. Unfortunately, that strategy always proved to be counterproductive whenever he was re-exposed to the wind. It invariably would provide a much stronger gust after a few good strokes and momentarily recapture the bow of the canoe.

Ben soon realized the wind was going to continue to

be a serious adversary in one way or another, and, like it or not, he would have to slow down to regain any measurable progress.

Ben's only real success was to override his impatience, take his time, and remain as close to the shoreline as possible. That internal struggle was ongoing as he pushed the boat like a Venetian gondola, managing only a few feet at a time. And when he bumped up against large groups of submerged rocks, it only made things worse trying to maneuver around them. Those were occasions he had to fight back his corresponding swells of frustrated tears and regroup.

Then came a time when he caught himself entertaining grim thoughts that this whole rescue mission could already be doomed. Even more harrowing was an unimaginable fear that both he and his dad might not ever be found alive in these woods ever again. The mounting pressure of an impending failure was beginning to grow until it was becoming quite possible.

Ben tried to cancel out his mounting doubts while pushing the canoe, but he knew the facts as they stood. He and his dad both were alone in separate locations. He had no clear idea of how to sort out his frustrating paddling predicament while trying to override his biggest fear of being alone competing with the hostilities of the dark.

Those facts kept his mind in constant turmoil. He desperately wanted to see an occupied campsite, not eventually, but immediately. His daring attempt to move downriver without a reliable navigational tool was fueling his belief that he might not ever be able to get help from anyone. His situation had changed so much that he had found himself regularly second-guessing himself with every push further downstream.

Soon Ben was confronted with the stark realization he was undeniably lost. That was the moment when he realized he was no longer on the main river, and his worst fear about his rescue attempt was at hand. Despite the ever-present darkness, he suddenly was able to see both sides of the waterway. *When did it become so narrow? It wasn't like that when we were on it before.*

The realization was like a sledgehammer delivering a devastating dose of reality, dashing his skull, when Ben discovered exactly why. Despite being mindful of his dad's earlier advice to stay alert, he had indeed entered a fork of one of the dreaded side tributaries and reached its vegetative dead end. At the discovery, he went limp. All he could do was wail in his head: *I don't believe this has happened. How can this be? This just can't be true!* But it was. The waterway he was on was done, and instead, he was caught amid a thick, swampy bog. It might as well have been quicksand; mentally he had been snagged and now was being sucked downward.

Because of the wind and rain, he had accidentally taken one of those smaller side branches and reached its abrupt ending. This meant a much greater loss of time, as he'd have to double back to find the river again and watch much closer with his flashlight to stay on course. Remembering his father's photo shoots along the way, Ben knew these narrow waterways varied in length, and he could have been on this fork the whole time. *This could be it. I'm done for.* The psychological sledgehammer's aim had been true, cracking his mind and his heart in unison. He couldn't swallow. His mouth had become bone dry. He couldn't even muster a tear to cry.

There he sat, frozen and dumbfounded, floating amongst what seemed like a sea of watery vegetation. Ben's worst fear of being endlessly alone in the dark had come to fruition. He was ready to surrender. He had become a zombie. He needed a mental rest—a big one, if he ever was to become himself again.

And there, while sitting all alone in what had now become a steady drizzle, having already screamed for help and used his whistle repeatedly to no avail, as a last resort, he closed his eyes and did something out of character: He began to pray in earnest for his own life. *Please help me. I'm lost and there's no one to turn to. I'm stranded on a cliff edge—not a swamp—ready to be pushed into the arms of whatever perils Dad warned me about.*

Ben's personal walls were crumbling as he waited for an answer of any kind. Attempting a last-ditch effort to calm himself down, he squeezed his eyes shut and chanted to himself: *It's going to be okay; it's going to be okay.* But this hollow mantra style wasn't working. The feeling of doom and gloom was still ever present.

During those chilling moments, with eyes closed, an emotion called "despair"—unbeknown to him—appeared in hls mind as a vague image instead. Remarkably, it had even transposed itself and had moved right square into his lap. When he opened his eyes, the illusionary thing was already staring him down and smirking with a provocative kind of look.

"So…what are you going to do about it, kid? Nothing? Well, tough luck, loser."

Ben couldn't even move to raise his paddle up to swat the figment away. He had become too stiff from the numbing shock of what it felt like to be a stranger to himself, disoriented in an unknown world, and trying to summon even the slightest vestige of the most basic survival wits. How on earth was he to reverse this tailspin?

What am I to do? Am I going crazy? Why is this nightmare continuing? Is God watching all this or even listening? As he waited for an answer of any kind, unexpectedly, he reversed course and thought about just surviving…at least until the morning light. Wondering how much longer he'd have to spend in this eternal darkness, he asked himself: *What time is it, anyway?* He was hoping it would be soon. *Just to be able to see…that would help me find someone.* He turned on his light and dared to check. *Oh, for God's sake!* It was only half past two. All this while, he had been out on the water for barely an hour. He snapped the light off.

Ben then tried his whistle again and blew on it several more times, wondering: *Where are the park rangers? Do they even patrol at night without a reason?* The noise of the rain helped provide the answers for him. All he was left with was his steady feeling of nothingness. He found himself raising a mental white flag of surrender with its emblazoned words, "I never should have left the camp and Dad in the first place." printed on it in big, bold red letters. Mired in self-pity, he said to himself: *This whole thing is all my fault.*

So, there it was: Ben was lost in a big way and completely uneducated for this kind of calamity, especially in the deep woods. That fact, combined with his increasing feelings of panic while snatched into nature's encompassing web, continued to challenge his very survival.

Being a fighter, Ben tried to think. It was all he had left, but at this point there were no answers coming. He silently sat like a hollow statue, bobbing, and rocking from side to side while an occasional brisk wind kept Ole Yeller penned tight against the tall bulrush reeds and surrounding lily pads.

As Ben remained frozen on the canoe seat, with the rain dripping off his hat rim and the canoe bottom filling with the chilling rainwater, numbing his feet, he discovered another new companion. This time it was a thing that felt like "anguish," and this time it wasn't an imaginary illusion. While he thought things couldn't get any worse, a group of nearby mosquitoes had found him. *What next?*

He managed a semblance of strength to reach for the spray bottle in his pack and lathered up as sparingly as possible. The spray gave him a small measure of relief, freeing his mind to turn an about-face of sorts and recenter upon rational thoughts that pertained to his predicament, his dad, and his family.

Then, without a compelling reason, he remembered the stone was still in his pocket, and how it had become a good luck charm of sorts for him earlier in the day. He rubbed the stone without bothering to take it out of his pants pocket and look at it. The rubbing provoked him to remember how his dad had explained what a stone like this had represented to someone ages ago.

Ben couldn't remember specifically all his dad had mentioned, but he began to grasp the stone's huge significance in a warrior's life and, more importantly, how it represented not luck, but raw courage for those warriors.

Comfort came with that thought, as his mind started to calm if only for a few minutes. At least, it was something. Whatever it was, the tag team of deep emotional despair and his physical anguish had noticed that he had found a slight countermeasure to their unwelcome presence: new thoughts focused on courage.

Even though his inner strength was severely drained, the mosquito reprieve filled him with more yearnings, more renewed thoughts about his family, his dad, and even God. They proved his resolve was not completely shredded and gone forever. The stone, coupled with images of back home, prompted Ben to clearly see a simple sign in his room with bright red lettering that he had made long ago and had hung over his bed's headboard, which merely read, "Persistence Overcomes Resistance."

As his dad would say, "Even a steady drip of water over the course of time will wear down the most hardened rocks." There—he'd had it all along, a mental safety net reminder that could hold him from being sucked all the way down his watery drain and out of sight. Ben repeated it to himself: *Persistence overcomes resistance. Persistence overcomes resistance.* Suddenly, he felt something positive inside himself begin to come alive.

As Ole Yeller continued to rock from side to side amongst the eerie forms of swampy vegetation and those extending into the forest, Ben knew that he could not quit. The motivational three words reminded him he was never a quitter, and it always helped him with his sports life back home. It was during this time his last reserve of adrenaline began to stir. It reminded him his dad was still back there, injured at camp, and depending solely upon him. Usually, it was the other way around, when Ben had been younger, but now the tables of responsibility had turned. Once again, he had to act. He could not quit.

Ben squeezed the stone in his pocket one more time, acknowledging with a symbolic gesture that at least something tangible was with him and on his side in this ordeal. Believing it had given courage to someone before him, he stiffened his jaw and decided to move on. He still had a chance of getting help if he went back to the main river.

Stepping out of the boat, back into the cold murky water, and into the soft, mushy shoreline, he turned the craft around. Maybe…this time…there would still be time for him to "shine in the big game," as his father had challenged. He knew there was nothing "half-assed" about what he would have to do from here on out. His persistence would be his will. The opportunity for a positive outcome was on the line. As his dad would have said, it was time to "finish the game-winning drive."

Once the canoe was reversed, he gritted his teeth and headed out from whence he came, away from his dead end. He was determined to do something—anything—even though he knew an ample amount of despair and anguish would still tag along as his steady canoe mates; however, he was determined to suck it up. This time he would take stock in himself and physically walk the canoe along the shore out of the inlet. And even though he was too tired to take any more chances pushing the canoe with a paddle, he convinced himself: *I'm not too tired to find help.*

So, onward he stepped along the foul-smelling marshy edge as he tugged against the suction of the gooey mud on the bottoms of his tennis shoes until the narrow creek feeding the inlet reluctantly, but gradually, had more of a sand-based feel to it. Despite the weather conditions, the creek was shallow, and as soon as he thought he could walk across the narrowest portion of the inlet, he braved the cold water and blustery wind to face his only option. He had to get to the other side.

Braving the crossing meant he'd have to walk to the opposite side, about thirty feet wide. With his light, the water still looked to be shallow and relatively solid. Better yet, stepping in, he found the depth no deeper than his knees. Fortunately, even with stepping ever so slowly, it only took a few minutes to cross. Relieved he had made it in one piece, without falling in or accidentally letting go of Ole Yeller, he was able to continue following the big river downstream. At least he thought he was back along the main flow. Without being completely sure, the return of a slight current with its floating debris was a good sign.

Even with this bit of uncertainty, Ben made sure he carefully walked the shoreline clutching the canoe's gunwale a little tighter with one hand and shielding his little flashlight with the other. There would be no more paddling of any kind tonight, and no room for a shred of self-pity. He had a mission to complete. Crossing the inlet was a positive booster and a good start.

Ben was glad to be moving again, and knowing he still had a shoreline to follow was better than sitting by himself, frightened beyond words, in his canoe stranded in the depths of a swamp. At least, he was headed in a straight course, step by step to a destination where he still hoped to find someone willing to help.

As fate would have it, and as soon as his thoughts had returned to hopes of running into that special Good Samaritan, he saw a flash of light coming from deep within the woods. He shook his head, then double and triple-checked to make sure it wasn't his imagination. It was well inland, to be sure, but it looked to be real enough and the first sign of civilization he had seen since he left camp.

Knowing the canoe was his only means of reliable transportation, he initially resisted his urge to leave it behind and go on foot inland to check out the light. Remembering his dad's deep affection for Ole Yeller, Ben hesitated for a minute more before he finally decided to pull his temporary life raft well onto dry land and try his best to securely tie it tight with his special triple "granny knot" to the nearest sizeable tree.

With trembling hands and chattering teeth, he managed to tie his unique knot as tight as possible. Despite the fact it was the only knot he knew; he trusted it would hold and gave it one more tug. Ben's mind was made up. He simply could not resist the temptation to check what the light source could be.

Before he moved away from the water toward the light, a true sense of renewed hope began to grow. Could it be that, finally, he had a visible source for a way out of this mess? Was this the occupied campsite for which he was hoping? Despite his initial hesitation, he knew: *I have no choice. I've got to check it out.* So, he turned away from Ole Yeller and its meager contents for the time being. Heading out on foot with his trusty light to do a quick investigation, Ben found he was also carrying a fresh spirit with the hope of ending this unmeasurable calamity and fulfilling an urgent promise.

Chapter 22

The Cabin Window

It was muddy footing in the swampy part of the woods, and hard going for Ben, who was already exhausted from an ongoing battle with a lack of sleep, worried beyond words for his dad, and not having the foggiest notion where he was. He stumbled and slipped on rotting branches and partially exposed rocks several times despite the aim of his flashlight.

While he was being drawn toward the mysterious light up ahead, he imagined being home again, and began to think of his mom. Even though his father was the one who needed his help, it was his mother who now occupied his mind as he faltered on. *How can I ever face her if I fail? Not to keep going will haunt me forever.* He was lost, but despite the odds, he was also mentally more determined, thanks to his newfound inspiration while sitting in the canoe and successfully crossing the inlet.

As he moved inland, brushing through the woodland entanglements, slipping repeatedly, and getting slapped in the face by clumps of low-lying wet leaves and an occasional pine bough, the distant light appeared to take on a square shape.

Ben began to believe what he was seeing could be a legitimate light suspended near what he hoped was a structure, like a tent or even a lamp post. *It looks like a crazy place for campers, but I don't know. Maybe, it's a ranger place. I just have to get there and find out.*

Just as hope was rising, he went down—hard, slamming his back and banging his head. *Holy cow! That's all I need...this close to help and stuck here with a broken back?* Ben had tripped and fallen from yet another leaf-covered slippery branch. This one caught him by surprise as he struggled to get back up on his feet and regain his balance. His low-cut tennis shoe treads were proving to be too smooth for these woodland conditions.

With more misery, the fall reminded him he had to slow down and be more careful. Despite the lay of the land and his wooziness, he had to keep going. The mystery of the light had to be unraveled. It could be the answer to his prayers. With determination, he steadied himself and stepped on.

The closer he got to the source of the light, the more he believed it could be coming not from a tent, but from a small building, and the beam being emitted looked to be a square shape like from what could be a real window. This was promising, because if the structure turned out to be a cabin, even if unoccupied, it might have a working telephone, food, or clean drinkable water. Maybe, even a towel or two to dry off with. Not only that, but a trail or a driveway could lead to a connecting road. It was beginning to look as if his decision to take the time to check out this mystery light might seriously pay off.

Despite all the melancholy conditions and unsure footing, spotting the light was strikingly good news. Added to it, the rain was letting up. As he got closer to the light, he could see it really was coming from a cabin, situated on a slight hill overlooking the waterway from which he had come. Like a luminescence-drawn insect with a buoyant spirit, Ben advanced steadily toward the lure of the light.

As he slid through the wet undergrowth, up a short incline to where the cabin stood, it was clear the window with the light projecting out of it was at the corner of the structure. There were no other lights, only the one from the corner.

Moving closer, Ben expected an end to his nightmare. Thinking of how most people tended to take things for granted, assuming their routine lives were the way they would always be until their world is suddenly turned upside down, Ben was grateful for the prospect his world might right itself within a few more minutes. All he had to do was reach the front door. Surely, there would be a trusting soul inside the place happy to help. With measured hope, he reasoned: *Why else would the light be on?*

Then again, if the cabin was unoccupied, he might have to break in. The use of a phone or devouring food of any kind compelled him onward. He was already envisioning what he'd say to the 911 dispatcher. He knew he wouldn't be able to tell them much except about his dad's injuries. Admittingly, there was little else he could say about his location, but he hoped the person on the other end of the line would instinctively know what to do.

When he was only a few steps away and could clearly see the details of the cabin's structure through the darkness, he couldn't help but wonder what kind of people owned this place. He ruled out the ranger aspect because even though it was wood framed, with a front porch, it looked old and run-down and even haunted. It had a dark, forsaken look about it. After a pause, he decided to ignore the twinge of fear he was beginning to feel. This cabin was his first great hope. There would be no holding back now.

Ben used all the energy he had left to get up the creaky steps up to the porch and bang on the front door, shouting, "Hello! Anyone here?"

Without a response from inside, he repeated the effort while he impatiently tried to open the door, only to discover it was locked. He banged again, with no sound of a response. Frustrated, he bolted from the door, along the porch, over to the lighted corner window, and looked in, only to see a scruffy-looking man, about sixty or so, still dressed in a V-neck undershirt and baggy blue jeans approaching the front door. Ben could hardly contain himself.

He waited until another light from inside the cabin, closer to the door, came on. Then there was a click of the lock and the knob turned. Once the door opened just a crack, there was a mutual look of surprise—one from Ben and one from a perturbed-looking old man. Ben was startled by the agitated look from the heavily whiskered guy, eyeing him up as a runaway kid, who appeared more like a mud-splattered, drenched rat. More surprising was when the man opened the door a little more. That's when Ben found himself looking down at a large blue barreled revolver pointed at his chest.

"Who are you and what do you want?" demanded the man on the other side of the door in a gruff voice.
Ben was taken aback and gasped at the sight of the gun. His face paled and his jaw dropped with utter shock. Despite the tone of the threatening question, the image of Ben's injured father was still burning strong. With this one chance, and out of sheer desperation, Ben took a deep breath and blurted out as fast as he could, "I'm Ben! I'm a camper from down the river and my dad is hurt. He's hurt really bad and needs help!"

Ben made another attempt before the man behind the door could slam it shut.

"Please, help us! If you can't, please call someone. I don't know what else to do," Ben continued.

The man paused a minute and opened the door a bit wider, but kept a steady aim on the pleading boy with his gun.

Able to glance inside the cabin room a little better, Ben hastily saw a couple of empty whiskey bottles, dirty dishes stacked high on the sink counter top, fishing gear leaning against the wall, and a deck of cards on a large wooden table, all within plain sight. Then, he noticed at least one other older, disheveled man beginning to stir from a dilapidated, oversized lounge chair stationed near the cabin wall closest to the door.

Ben tried his best to ignore the gun, and instead, took stock in his fleeting opportunity and said, "Please mister! I've got to have help! It's for my dad. He's back at our campsite and unconscious from a fallen branch in this storm we had! Please!" Ben was wavering between the edge of hysteria and a glimmer of hope.

As he spoke, he continued to size up the inside surroundings, trying to judge what kind of problem he may have stumbled upon. *Are there more people in here? What are they up to?*

"What do you want, kid? What's your problem? It's in the middle of the night. We're trying to get some sleep," responded the man at the door, still holding the gun on him and acting as though he hadn't heard a word Ben had already said.

"Who's with you?" the man continued.

"No one! I'm by myself. I just need help in the worst way."

"What's…going on?" said the second man inside the cabin. He was trying to emerge from a deep sleep or stupor and rise from his creaky old lounge chair.

Appearing still half asleep, with only one eye open and highly irritated at the sight of the boy barely visible outside the door, the man struggling to get out of the chair yelled, "Shoot him, Dan!" slurring his words while still struggling to stand up. "He's trespassing! Just shoot…and get it over with…we don't need anyone snooping around here."

Both men looked as though neither had had a warm bath or a close shave in many days.

Not to be deterred, Ben shouted, "It's my dad! Don't you understand? He's hurt bad! I don't know how bad he is, but a good part of a tree fell on him. I've got to find help and soon. Do you have a phone in here?"

The man with the gun, who was big and stocky, stood his ground in front of Ben. However, he looked as though he was starting to understand the earnestness in Ben's high-pitched voice. For a moment he looked sympathetic but confused.

"Hold on a minute, kid. Let me think," Dan replied. "There are serious woods out here. Where the hell did you come from?"

Torn between relief from having found a person who might listen and help, but with great apprehension about the gun still pointed at him, all Ben could rightly say was, "I don't know. It's somewhere down the Pine River."

The other man named Gus, who was shirtless and much smaller than Dan, but covered in a variety of tattoos, piped up in a barely coherent voice, "Get him…outta here! He's trouble."

Instead, Dan opened the door and motioned Ben in. When Ben was inside, he shut the door behind him and relocked it with a clear sounding metallic click.

Ben realized he was potentially caught in a place of danger, reeking with a nauseating mix of offensive smells: powerful mildew, strong whiskey, stale cigarette smoke, and penetrating body odors, all rolled into one. Once again, he managed to ignore the bad impression and continued his pleas.

"Please help me," Ben pleaded with tears welling in his eyes. "It's my dad..."

Dan didn't answer the pleas, but his facial expression appeared to Ben that Dan considered him not to be a threat; instead, a big nuisance that needed to be addressed in one way or the other.

As Ben's tears continued to roll, Dan slowly lowered his revolver and placed it on the table within quick reach. Despite Dan's response, Ben remained close to the door in case it became obvious he'd have to make a run for it.

Then, it was Gus who said, "What the hell you doing? Get rid of this kid! We don't need his kind of trouble."

With a furrowed brow Dan reacted, "Okay, kid. Calm down. Can't you see you're irritating my partner? Now, where is this dad of yours...who supposedly needs us?" That was about all the compassion Dan could produce.

Ben took another deep breath and, as tired as he was, tried to explain once again.

"I told you; I don't know. We were on a fishing trip...camping along the river not too far from this cabin but a lot more down the way, the Pine...I think. I paddled this far in the dark and saw your window light, but I'm lost."

"Well, that water down there still is the Pine, but there's no other people who live anywhere around here, and Gus likes it like that."

"Do you at least have a telephone I could use?"

"We have no phones here. They cost money and we don't need one," Dan replied. His tone turned sour. "We don't need any more people like you around here bothering us and asking questions, either."

Gus stirred again. He was becoming a bit more awake and looked to be more threatening as he tried one more time to get out of his chair. As he staggered upright and regained his balance, he refocused on the other two.

In no time, he bellowed out, "What did I tell you, Dan? Where did this kid come from…and why are you fooling around asking all your dumb questions? Who cares? If we wanted a goofy looking early trick-or-treater around here, we would have set up a candy dish. I'll tell you what I'm going to do. I'm going to shoot first and ask questions later…that's what I'm going to do. Where did you put my gun, you big moron?"

"It's on the table," Dan replied curtly, "but you don't need to shoot anybody just yet."

"The hell I don't," Gus huffed.

The men hesitated for a moment to see if this was just a drunken bluff between each other, and then they both went for the gun. Ben was petrified, and by this time, knew full well that being trapped any longer in this place would be a huge mistake. There was no phone, and it didn't look like there would be any help coming from these two.

As the two burly men were distracted struggling for control of the gun, Ben reached for the locked door. It was an old sliding bolt lock, and he moved it and turned the doorknob. He raced out the door and didn't look back when the gun discharged. He heard Dan yell, "What the hell are you doing?"

Gus shouted, "We can't let that kid get away! He might say something."

Ben didn't know who had pulled the trigger or if

anyone was injured—it didn't sound like it—but leaped from the rickety porch as far as he could. The mud cushioned his landing to a certain extent, but his raincoat length had obstructed his view. He hit the slippery ground awkward enough to roll his ankle. He went down in a heap.

In extreme pain and with flaring nostrils and trembling hands, he tried to get up. *I'll never get out of here...I'm hurt bad.* It was a struggle to get back up, but there was no time to waste. Once finally upright, he found he couldn't put any weight on his foot to take another step. *Oh God! Not this! I've got to get away! That gun is loaded! I can't believe this!*

With grit of steel and clenched fists, he absorbed the pain and hopped on one foot as fast as he could, managing not to fall again while watching the porch door. Once he got to the closest underbrush, he dropped down, moved his raincoat aside so he could crawl, and moved far into the thick cover. All the while, his ankle stabbed with pain. Before Ben could calm down and tend to his injury, the two men burst out of the cabin where their yelling and cussing resumed, another struggle began. They had taken their fight onto the porch.

In another second, they pulled each other over and slid down the steps, still struggling over the gun. Then, bang! Another shot went off. Ben wasn't sure if he should try and move or stay put. One thing for sure, the terror he was feeling made him think he was going to lose his spaghetti-and-meatball dinner. It took all his self-control for that not to happen, or even to bolt away on his hands and knees from the hair-raising threat that was happening only a few yards in front of him.

Will they be able to see me here? Ben wondered. It wasn't long before they stopped, waved their arms in his direction and went back into the cabin. Ben held his breath. *Do they have flashlights in there?* He was hoping they would stay put, but then, sure enough, out they came. It was like they had read his mind. One of his questions clearly had an answer. Instead of flashlights, they had a large gas lantern and were headed his way.

Big Dan, who was holding the lantern, slipped and went down and another flood of loud cursing began. Gus, who had possession of the gun, picked up the lantern and headed Ben's way, while Dan hobbled back to the cabin.

Without a word, Gus fired a shot in the air, showing he was serious about trying to flush Ben out. Frantic, Ben froze and held his breath. *How long should I stay put? How can I even move? What am I to do?*

Ben's knuckles were turning white from gripping his fists so tightly. Fortunately, his answer came quickly, in the form of renewed rainfall. It was as if a faucet in the sky had turned on, making the lantern's wide viewing distance, less so. As the thoroughly wet gunman approached, about halfway to Ben's hideaway, he veered off and began to waver from side to side. Ben marveled that he was able to walk at all in the slosh and mud after how groggy he had appeared in the cabin.

Ben figured both guys had been drinking, and in the case of Gus, well beyond rational thinking. Ben had seen this behavior once before at one of his friends' overnight camping parties, while his friends were experimenting with beer and hard liquor. It turned out to be a bad scene. With that in mind, watching Gus about to lose steam, Ben knew it was best to stay put and not make a sound.

But Gus pressed on until, for no reason, he paused to reorient himself, swaying back and forth. When he continued again, he headed off course while trying to keep his balance. Instead of heading straight toward Ben, he made a couple of wide circles, then a staggering zigzag step or two before he finally steadied himself, turned, and headed back to the cabin porch. *He looks like he's given up. Keep on going, you creep!*

Ben let out a huge sigh. But his ordeal wasn't over. Gus fell on the steps and heard his gun hit the porch. After another swearing episode, Dan came back out and dragged his cohort inside. To Ben's horror, he saw Dan return outside the door, but only to retrieve the gun. Ben stayed frozen, trembling from the drama played out again right in front of him. He was glued to the ground, shivering in the brush thinking: *Is there more to come?*

Ben knew they both could easily return in a few minutes with a bigger light, raincoats, and more determination to continue their desperate search. Except for Ben's ankle, his body had already turned to stone. He paused and closed his tear-filled eyes. They had seen enough.

After a moment fighting the return of his demons, Ben regained his wits and tried to refocus on the cabin, but his ankle needed attention. He took a risk and took out his little pocket flashlight. He bravely turned it on.

Checking on the condition of his ankle as quickly as he could; it was obvious this was a severe injury. His ankle area was already swollen, black and blue, and throbbing from his heel all the way up to his knee. The intense pain reluctantly forced him to take the time to gingerly take off his shoe. He had no choice but to try to help relieve his agony.

With the help of the light, he untied the laces and managed to get the shoe off, but it didn't come easily. The effort verified that his physical appearance matched his mental state. One thing he knew for sure; his injury was a serious setback in his quest to save his dad. As soon as the shoe was removed, he snapped the light off.

Ben was truly afraid, but he couldn't move. Other than his leg, he was numb from sheer exhaustion and mental fatigue. *What a huge waste of time this cabin thing turned out to be. I can't believe it.*

He covered his face with his hands and shook his head. *I don't believe this. That was a close call. What's with the gun? I've never had one pointed at me before. Who are these guys?* Ben was grateful for his good fortune to have escaped from a dangerous situation. *Why are they so upset? Were they really going to shoot me? All I asked for was help for my dad.*

Ben wished he hadn't left his backpack in the canoe—or the first aid kit back at camp, for that matter. *Even a few bandages on the blisters on my hands right about now would help.* All he still had with him besides his hat, the whistle around his neck, and the clothes under his raincoat were in his pockets: his dad's knife and the stone.

Ben gratefully thanked God for his escape and thought he could get by without going back to the water if he had to. He was just thankful to be out of that evil place, even if it meant an injured foot. *Who knows what that Gus might have ended up doing?* He shuddered to think about it. *I absolutely have to get away from here. I'm not out of danger just sitting here...not by a long shot.* However, the rain and the darkness, for a change, were now his new-found allies. He was out of view. *All I need to do is stay alive and move away as quick as I can.*

Ben decided to stay low to the ground, hiked his raincoat up to his waist, and as best as he could, crawled a little further away from the cabin. The effort took about all he could withstand before he had to stop. His ankle made it so. As he lay quietly with his injured leg extended, he tried to think logically. *There must be a trail or a driveway that should lead to a decent road. How else did these maniacs get here?* He was not going to be able to go back down to the river with his injured ankle. *Anyway, didn't I already tell them that's how I got here in the first place?*

Besides, the river route had already proved to be a hopeless situation, fighting along in that vast watery world of endless shoreline and lapping waves. *There really wasn't anything worth going back for, including Ole Yeller, except for the mosquito spray.* Leaving that little bottle of repellent behind was bothering him in a big way. He knew he might have to pay a big price to Mother Nature for that decision, if the rain ever stopped, but it was a risk he would have to take. His ankle was screaming at him...*No way!*

While his thoughts shifted from the possible terror of hordes of mosquitoes to those of his father, and whether he would ever see him alive again, the lights inside the cabin window suddenly went off. The entire cabin went completely dark and still. Without the window light, he could barely see the cabin at all. However, he judged the immediate threat of the two drunken brutes might be over, at least for now. *Hopefully, they're passed out and won't even remember I was here.*

He waited until he was sure all would remain quiet, then used his light again to check his watch. It was a quarter to four. It must have taken him longer than he thought getting into and out of the cabin. He said a short prayer with more thoughts for his dad.

Finally, he gathered up the last bit of energy he could muster, grabbed his useless shoe, and decided he would have to continue to stay low. Walking would not be an option anymore. So, on his open blistered hands and only the paper-thin nylon pant material covering his legs and knees, he began crawling through the wet underbrush, directly in the opposite direction from a kind of danger he never knew existed in real life.

It was tough going, trying to remain quiet and out of sight as the patter of the night time rain bounced off his raincoat while he made his way further from any more cabin-related harm in search of a simple path out of the forest.

He crawled along through the dense undergrowth, occasionally scanning the woods with the aid of his pinpoint light and hoping to get a safe distance before deciding what to do next. With every forward movement, he could feel the shaman's stone in his pants pocket bumping against his thigh. The constant patting against his good leg temporarily diverted his thoughts to a wider diverse of rambling questions: *Who was the person who had this stone before me? What was he like? What dangers and battles did he have? Why would he ever give it up?* There were many others as he moved along and tried to forget about the terror he had just experienced inside the cabin and his ongoing escape.

Unfortunately, the stone was only a brief distraction; it revealed no secrets. With no answers, the bizarre situation Ben had just been a part of forced him to realize he would have to keep his wits and trust in himself to face whatever else lay ahead. There would be no turning back. But for some inexplicable reason, having the weight of the stone close by, along with the memory of his dad's words still attached to it...helped.

Chapter 23

The Search

Ben listened for any more impending danger coming from the cabin. When he felt he was far enough away and safely out of sight, he stopped and took a few seconds to reexamine his throbbing foot without the aid of his light. Carefully, he touched his ankle to check on the swelling. *Man, oh man...it feels huge. It must be broken.* The slightest touch sent a renewed pain shooting up his leg, enough to provoke a yell—but he wisely held his tongue.

Ben's injured ankle was a serious problem, but resting it gave him time to reconsider having left the river in the first place. He reminded himself: *This is the second time I have gone out into unknown danger. First, it was leaving the campsite and reaching a dead end, and now, it's which way is the best way out of here. Is it through the woods or by the river? OleYeller is still waiting for me* back there in the swamp. *I just need to be sure what I'm doing makes sense before I go too far ahead.* What would Dad do? With Ole Yeller involved, that question lingered far too long.

Despite being riddled with doubt about how to safely get further away from his current predicament, one thing was for sure: he'd have to do it without banging his ankle any more. *I can't take much more of that.* Ben was hoping for a trail or something better instead of the swamp. *A driveway must be somewhere nearby.* Even the option of searching for a well-traveled path meant trying to stand up and using his dad's camp flashlight a little more than necessary to see any distance. This little device had become precious. It was his one reliable tool for any chance of escape, at least until sunrise.

Ben rationalized; *I don't think those guys would have used a boat to get here. But who knows? There must be a way to the cabin from an established path or road, but where would it be?*

Nothing was clear from his vantage point surrounded in dense brush, and without the aid of the cabin lights, it was hard to keep his bearings or rationalizing straight.

Ben's second-guessing was becoming an ever-present obstacle. While a good share of his earlier decisions along the way and their outcomes had not worked out for the best, he reminded himself: *I made it this far. I'm still lost, but I'm also still alive.* Armed with that mindful resolution, he fought away any more negative thoughts.

Knowing he had to move on while he could, Ben turned his light back on, raised himself up on his good knee above the brush level, and scanned the immediate area, while staying focused for any ominous sounds coming from the cabin. As he did, he spotted a narrow clearing that might have been an old grassy driveway leading away from the cabin. It looked overgrown with a few small emerging trees and smaller sized shrubs but not passable with a vehicle. However, it may have been a wide enough trail—six feet wide—at one time or another. *Should I try that pathway? I've got to get out of here. I've got to believe Dad would already be gone by now.*

Ben quickly turned his light off again and sat there all alone in the darkness. He could feel the increasing pressure to get help as quickly as he could. He had to act. The violence at the cabin was pushing him toward the road concept. It seemed more logical. Talking to himself, he rationalized: *I already know how far back it is to the water, and even though it was not a great distance away, the combination of confronting more slick leaves and forging through more muck along the shoreline means I'll have to risk damaging my ankle even more.*

On the other hand, if this is the pathway, I'll be able to move along much quicker. Maybe, the trail or a driveway won't be that long. But...maybe it is. I believe those two old drunks wouldn't like walking any longer than necessary. I'm figuring the chances are more than likely that a clearing could be the trail through those woods that they used.

Ben visualized himself reaching a road and flagging down a passing car. *I could be done with all of this well before the light of day, surely quicker than the water* route. *More than anything else, I can't afford any more setbacks. I'll crawl the whole way if I have to. Dad's life depends on me. I just hope to God he's still alive.*

That hopeful reasoning was strong enough. So, without any further self-debate, Ben chose the mental image of a nearby road over an elusive river campsite. His decision became more immediate when a light in the cabin suddenly came back on.

Oh, for God sakes! The light reminded Ben of his own light, and he immediately cupped his hand around it and turned it back on to check the time. *How much time have I wasted? How much longer until dawn?* It was ten to four. Knowing that, he clicked it off. Dawn was still a long time away, but it had been less than five minutes since he had sat frozen, considering what to do next. So far, his indecisiveness hadn't been too costly, but now, something was up. His action to escape had to continue right now.

Whether Ben was suffering from shear exhaustion and stress didn't matter anymore. He sensed something more dangerous was about to begin. With Ben's escape direction resolved, his most overriding problem was how long he'd be able to last with his ankle throbbing and aching the way it was. Earlier, he had said to himself that he would crawl the whole way, if he had to, reciting to himself his key motivation: *persistence overcomes resistance.* His will and tolerance of pain would now be put to the test.

To Ben's chagrin, he still had no idea what those guys in the cabin were up to or where he was in these never-ending woods. He wasn't even sure he was in the national forest anymore. He only knew where he needed to be and desperately hoped finding a nearby hardtop roadway would be the answer. To prolong this night with any outcome other than his dad's rescue would be an unforgivable failure. His will was being driven for that not to happen.

With his eyes glued on the cabin porch, he tried to put his shoe back on, but the effort was excruciating and futile. He would have to save his tennis shoe for another time, perhaps as a protective glove for his open blisters from the sharp unseen ground objects, in case walking later proved not to be possible.

In a desperate attempt to move along quicker, he turned his light back on and decided to try a last-ditch attempt to stand up to see if hopping a little way would ever work. It was a no go. Each time the tip of his big toe accidentally bushed against a shrub or scraped the ground, huge waves of fresh and more intense pain flashed all the way to his hip and beyond. It was a dumb idea.

Even though he was a relatively tough athlete, he couldn't bear this kind of torment and he couldn't risk slipping and falling again. *I really will have to crawl my way through this thick stuff.* Back down on his all fours with his injured foot bent over his knee, he started a course that was based only on a raw gut feeling.

With his light guiding the way, he made his awkward crawling moves creeping further away from the cabin as quickly as he could manage. As he crawled along, he looked over his shoulder hoping Dan and Gus would stay put. So far, so good.

As Ben moved along, the wet sticks and random stones were proving to be sharp on his shoeless hand and both knees, and occasionally, he had to stop and rub them down. He thought about using his other shoe, but for now, he wanted one hand free to be able to move the brush away from slapping his face. Still concerned about his light's battery life, his brief rest stops from the rough terrain were taken in total darkness.

It was ever so creepy moving slowly in the forest all by himself, and especially, knowing there was still a real possibility of imminent danger still dwelling within the cabin. His agonizing pace allowed him to analyze all his sounds and those nature was providing. Cracking sticks under the weight of his hands and knees, coupled with the eerie pattering of the dripping rain from overhead branches, did not help. Resting under those nighttime circumstances were proving to be highly stressful events.

Thankfully, the absence of any other outside sources of light pointed in his direction allowed for a small measure of relief. However, a different problem was becoming another concern—accumulating mosquitoes—that had suddenly begun to take notice of Ben busily disturbing the forest's low-lying vegetation.

Despite the rain's drizzle, the invaders began hovering around Ben's ears and face with their high-pitched whiny sound that only mosquitoes can make. There weren't many at first, but they kept him motivated to hurry up and keep moving. Eventually, they forced Ben to pull his hat down as far as possible and tug his dad's raincoat hood over it. As an extra measure, Ben drew the hood's drawstrings ever so tight around his exposed face, covering all but his eyes.

To a certain extent, his preventive actions helped, but thanks to the thinness of his canoe pants, his calves and thighs were still at the mercy of the flying devils. They were another reason Ben desperately hoped his decision to crawl back through the woods for his eventual escape and rescue was not only correct, but also short.

Ben's anguish continued with his on-and-off crawling struggles through the underbrush. It was slow work, and often resulted in hard scraping against his elevated ankle. Ben also found himself spending more time slapping away the hungry mosquitoes.

Toiling along, he found he had to stop and rest for longer periods of time, and as a result, endure more of the hovering mosquitoes' relentless kamikaze-like attacks when he was still. During one of these stops, while wondering how far he had managed to make his way from the cabin, his heart nearly stopped when he saw flashlight beams and their reflections piercing through the tree branches, bouncing off their neighboring trunks.

Pure unadulterated panic enveloped Ben. He forgot all about the mosquitoes. His heart began to race. A cold sweat enveloped him. *Why are they so determined to get me? Why is this still happening?* Wild-eyed, pure panic jump-started his effort to move on. Fumbling along, he moved for as long as he physically could stand until he could go no further. He had to stop one more time to rest and catch his breath despite the ever-present danger that had stretched not far behind.

The sporadic flashes of beams continued. He moved

until he had to take another rest stop. The only redeeming factor as he tried to catch his breath, was that he had time to access his progress. With the aid of his trusty light, he managed to notice the trail becoming less and less overgrown. *Thank God!* Even the tall weeds up ahead were showing freshly crushed fern pods and flattened switchgrass blades.

Encouraged that he may have made a good choice to go this way, he tried to mentally recollect himself and regain the feeling back in his hands and knees. He checked the trail behind him. *Are the lights getting any brighter? I can't tell.*

After waiting a moment with nothing apparent, Ben rechecked the watch. At his pace, he figured he was averaging no more than five to ten minutes before he simply couldn't go any further without a rest and a chance to swat away the most aggressive mosquitoes.

The time stood at a quarter to five. *How much further can I go on? These mosquitoes are driving me crazy!*

Swatting the pests didn't keep Ben from hoping the end of his nightmare would be just beyond the reach of his own light beam. His effort, so far, had become a continual marathon of tension, frayed nerves, and not knowing what was coming next or how far he was away from the cabin. And even though he felt he had hit his "mental wall" way back down in the abysmal swamp, he was fighting for a few more doses of physical energy to reach an undefined finish line drawn many unknown yards away.

And tonight, for the first time, Ben's sense of a typical finish line had dramatically changed to any kind of ordinary, well-traveled road without the slightest hint of someone like Dan or Gus anywhere near it.

    Ben's next rest stop was longer than usual, despite the bugs. Ben was getting desperate to do something about his ankle. Besides the fact it felt twice its normal size, it was killing him from extended branches recoiling against it during his short but grueling crawling periods. The mosquitoes didn't help. To their delight, they were taking advantage of the exposed injury. Trying to relieve the itching, while enduring bush slaps, was becoming a major challenge. *What can I do? I know one thing; I will never forget to bring mosquito spray out in the woods ever again.*
    Then, he had an idea while he remained alert for any hints of human voices. With the light beams in the trees momentarily gone, he quickly stripped off his canoe pants. Now, he was down to his briefs. *I hope this works.*
    He pulled out the drawstrings in the waist and carefully wrapped his pants around his foot. To keep the wrap in place, Ben lightly tied one end of the string around the arch and then wrapped it around his calf all the way to the bend in his knee. He tied it like a shoelace bow. It was painful at first, but he hoped the makeshift nylon cloth boot would help insulate against any further brush scrapings and mosquito bites. The problem now was his other leg would be an easier target for the accompanying flying varmints. There was no choice. Ben's good leg had to be the next fleshy sacrifice.
    Before straightening himself back on his knees and

trying his idea out, he bravely surveyed his immediate area with his light. To his surprise, the trail's surface was improving for the better. It showed more open portions that looked like an ancient grassy road that had been used before the days of paved or graveled roads. Ancient tire depressions were still visible. However, over time, the pathway must have become impassable. Without regular use, small-sized trees had taken advantage of the space and freedom to grow.

Even though he had no idea how far he had gone to get to this point, even if it was relatively short, this new evidence, coupled with his insulated ankle, buoyed Ben's spirits. The sight re-created hopes that he could really escape. The reality of a nearby road might finally be within his reach.

With lifted spirits, Ben crawled on. All the while, he tried to ignore his constant pain, and the off and on terrifying dangers that Dan and Gus still represented. His nightlong ordeal had pushed Ben into a semi-conscious state. His mind wandered and was becoming occupied with random visions of his life back home. There were flashes of his brief time with the Boy Scouts and his weekend family vacations. Then, there were the memories of his sports teams, and the countless hours of practices and games he had been a part of.

His resting episodes, balancing on the edge of terror, jolted him with renewed thoughts of his helpless, blood-soaked dad. Wrapped in his dad's raincoat as he was, he was continually on his mind in one way or another. He hoped he was still alive, and the coat helped embrace his fond remembrances of him and his hopeful will to make them a team again. Besides the abundant sports memories, there were others. Fred's love of classic rock 'n' roll was one. His goofy dancing moves at wedding get togethers always seemed to help make his mom and sisters love to make fun of his dance floor antics. That vision generated a whirl of more family memories, strangely, all pleasant as he slowly moved through the soggy trail. He hoped there would be more.

    At another quickened rest period taken solely to rub down his raw, bloody knees and forgetting for a moment the ongoing threat of Gus and Dan following his trail, his idle thoughts reappeared. Only this time they centered on his treasured stone.
    He patted it from its secure pocket location and resisted shining his precious light on it one last time, but it again was calling to him as an inspiration of sorts. Worried it might somehow get damaged in his pants, he responded by turning on his light, checking its condition, and transferred it to his raincoat's deeper side pocket. For now, his immediate world included the stone.
    As he moved along as best as he could in the night's eerie and damp stillness, the stone's presence brought reoccurring thoughts of his dad's words about the power and encouragement the stone invoked for the Native American warriors, especially before entering a fearsome battle. Surely, the person who had lost this stone must have believed a higher being was behind that pervasive power, and Ben wondered if God was watching him now, as he struggled along, alone on a wet grassy trail.
    Thinking for a moment of God as he was, Ben felt

guilty he hadn't been a fan of going to church on a regular basis. He hoped this wasn't to be his last day on earth. To his credit, he reminded God that he was familiar with a couple of traditional prayers—the Lord's Prayer and Psalm 23 plus a couple well known hymns. His wide-ranging thoughts of the stone and God brought him back to his times sitting in the pews back home with Mom and Dad. He wished he could be there now.

Looking past his shoulder for any more imminent danger, Ben was trying his best to be optimistic. The comfort of having the stone with him and his newfound relishing of his fond memories back home helped make his struggles to get away almost bearable. No longer was it just his dire hopes for saving his dad that drove him on to reach his prospective road home. He felt a building up of gratitude for things now lost, but hopefully to regain and fully appreciate.

Reflecting as he was, Ben made sure the stone was still securely placed deep within his raincoat pocket, took a deep breath, and uncharacteristically said a long, silent, and ever solemn prayer. In it, he made some strong promises like he had never made before. He even invoked Psalm 23 at the end. *The Lord is my shepherd; I shall not want...*

With that important prayer finished, he grimaced and groaned as he moved back onto his hands and knees, then pointed his little flashlight straight ahead, and switched it back on to face whatever new obstacles lay ahead. Behind him...mentally focusing well beyond the back of his shoulders...and into a blurry future, fate's answers remained unknown.

Ben had moved no more than a couple more yards when he accidentally broke another stick, and it poked his lower thigh. *Wow...that one really hurt! I wonder if it's bleeding.* He turned his light on and checked. *No blood...just another problem. I wonder if God is listening anymore.*

When he turned to sit and rest to collect himself, with the light still on, he rechecked his location. As he did, he spotted the distinct reflection of a long silver vehicle bumper on the grassy trail. It made him curious enough to ignore his ongoing stresses and restart his grueling ordeal to check it out. *What's this all about?*

The effort to get closer and figure out what he had discovered was longer and rough enough to remind him of his past grueling football practice drills requiring a major amount of sweaty work. However, the closer he got, the clearer it became that he was correct—it was a bumper, and it was attached to an old vehicle of some sort. *This is incredible!* Tears welled up, and any lingering doubts about taking the wooded trail instead of the river vanished. A vehicle had to mean a road was nearby after all. His silent prayers had been heard. *Thank you, God!*

Now Ben was inspired, and moved as best as he could without any more rest stops. When he was close enough to the vehicle, he realized it was an old pickup truck. From a distance, it looked as tired and worn-out as he was.

Nonetheless, he instantly imagined the keys still in it, backing the thing out of the woods, and driving it down the road. As he got closer, he confirmed it was old, all right. He was sure his friends would have called the thing a "beater," with plenty of rust, faded paint, and open spots visible along the fenders. It could have been completely rusted-out and dinged all over, but Ben couldn't have cared less. He was still thinking: *Keys.*

Once he reached the truck itself, and making sure the previous streams of light behind him were not visible, he used the slippery front bumper to steady himself and get to his feet. He had to stabilize himself first, but when he was ready to continue, he used the frame as a support to shuffle his good leg to the driver's door. Without a minute to lose, he grabbed the handle and pulled. It creaked ajar with ease. When Ben was able to maneuver himself and pull a little more, the door swung open wide, and the inside light came on. *This is too good to be true!*

Next, he checked the ignition switch, but it was empty. Then, he checked the front seat and underneath, including the filthy floor mat, for a hidden spare key. No luck. Next, he checked the glove compartment—no key there, either. However, he found a truck registration mixed in with various old receipts and other miscellaneous items in the box. Ben checked out the registration. The name listed was Gus T. Murphy. *That's interesting.* He folded the registration and put it in his raincoat pocket along with the stone, thinking: *I might need this.*

He continued his search, but there was nothing worth noting. The back seat and the floor were mostly filled with the trashy remains of fast-food paper waste and what Ben considered useless garbage. The outside bed was empty except for a badly worn spare tire.

Satisfied that no keys were available, he double-checked his raincoat pocket to make sure the registration was still in there and not lying on the rain-soaked ground. It was, indeed, in the pocket. *This information might one day give me a clue why these guys were so hostile when I asked for help and wanted to cause me serious harm. At least, Gus did. I'm sure of that.*

Ben was more than encouraged that a road should be nearby. This truck proved there had to be a drivable road somewhere up the trail. There was no other explanation. The trail directly behind the truck also looked to be much better, like an old grass covered logging road.

However, no sooner than he was ready to move on, the flashes of light behind him had returned. *Oh God! They're coming! What the heck? Why are they still in these woods? Are these creeps for real?*

Ben wasted no more time and dropped back down to his hands and knees. His sense of urgency helped him crawl on steadily, thanks to the benefit of the rest while searching through the truck and the momentary reprieve from the growing intensity of the accompanying mosquitoes and his damaged ankle.

Ben realized his discovery was a bittersweet one as he tried to wipe away his tears of joy with mud filled hands. Knowing his decision to come this way was correct kept him inspired and moving. He even began to imagine his winged adversaries (in a demented way) were also helping him along by forcing him to press on.

Maneuvering around large muddy puddles and hidden stones, with deliberate and cautious moves, was harder than he would have ever imagined, but fear was proving to be another great motivator. Alternating his spare shoe on his hands helped, but his knees were a different story. With each "step," he hoped for more extended patches of grass to help keep his knees from being mistreated anymore. All the while, the streams of light beams were flashing by him more frequently.

Then, the trail merged with another, and instead of more grass, the combined trails' surface became a clay and gravel mix. To Ben, this was a sure sign he was getting closer to civilization. To him, it looked like it was surely drivable. Although encouraged, it forced him to crawl away from the sharp-edged rocky surface and further into the trail's shoulder with its rougher thickets of underbrush.

This new section proved to be even slower going and maddening to get through. The general woodland vegetation and other mid-level stiff shrub branches were miserably wet and harder to move away with just one hand. Frustrated with his slower progress, he stopped, gasped to catch his breath, and rechecked the time. It was five-thirty. *Thank God. It'll be daylight soon.*

He hadn't inched much further down the open trail when suddenly, he heard the old truck's ignition attempting to turn the engine over. *What? What was that?*

Despite the truck's dilapidated appearance, the old engine was responding to a lively battery and sounded strong. *Holy cow! They did have the keys and they're not giving up. I've got to get off this trail.*

With Ben's spirit deflated, it was an immense physical

struggle to crawl deeper off-trail. The vegetation here was unrelentingly thick. With bulging eyes and a dreadful vision of being shot, he realized his crawling time had run out. All he realistically could do was lay down as flat as he could, right where he was and wait for what was to come. More frightful, he had managed to be only a couple of yards off the trail before it had become too dense. His predicament had become unbearable. With what looked to be "a moment of all moments," he said a final prayer and gingerly lowered his ankle. With his head flush against his folded arms; he held his breath.

Unbelievably, no sooner than after the old engine had turned over, was revved-up and in gear, its high-pitched transmission sounded as if it was moving in reverse, backing up. *Oh my God! Here they come!* Ben heard the truck stop, pause for a minute, and then begin to move again in the same reverse manner. This time it was close enough where he could see another flashlight beam ricocheting, in a wand-like manner, over his head into the brush well beyond him. *For God's sakes! They're going to find me!*

Ben stayed ducked down, and pressed the side of his face down to the wet ground as flat as he could. The old truck was slowly rolling closer towards him. It wasn't long before he could clearly see the red tail lights through the brush, while the flashlight beams continued to bounce and wave overhead.

The tension caused Ben to feel as though his blood had changed from a warm red into a stone-cold blue. His heart was saying it had more than enough and was already on the main street of "heart attack" city. *Oh my*

God! What am I going to do?

On the truck came, still in reverse, until Ben could see the worn tire treads and tarnished hubcaps only a mere few feet away from him. The truck, ever so slowly, gradually passed him by. Miraculously, it did not stop. It continued to roll with the flashlight beams still scanning the woods just beyond his hiding place. Ben remained frozen until the truck came to a rolling stop close by. It idled for a minute. *This is it...they saw me. I'm done for.* However, instead of anyone getting out of the vehicle, the driver began to attempt to turn the truck around where it was in a wider area of the trail. It took two back-and-forth turn around maneuvering turns, but once the truck was repositioned, it began to move forward further down the trail until it was out of sight. *Thank God!*

Although Ben couldn't see who was behind the wheel, he hoped both lunatics were in the truck and were finally gone, but he couldn't be sure. *They had been fighting before; maybe they still were. I've got to stay alert and not move in case one of them is on foot following the other. I can't believe all this.* For now, all was quiet except for the ever-present dripping from the tree branches high above.

Ben took a deep breath and tried to regain his shattered wits. Besides having been completely terrified, at least Ben knew there had to be a better road further down the way. In his hair-raising meltdown, he had also forgotten about his stone. Trying to calm himself down, he reached into his raincoat, found it was still there and gave it a healthy squeeze. Perhaps, it had helped him stay put.

As he did, he tried to give himself the semblance of a pep talk. *I'm going to need all the stuff this thing has. That was way too close. The way things are going, I'm going to need to get out of here somehow a lot faster…before I can't. I don't know if I can take much more of this. All I know is Dad needs me, and that's what matters.*

It wasn't much of an optimistic self-talk, but it was enough. As soon as Ben thought the coast was clear, he left the stone where it was, got on his knees and crawled back onto the side of the trail. It was then he realized the rain had stopped. Taking heart, he began crawling in earnest, fearing his renewed blast of energy could very well be his last. *How much further can I go like this?*

It was clear he was going to have to struggle some more before reaching the end of himself or the end of the woods. *How much more?*

He had fought a gallant fight, but with a body that was beat down and begging to quit. The only thing that remained and pushed him on was his solemn promise to his dad he would return. It was one he had to keep.

It was at that very moment Ben suddenly heard "It"—the sound he'd wanted so desperately to hear all night long. It was the common sound of people on the move, with the associated high-pitched hum of their vehicles' hot wheels meeting a stretch of smooth black asphalt.

Judging from the sound, Ben figured he had to be fairly near a town road, or better. Focusing on the image of a nearby road brought on an indescribable surge of joy to his heart. Ben thanked God repeatedly for that one beautiful sound. He knew he was close to the proverbial football goal line—deep within the red zone. He was more than ready to spike the heavy ball he had been carrying ever since finding his dad injured.

With the invigorating sound and vision of a rescue planted in his mind, Ben persisted with his newfound surge. He used every ounce of the energy he had left and crawled nonstop until he emerged from within the thickness of the dark woods, and saw with his very own eyes, the straight edge of a finely paved blacktop surface. It was complete with its firm level shoulders, short white lane divider stripes, and finely graded gravel lines, and littered with wet leaves and small branches from the late-night storm. All that was between him and his finish line was a choice between a rock laden culvert, or a long ditch filled with a heavy green-looking mix of water and weeds.

Regardless of his choice of obstacles, he had done it. He had arrived. *I can't believe it! I just can't.* Tears of joy flowed at the sight of that plain country road. It was enough to make him pause, cover his eyes, and give a huge sobbing thanks. *I just can't believe it…I'm still alive. I hope it's not too late for Dad.*

And even though the blacktop had the appearance of an ordinary road, he figured it would be only a short matter of time until another car would come along. The road sighting and an image of his father being rescued released his deepest doubts of the night. *I made it!* He was no longer afraid.

Gone also was the fear of that old truck returning. Whatever Dan and Gus did from here on did not matter anymore. Ben was numb, and simply had to take this one big chance to flag down anyone who might help. Hope and courage were with him.

Of course, he couldn't get to the road fast enough. He even tried getting up to stand and hop there quicker, but that was a mistake. He couldn't hold his balance, and the joggling motion on his leg was excruciating. He ended up back on his knees, swearing at himself.

At the culvert, the rocks were proving to be far too big and sharp. Instead, he was forced to cross the foul-smelling ditch on all fours. Yet, as he did, he was still grateful. The ditch approach was direct and softer. The cold foul-smelling water didn't matter, either. He was able to rinse off his itchy, grimy hands and legs as he made his way through the shallow water.

When he finally passed through the ditch and reached the edge of the dark pavement, he took a well-deserved rest on the roadside shoulder. There, he situated himself on his buttocks with both his legs stretched out, dripping a steady stream of green water off his whole body. It was an awkward position, with one foot still wrapped-up in his long pants, sopping wet, and trying to stop his continual shivering within his filthy raincoat. Awkward or not, it was the best position for the relief he had to have. He didn't dare sit in the road itself for fear of being run over. The finely graveled shoulder was certainly good enough.

As Ben patiently sat there all alone resting, he understood his appearance might be a terrible sight. His raincoat was covered with batches of string-like green algae. His saturated hat brim, barely protruding out of his raincoat hood, partially covered his face. Even the fact that he was sitting with only one shoe on and the other laying nearby had to be questionable to a degree to any passing would-be rescuer. Even the pesky mosquitoes seemed to have become wary of his appearance in the daylight by remaining within the cover of the woods.

Staring blankly at his new surroundings and himself in the emerging light of day, Ben resolved his appearance couldn't be changed. He was freezing. His teeth chattered. He could do no more. His ankle, discolored and swollen, echoed the look.

During his brief self-assessment, he noticed his silver whistle still hanging around his neck. He recalled what his dad had said about the whistle's ability to carry over long distances. As a distraction, he mustarded enough energy to test it out. After a first spray of water cleared itself out, it was found to be still loud and sharp. He blew it again, only this time, three blasts in case someone within earshot could hear his SOS. There was no immediate response, nor did he expect one. However, he was elated and ready to use it again for the next passing vehicle, no matter what.

It was to become a long, quiet wait, as he watched the early golden colors of a new day's sunrise appear. Ben had to continually shake his head to keep himself awake. He even talked to himself, rehearsing over and over what he would say to the first friendly person who might happen to stop and offer him the help he needed.

The minutes that dragged by each felt like their own version of an eternity. His bouts of anticipation became tempered by the creeping return of uncertainty and worry. *What if those bad guys do return? And what if after all this, I'm shot dead right here?* Staring blankly at random puddles scattered amongst the wet pavement, he was mentally too drained, and dismissed those lingering thoughts any further. *This is my spot…I can't worry any more. This is where it ends…one way or the other.*

Despite the gloomy clouds that had provided the night's mostly steady rainfall, the early sunlight had changed the sky into a brighter red and purple spectrum, matching Ben's discolored leg. As beautiful as the morning sky looked, none of it helped speed up the clock or lessen Ben's overall misery. Not even the cardinals and robins chiming in with their early-morning calls softened his impatience. *What on earth is taking so long?* Ben had no idea, but he had experienced enough of the wait, when he heard the magical sound of another set of high-pitched spinning wheels humming along the blacktop. Another "It" moment was coming his way.

And when the source of the approaching sound appeared, he was thunderstruck; his situation hadn't worsened with a sighting of the beater truck. *Thank God*!

In fact, it wasn't a truck at all. It looked to be a big blue passenger car with two people in the front. It was moving fast. He grabbed his whistle and blew it as much and as hard as he could, but they never slowed down, not one bit. They were in the opposite lane and must have been distracted talking to each other, with their windows rolled up. They did not appear to acknowledge his whistle or notice his frantically flailing arms. They passed him by with ease. *How could they not have seen me? Is this how it's going to be?*

Ben's heart and hopes sank faster than the speed of that car. Ben prayed again and made a few more promises. He even took out the stone, only this time, not to just look at it. This time he was thinking about giving it a long heave-ho back towards the woods.

At that same exact moment, however, he heard another approaching vehicle. It was in the far lane, same as the earlier car, and looked to be another passenger sedan with only a solo driver. He unconsciously returned the stone to its home in his raincoat, and refocused. This time he used all his remaining energy to muster up another continuous stream of whistles while he waved his arms.

This car, too, passed him by—but not for long. To his surprise, its brake lights came on and it began to slow down, then stopped and turned around. In a matter of a minute, it had come to a complete stop just before the spot where he was sitting.

Ben could feel the engine's heat; it was parked and idling that close. Suddenly, blue and red flashing lights came on, as the engine idled on. The vehicle had looked ordinary at first; however, the flashing lights told a different story. The person who opened his door and stepped out onto the road moved toward him around the front of the unmarked vehicle. It was a sight for Ben's sore eyes—a fully uniformed police officer. *Thank God!* Ben felt relieved, even though he saw the officer had his hand on the ready with his weapon unclipped in its holster. Ben understood the situation. This stop was business.

But before Ben could positively react to the uniform and the badge, the bright strobing lights, or negatively to another person with a loaded gun casting his long shadow over his weakened frame, he uncharacteristically froze. The stern-looking officer paused a few seconds, as both sized each other up. Then the officer stepped a little closer. After appraising Ben's haggard condition, blank stare, and overall bizarre appearance, he leaned over and said in a stiff and authoritarian tone, "What seems to be the matter here, son?"

Chapter 24

Deliverance

The name on the silver name tag pinned over the officer's uniform right pocket read, "Officer James T. Delaney." Officer Delaney looked to be middle-aged, of average height, had a well-trimmed mustache, and was dressed in his nicely pressed uniform and polished black boots. He didn't look to Ben to be overly threatening, but the officer's question was more like trying to respond to a pushy TV sportscaster, who had just thrust a microphone in his face and asked him what it felt like to win the Super Bowl in front of millions of people. There was so much joy in Ben's heart, overwhelmed that his ordeal was finally over, he became…for that moment…speechless and dazed.

Despite Ben's earlier mental rehearsals for a coherent response, he was overcome with emotions. He couldn't prevent the sea of tears, already welled-up in his eyes, from freely cascading down his cheeks and spilling onto the ground.

The officer, realizing Ben's reaction was extraordinary, tried a different approach with a little less authoritarian tone and a little more sympathy in his voice, but remaining official.

"Do you have some identification, son?"

Ben still didn't know what to say and then blurted out what he had been thinking during most of his overnight ordeal.

"It's my dad. He's hurt back on the river. I've been trying to get him help all night long, but I'm lost. I hurt my ankle…I can't walk. My dad's hurt, too—only worse."

Officer Delaney moved in a little closer and bent down next to Ben. "Now, slow down, son. Let's take one thing at a time. I take it you don't have a valid ID with you." He paused for a second then said, "What's your name?"

"It's my dad! We've got to get back to help him before it's too late!" Ben insisted without any thought of what he had been asked.

By this time, Officer Delaney had sized up this situation. "Okay, let's slow down. I hear you, but you're a mess and you look like you have serious injuries of your own. I'm going to help you get into my patrol car and see if we can't talk a little better inside where it's warm and dry, instead of on the side of the road with you sitting here, soaked and all."

Officer Delaney stood up and turned to the back door, opened it, and began to help Ben up into the secured back seat. As he did, Ben continued where he had left off.

"We were on a fishing and camping trip, and during last night's intense storm, a large branch fell on my dad's tent. I tried to help..."

Officer Delaney took in his words as he tried to avoid touching the wet raincoat and helped Ben lean into the seat and said, "We're going to get you to the local hospital not too far from here to check you out. I will notify the park rangers of the accident, but you need to try and calm down. Believe me, we will do whatever it takes to help your dad. Unfortunately, all our local ambulances are aiding those injured in last night's tornado. It'll be quicker if I take you there myself."

The process of getting Ben completely into the patrol car was a slow one, partially because Officer Delaney was trying not to soil his clean uniform so early in his morning shift by accidentally rubbing against Ben's filthy raincoat and exposed extremities. As Delaney stretched and strapped the rear seat belt around Ben, Delaney was mindful not to bump Ben's injured leg or touch his bloody knees. Once Ben was safely secured and before Delaney put his patrol car into drive, he radioed his dispatcher.

"I've got an unidentified teenage male with a significant leg injury and other assorted medical issues I found sitting next to the roadside on Route 131. I'm transporting him to the closest hospital myself. Looks like that's in Cadillac. Please let them know of an approximate transport time of about twenty minutes. Also, stand by for more information regarding an adult male with unidentified injuries situated somewhere along one of the rivers inside the park."

Officer Delaney paused his radio and checked into the rearview mirror. Looking directly at Ben he said,

"Okay, son, I'm taking you to the hospital for an examination, especially for that leg of yours, but I need to know you and your father's names. The rangers will be at a great disadvantage in finding your dad if they don't even know who they're looking for."

Ben tried to remain coherent and responded with, "Ben and Fred Nelson...I'm Ben. We were camping...and early last night a tree branch fell, and my dad got hit on the head...we were in separate tents. He was bleeding bad, and I tried to help him, but he was unconscious. I didn't know what to do...I went to find help, but I didn't know where I was...I just hope he's still alive..."

Ben struggled to finish his last sentence, but his voice tailed off as more tears began to fall.

The officer tried to reassure Ben. "We'll do all we can to find and help your dad, but I'm a little concerned about you as well. Do you know what river you and your dad were on last night? There's several of them out here."

"I'm pretty sure...it was the Pine. That's where we were...but I'm lost. At least, that's where the two men I met a few hours ago said I still was."

"Wait a minute. You talked to two men in these woods?" Officer Delaney raised an eyebrow.

"Yes." Ben's voice gained a little more acceleration and intensity. "But you don't understand. I found an old cabin back there—he pointed—with two bad guys in it, but they had no intentions of helping me, anyway. They acted like they were drunk, and one even had a pistol pointed at me the whole time I was there. I thought one of them was really going to shoot me…I got away…but not before a shot went off. That's how I hurt my ankle when I jumped off their slippery porch. My dad said it was the Pine…much earlier. I'm sorry…that's all I know."

"Take it easy, son. I'll get more information from you later. Just try and rest a bit. I think we have enough to go on for now." Officer Delaney mentally processed this latest information. "Two men, you say. And a shot?"

"Yes, actually there were two more shots when I was hiding."

Delaney frowned, but didn't ask any more questions, as he could see for himself his passenger was exhausted, still shivering, and even slurring his words to the point of becoming partially delirious and hard to understand. He pulled away from the shoulder of the road, turned his vehicle back towards town, and reconnected with his dispatcher once again with Ben and his dad's names and the vague location of the campers' whereabouts along with the information about the two other adults.

Consequently, there were several more radio exchanges with the dispatcher back and forth as the patrol car rolled down the quiet, heavily wooded road in the bright early-morning sunshine. As Ben stared out his window at the glow of the sunrise, he couldn't help but find a brand-new appreciation for this new day's morning sun. It was starting to stand for hope…real hope.

Delaney checked in his mirror to keep a watchful eye on his passenger as they sped down the road to the hospital. Sometime while in route, Officer Delaney casually commented, "You know, I almost missed spotting you out there, sitting on the road like that. Luckily, I had my window down a bit, and I heard that loud whistle of yours. That was nice thinking."

Ben eked out a slight smile. Delaney returned the smile in the rearview mirror. With that momentary relief, Delaney felt it safe enough to inquire about the two mystery men who had threatened Ben earlier.

"So, what about those two men you met out in the woods?"

The question came too late. Ben's eyes were closed, and he did not respond. He was spent. He had reached the goal line, and the proverbial ball had already been passed on to the referee. He needed total relief from the intensity of the "big game" that had just taken place in the woods. His answer would have to wait until a better time. Delaney let him sleep.

Ben felt he had just closed his eyes when he stirred and became partially coherent, finding himself in a hospital gown and being wheeled down the hallway on a stretcher by a nurse's aide. In a matter of moments, he was brought into a small examination room. In a sense, Ben was still lost, as he had no idea where he was.

Before long, a young man with the traditional white coat and stethoscope around his neck walked in with a nurse right behind him.

He smiled and said, "Hello, I'm Dr. MacFarlane. I heard you had a bit of a rough time last night. I'm sorry about that, but we're going to give you a once-over and take a good look at that injured leg of yours. Don't worry, we'll get you on the mend as soon as possible."

Ben nodded. "Have you heard anything about my dad?"

"No, but Officer Delaney wanted you to know that the park authorities have been notified, and despite a significant amount of storm damage sustained in the area, a full-scale search and rescue effort has begun. He'll be back here soon to interview you after we get finished to find out a little more about your circumstances and notify your family as to your situation and the rescue efforts out in the field."

"Now, let my nurse take your arm and we'll get your blood pressure read first. We'll check out that ankle and take a few X-rays as well."

Ben merely stared and nodded in response.

Dr. MacFarlane diagnosed Ben with torn ligaments in his upper right ankle and suffering from hypothermia and general exhaustion. He was put on warm fluids and IVs and readied for a cast to immobilize his foot. The cuts and scrapes on his raw knees and large burst blisters on his hands were cleaned and treated. He was also given a sponge bath with antiseptics to soothe the multiple insect bites, but beyond that, there was nothing more the medical team could do for his ongoing concerns about his dad.

Ben still hadn't talked to anyone in his family, but he was informed that Officer Delaney had returned and was waiting outside his room to start the process going. Things were happening fast—it was still early morning—but not fast enough for Ben.

Once Dr. MacFarlane was satisfied that Ben wasn't in any further pain and was comfortable with his new cast and overall well-being, he allowed the officer into his new patient's unit situated just off the emergency room.

Before the two men traded places in front of Ben, Dr. MacFarlane assured Ben that his ankle would be fine in about six weeks. He instructed him to keep off it for as long as possible to aid the healing, and to be sure to get plenty of rest while he was here and when he returned home.

"Now, don't try and be a hero and walk on it anytime soon. According to the X-rays, you don't have any broken bones. I'm assuming you received serious ligament damage in the form of several tears. These tears can at times be worse than a bone break. They'll need ample time to heal properly. My advice is not to rush to get back to normal. And, when you're back at home, your family doctor will reexamine your ankle and give you more information. In a few weeks, your cast will be removed, and you'll receive a walking boot, but in the meantime, we'll provide you with a pair of crutches before you leave. I don't think I can state it too strongly…stay off that foot."

He continued, "I'll stop in later in case you have any questions. Take care, Ben. I hope your leg heals soon. And rest assured, our nurses will give you the best of care. In the meantime, Officer Delaney is waiting to see you."

Dr. MacFarlane left and within minutes Delaney entered.

"Hello, Ben. It's good to see you're looking better, and I hope you're feeling up to all that I need to discuss with you this morning."

Ben responded, "Have you heard anything about my dad?"

"Not yet. The rescue teams in the park are on the water and canvassing the full length of the Pine and its tributaries. When there is further news, I will let you know the minute I get a report. In the meantime, I need your home phone number so I can contact your family and apprise them of your situation. I have a pen and paper here, so give me your mother's name and we'll get that done right away."

Ben complied. Then Delaney said, "I also need to ask you about those two men who threatened you, as it sounds as though they may have committed a serious crime. Are you up for that?"

Ben shook his head. "I'd like to talk to my mom, instead."

"I'll notify her first, then we'll set up a time for you to talk with her while you're still here at the hospital. I'm sorry, but I have to follow policy in this case and contact her beforehand."

Ben nodded as he fought his ongoing battle with intense drowsiness and fears of possible unwelcome news. Having supplied his mom's name and number, he asked the nurse who was checking his medical machine readouts, "Do you know where my clothes are? You know...the ones I had on when I came here?"

The nurse replied, "They're being cleaned, but we have all your personal items in a plastic bag on the chair in the corner right over there."

For a second Ben envisioned his pocket items being

lost or ruined but was relieved when he looked over to the chair and confirmed they were where she said.

"Would you mind bringing my stuff over to me...when you're done. I really need to see them for a minute."

"Of course." She was a little perplexed but stopped what she was doing and went over and brought the bag to him.

Officer Delaney was equally perplexed and waited while Ben verified that his trusty flashlight, the stone, his knife and whistle, and the truck registration were all there. Carefully, he picked out the wet, folded piece of paper and opened it. He confirmed it was still legible and handed it to Delaney.

"Here, this might help you find out who one of the two guys were. I found it in a truck not far from the cabin. It was in the glove compartment when I was looking for a set of keys to try and drive it away. One of the men called the other Gus, and that's the same name on the paper. That's all I know about them."

Delaney was surprised when he looked over the soiled registration. He thanked Ben once again for his good thinking.

Encouraged, Ben struggled to continue with a little more information that he hoped would help.

"I found the truck on the trail that led to the cabin...where they were. Where you found me is where the trail came out of the woods...I know they were looking for me. I could see their search lights flashing all around, but at least one of them took the truck and finally left. I don't know who was in the truck. They both could have been in it...I couldn't tell. I was hiding near the edge of the trail, but was too scared to look. After I was sure the truck was gone...I followed the same path they took. It wasn't very long. Once I saw the road...I went straight through a big wet ditch. Anyway, I hope the registration didn't get too messed up. Maybe it will help."

Delaney didn't respond, but realized he had a major clue in his hands to help find these suspects, and was eager to follow the lead after he first contacted Ben's family. He graciously wished Ben a speedy recovery and told him he'd return with more information as soon as he had it. He assured Ben he'd personally contact his family first and left the room.

After Delaney left and before the nurse could return the bag and its remaining contents, Ben took the stone out and clutched it firmly. Grasping for hope, he said a silent prayer for his dad's safe return.

Ben was eventually moved to a regular patient care room and treated with a meal of French fries and a vanilla milkshake, per his request as off-menu items. It wasn't the best start for solid food, but it was substantial enough and all he was in the mood for.

He had gotten only halfway through his treats when he dozed off again until his attending nurse woke him up for another dose of meds and news that his mother and the rest of the family were in transit from Ann Arbor. They would be here in about three hours. It was news worth waking up for, but he was disappointed that this small rural hospital didn't have the recent technology of a cellular phone system for Ben to talk with her himself. Worse yet, the violent stream of storms overnight had knocked down many trees, temporarily leaving the facility with no regular phone service.

With the power lines included in the mix of tornado damage, a few portions of the hospital had to run on auxiliary power. Communications had been a casualty all around the area. His nurse assured him that once the lines were up again and service restored, she would personally try and contact his mother for him. She had been advised that her patient's mom had a new "black bag" car phone with her.

Ben's deep concern was that she needed to know he was okay directly from him. The nurse said she knew Delaney had already passed that official information along. Ben resigned himself that would have to do. Since there wasn't any more that could be done, except to wait, his disappointment changed to relief. His mom was, at least, informed and on her way. The news helped him drift back asleep.

It couldn't have been more than an hour later when his unit's care nurse came in once again and abruptly woke him up. Now, he was getting irritable and made a face that reflected his thoughts. *Didn't the doctor say I need lots of rest? At this rate, it will take forever for me to get caught up!* She at once understood his expression and apologized for disturbing him again so soon, but he had an important visitor. Ben at once thought: *Is Mom here already? Did I sleep three hours that fast?*

Ben was still groggy, but the anticipation of seeing his family again perked him up. He glanced over to the doorway. And sure enough, it was family—but to his amazement and sheer delight, there was his dad, the old professor, sitting in a wheelchair at the doorway! He looked banged up, but it was his dad...Dr. Fred Nelson himself.

Ben couldn't believe his eyes. "Daaaaad!"

There he was, complete with several bandages patched around his face and wrapped around his head. With his face partially distorted and swollen, he looked as if he had returned from an active war zone. Despite Fred's appearance, there were no other words to describe the reunion as the nurse wheeled him over to Ben's bedside and the two reached to embrace, with Fred managing to momentarily stand up from his wheelchair for a long, grateful hug. There were plenty of tears of joy coming from both sides. Fred was first to struggle a few words out.

"I guess we've got some catching up to do. What do you think?"

"Boy, am I ever glad to see you!" Ben responded. "I can't tell you how much I hoped to see you again. It's just unbelievable...I don't know what else to say. I can't believe we are here...at the same hospital. Officer Delaney must have made the connection. You're really here..."

Ben's voice trailed off, so full of emotion he was barely able to utter, "I can't tell you how I thought I might not ever see you again."

The nurse who had wheeled Fred in was still present and almost overwhelmed by the sight of the emotional reunion. Gathering herself, she interjected that she would leave them alone so they could get readjusted and fill in the missing pieces of their two divergent stories in private. Before she departed, she reminded Fred he should return to his wheelchair and informed them she'd be just down the hall if they needed anything more. Without any fanfare, she left them alone.

"You know Mom is on her way, right?" asked Ben.

"Yes, one of the nurses let me know right after I was admitted," answered Fred. "They also told me you were already here, and that's why I insisted on getting over to your room right away. I'm not fully treated yet, but the staff understands. They're busy treating plenty of other storm casualties, anyway. So, what happened to cause you to be here, too? Where did you go?"

Ben took a deep breath to gather himself and said, "I went to find help in the middle of the storm with the canoe. I couldn't wake you up and you looked hurt…bad. I didn't know what else to do! Fortunately, after I got completely lost on the river, even with your map, I saw a cabin light deep in the woods. I thought there would be someone in the place who could help, so I left the river, but that didn't work out. Plus, I twisted my ankle." He pointed to the cast.

"The guys in the cabin weren't happy to see me at all, and I had to make a run for it, but I slipped in the mud. It took a while…but I made it to a road and Officer Delaney found me and brought me here. He called Mom, too. It was a real long night, but I was mostly worried about you."

"Well, that was a bad storm, all right," Fred said. "One of the worst I've been through in my all my camping adventures. I heard from one of the nurses that a tornado actually touched down somewhere around here. Anyway, even though I was unlucky with that branch falling where it did, I was fortunate in that it could have been much worse. Thankfully, I didn't take a direct hit and it must have just grazed me. It had to be one of the side branches that slammed me against the ground and knocked me out for a while."

Ben waited for the rest. Fred continued, "More importantly, I have you to thank for putting up that post with the flag and the makeshift 'help' sign on the ground. That's what saved the day, because it must have not been too long after you left, a couple of old crusty anglers spotted it with their headlamps as they were casting toward the shore after the rain had slowed down and the thunder and lightning had stopped. I can't believe those guys, Bill and Pete, and people like them who love to fish that much, but I'm glad they were out there, nonetheless. Anyway, they saw the sign and stopped and checked it out. They were there when I was just coming to."

Fred thoughtfully paused and said, "Am I talking too much?"

"No, Dad. Keep going. I want to know what happened."

"Well, I know they were concerned about the way I looked, with the amount of blood on my head and face and all, but I think the injuries looked far worse than they really are. Plus, the big bruises on my legs, and my nose all screwed up and all...I'm sure it was a bit frightful to them, too. I'm sure my nose still is, but once they were able to ask me some questions, they got me up and into their boat and cleaned me up. They even fixed my crooked glasses with the tools they had in their tackle boxes."

Fred paused to swallow hard and continued, "I really appreciate what they did...I hate to have messed up their fishing time, but with the way I looked and after I complained about a terrific headache and dizziness, they knew they needed to get me to a hospital. They insisted I go there instead of diverting anywhere else to look for you. With the sign, and your pack and the canoe gone, it looked clear enough that you had already left."

"Then what happened?"

"Well, it took a long time to first get back to their fishing camp with the small electric trolling motor they had, then even longer to get to their truck back to the road. I was worried sick about you all the while, wondering what on earth happened to you. The problem is these guys didn't have a mobile car phone, so I was completely in the dark until I talked to your mom about thirty minutes ago. There was a county patrol officer here when I arrived, and he was nice enough to let me use the phone in his vehicle...a nice man. He's the one who told me you were here already and how he found you along the roadside."

"And you talked to Mom?"

"Yes, and of course she's more than relieved to know we are both alive and here. Until I talked to her, she only knew about your status, not mine."

"And you're going to be okay, right, Dad?"

"I would expect so. My initial exam verified that I have a broken nose and they fixed that already, but they are going to keep me here a while to watch for the aftereffects of a concussion. But cuts and bruises are nothing compared to knowing you are going to be okay, too."

Before any more was said between the two new patients, the attending nurse came in and said, "The doctor on duty will be ready shortly to finish his examination with you, sir. Also, the police officer connected with the rescue effort of your son is in the hallway and requesting to have a short interview with you both."

Ben and Fred looked at each other and both nodded in agreement.

"At the very least, he needs to be thanked for all the help he has given us today," Fred said.

The nurse relayed the sentiment, and Officer Delaney entered. Understanding that this was a special reunion time for the two patients, he tried to be as brief as he could be.

"Ben, I hope you are feeling better. Same to you, Dr. Nelson. I know you also had a terrifying ordeal last night. I'm glad you two made it out of the woods and are going to be okay. I just need to clear up a couple loose ends here. I'll be as quick as I can."

Ben and Fred gathered in their emotions and moved away from each other for the moment. Both were ready to listen intently to what Delaney needed to clear up.

"First, the park rangers have been notified of both of your rescues from the camp and you're here in town being treated. All your equipment, including your canoe, has been recovered. Second, I want you to know you have a remarkable young man here, Doctor. I just hope my two boys turn out to be as resourceful and clear-headed as he has been.

"Thanks to Ben's efforts with the truck registration recovery, we were able to track down and apprehend the two suspects your son encountered during the night. Both were wanted on several outstanding warrants, the most serious being an attempted armed robbery a few weeks back. Mr. Gus Murphy also was involved with several domestic abuse and assault and battery charges. These two were on the run, and apparently had been in hiding in that abandoned cabin that your son stumbled upon."

Officer Delaney's eyes turned to Ben and said, "Young man, you're to be commended for providing a key piece of information resulting in their capture. I was also personally impressed with your use of that whistle, which alerted me to your situation by the road. With so many people involved in the aftermath of last night's storm, you might have not been found for a good while had I not heard that shrill sound."

All three of them smiled with that.

"Anyway, I don't want to take up any more of your family time, but Dr. Nelson, if you want to press charges for the assault of a minor with a deadly weapon on your son, that's a possibility for you to consider. That's all I have, other than to take care, gentlemen. It's been a pleasure to have been of service to you both."

They all shook hands, and Ben and Fred expressed their utmost gratitude in return. Ben, with a sizable lump in this throat from realizing he might not ever see Officer Delaney again, paused as he thought about reaching out and uncharacteristically giving Delaney an emotionally ever-thankful hug, with a promise to stay in touch, but he was still mentally exhausted and a little embarrassed by the thought, so he let it slip with just another appreciative nod and a smile.

Officer Delaney, for his part, was pleased with the outcome of the events and gratified to have been able to help. However, while he was trying to keep an official demeanor, his body language betrayed him. It was clear to Ben he had lost the authoritarian persona he had displayed at the roadside when they first met and wanted to prolong his last good-bye and savor his part of the reunion with the two camp survivors. Ben remembered he had said he was a father, too. So, for just a split second, Ben suspected Officer Delaney had a similar lump in his throat by the look on his face.

However, thanks to his many years of experience in the county sheriff's department, Delaney recovered the quickest and regained his official "game face" demeanor. Ben understood the look. So, without any more discussion, Delaney raised his hand as a signal for a silent good bye to them both and promptly left the room.

Fred, after seeing his son's emotional display and the officer's reflective response, remarked, "Now, there goes a special man, Ben. I'm glad he was the one who found you."

Ben nodded in agreement and said, "That's for sure."

Fred asked, "Say, what's that assault charge all about?"

"Well, I think the guys I ran into at the cabin were thinking about shooting me, to tell you the truth. One had a gun pointed at me the whole time I was there. It went off three times after I bolted from that awful place. The first two could have been an accident because I don't know if they ever shot directly at me; I really don't know. I do know the third shot was intentional. It was like a warning shot outside their cabin to try and flush me out of the brush. That one I saw. I gotta tell you, both those guys were very scary."

"Gee, Ben, I'm incredibly sorry you had to go through all that you did last night. Finding me unconscious the way you did and traveling alone through the forest, not knowing where you were, soaked in the storm, makes me feel just awful. It's hard to imagine how you persevered through all that. I don't know what to say. I'm just so thankful you made it back safe and relatively sound."

After a long pause trying to restrain his emotions, Fred added, "So you used your whistle, did you? And you made a rescue sign for me. On top of that, you helped Delaney get a couple of criminals off the street. Ben, that's so incredible. To think you did all that while enduring a night full of suffering and sacrifice on my behalf."

After a long emotional pause, Fred was able to continue.

"Ben, I can't tell you how proud I am of you. You really performed in what I would say in a most heroic fashion. I just hope this sour experience on the river isn't going to scar you for life against me. You know...against camping in general, or any future experiences with me or anyone else."

Ben was still tired and groggy, but tried to give his dad's concern time to sink in, and finally replied in as thoughtful a manner as he could muster under the circumstances.

"No, Dad, I don't think so...I know accidents happen and they can happen anywhere. The roads where we live are full of them...especially during the winter. We see it all the time. If camping is the issue, a shorter camping trip closer to home might be much better. I guess...it's like you've always said before, 'It's not the situation, it's the response.' You know...it's how you respond. Right?"

"Well, you responded in the most admirable way, and again, I can't tell you how proud I am of you."

"Thanks Dad. I know one thing...I'm going to appreciate things a lot more than I ever have before. That's for sure. And, just one more thing...before I zonk out. I want to thank you for teaching me all about that shaman's stone stuff. You know, I can't explain it...but I have to say that while that stone was one of the few things I had with me the entire time, I felt it gave me an extra push, an inspiration every time I thought of it or touched it. I don't know what it was, but I feel bad for the person who lost it in the first place. I hope everything turned out okay for him, too. You know?"

"I would believe so, Ben. More than likely, he was able to replace it before too long. No brave on a dangerous hunt or a warrior on a bloody warpath in that dangerous world would ever want to venture into one of those situations without one. It helped to alleviate their immediate fears. While stones like that didn't prevent fatalities, they supplied hope of good outcomes provided by their spirits. In a sense, they supplied a certain amount of confidence despite all the odds. I call it courage…plain and simple. Truth be told, a good medicine bundle was essential to cope with about everything that occurred during everyday tribal life. With it, a bundle contained a special, indispensable item that helped ward off all the 'bad medicine' people, who lived during those historical times, were forced to confront. In this case, a stone such as yours was somehow destined to be here with you and all that you faced last night."

Ben acknowledged the information with a humble smile, and with that opening, Fred seized the opportunity to add more to the moment while he could.

"Ben, there's one more thing I want to tell you before my nurse comes back. This is hard for me to say…but it's something I've been thinking about for a good while. For whatever reason, I just couldn't man-up and face it. For a long time, I was feeling I had been losing touch with the family. I guess a part of the stone's influence for added courage may be rubbing off on me today as I say this, but this is as good a time as any to start making a change.

"This unfortunate camping episode, starting with my rescue and the long boat ride back with Bill and Pete…and especially, not knowing how this would end…I came to question what I could have done differently to prevent my reasoning that a one-time trip would be a cure all for not being around the house with you and your mother more often. To be perfectly blunt, I think part of my answer was my career and unconsciously taking you two for granted.

"While I was worried sick about your whereabouts, I was wondering how I could have been so neglectful, and if I were ever to get a second chance, I would make some serious changes. It's kind of like Charles Dickens' Christmas story with me being Mr. Scrooge after finishing seeing himself with the three ghosts of Christmas. It wasn't pretty and it has to be addressed."

Fred pressed on. "Occasional trips such as these really can't make up for lost family time. Looking back, I feel as though…I have neglected you in a most startling way and I can't take it back. I guess this trip has brought that stark acknowledgment forward in a head-banging way. No pun intended."

Ben looked surprised and started to speak again, but he held back, figuring his dad would have more to say. He was right.

"Ben, I do want to thank you again for your colossal effort to help rescue me. I'm sure your being lost in a forest, all by itself, was an all-consuming and terrifying event, especially at night. And that's why I want you to be the absolute first to know…that I've decided to do something about what I'm saying. I'm going to start with taking an early retirement and resign from the university as soon as I can. While I love teaching, there are other ways to get that done. I'll find something less taxing, so I can redirect my focus on what really matters to me. That's you, your mom, and your brother and sisters."

"Gee…Dad," Ben was startled with that announcement. It sounded too good to be true.

"I don't know what I'll do next… Maybe, I'll write a book or start a small outdoor recreational business. Your mother and I have saved our money, so we'll be okay. Anyway, I haven't got that far yet with any specific details...but who knows? Maybe together, you and I can sell some canoes like Ole Yeller. Maybe, even a few kayaks or an array of fishing gear...as long as it doesn't take away from a family focus."

"Really?" Ben still couldn't believe his ears.

"Really...and I'm dead serious. I suppose I could write a sequence of archaeology adventures or a series of fictional camping tales. You know what I'm getting at? I have really come to believe I've been a hard pill to swallow for the past few years. You know?"

There was a mutual return of smiles and glassing of the eyes between the two with that last side comment, but Fred's heartfelt words recaptured a feeling that life might get much better—and even the rest of Ben's world, for that matter—if he only could believe what he was hearing. *I want that.*

With tear-filled eyes, Fred uncharacteristically uttered, "I've made a bunch of serious mistakes. I hope they aren't long-standing."

Realizing he still had a few more minutes, he continued, "I also want to say here and now that during that long agonizing trip out of the woods with Bill and Pete, and all the way here, I came to realize I have been overly consumed with my self-importance for a long time. More specifically, as it applies to our trip together, when I should have been more attentive to you and showing you some basic camp skills, instead I was preoccupied with spewing out my know-it-all facts about everything else.

"Not only were you totally uneducated for what lay

ahead, but I was also unprepared for this trip. Because of my negligence, neither one of us was ready for anything like what happened overnight."

"What do you mean by that?"

"Instead of just getting a new fishing book, I should have also brought along an emergency medical book for campers. Not only could I have shown you where I had it, but we could have gone over it together before the trip. And, instead of lecturing you about nature's hazards, I left you largely unprepared with just a silver whistle. As far as hazards go, I clearly should have never pitched my own tent under a tree with an assortment of dead branches, and more than likely, none of this would have happened.

"Truth be known, I brought a survival kit along with a compass, waterproof matches, and all that, but here again, I neglected to share that information with you. Instead, I bragged it up about the possibility of seeing a wandering bear or hearing a wolf's howl back there. Ben, I'm awful sorry for what happened to you, when all the while it was you who was out there being tortured without as much as a decent headlamp while trying to rescue me."

Ben was still astonished at what he was hearing, all this coming from his experienced camping partner.

"And you know…and I must confess this to you…to get this out to clear all the air before I have to go. A few months ago, I was called a pompous ass in one of our staff meetings by a seasoned university colleague, whom I respect greatly. But I laughed it off. However, I realized she was right back then, and now, even more so today. I would say my behavior on this trip has made words like that ring true more than ever. In the end, it has been you…who has finally taught me, as a severely misguided professor, a powerful lesson…in resilience, courage, and hopefully…forgiveness."

There was a brief silence after Fred's voice tailed off. Neither one was able to speak further. The lumps in each of their throats were long lasting, but the simple power of Fred's heartfelt confession cemented into Ben the idea that despite his dreadful all-night experience, in the end, somehow it all might have been worth it. There could be a positive aspect to his tragic suffering if his dad's words really would come true. Mother Nature may have not only taught Ben the value of persistence and coming to grips with his innermost fears; she also may have touched and affected his father's heart with a more powerful and lasting blessing.

Ben wiped away his eyes first while thinking, *I can't believe my ears.* Only a moment more passed before Ben was able to say, "Dad…you don't know how much I have wanted to hear…something like you just said. Maybe someday…if you want…we could make a trip to the bakery…you know…to get one more Sunday paper."

Fred caught the hint and said, "Sure, Ben. I'd like that."

After a short pause reflecting on what had just been revealed between the two, coupled with a full measure of gratitude for having their individual prayers answered, Fred finally wiped his swollen face and tried to regain his composure by bringing things a little closer to home by adding, "And let's hope your mom…gets here soon, too."

"You can say that again, Dad."
"Okay, Bennie...let's hope your mom gets here...soon."

As timing would have it, when Fred and Ben looked up, they saw a young nurse's aide standing silently at the doorway. Her presence cut through the room's heavy atmosphere.

"I'm sorry, Dr. Nelson, to interrupt your valuable time with your son, but I really need to return you to the examination room to finish your treatments. The doctor will be ready in a few minutes."

Fred said, "I understand. I think we are good here for now, but if you don't mind, I'd like to make a quick stop at the restroom beforehand— he pointed across the room — if I could."

"Of course. Let me wheel you over there."

Taking advantage of the situation, knowing Fred would be busy by himself for a few more minutes, Ben did what he knew he had to do. Once the restroom door closed, he motioned for the aide to please come over to his bedside. Moments later the aide was back assisting Fred safely back into his wheelchair and headed for the door. But, not before Fred said to Ben, "Now, get some rest while you can. I'll see you soon."

After wheeling Fred back to the examination room, the attending aide stopped and pulled an object from the front pocket of her clinical gown and said, "Your son asked me to give you this. He said you'd know what it's about and could put it to good use. I'm not sure, but I think he called it a shaman's stone...whatever that is. It looks like an arrowhead to me. Anyway, it really does look pretty cool."

"Yeah," Fred replied. "I guess it really does. Even more so…when you know there's a message attached."

There was a collective raising of the eyebrows questioning Fred's response from the others in the room. They were focused and anxious to get restarted with their unfinished medical work, while their distracted patient had to first clear a certain choking in his throat and suppress a fresh welling of tears.

As Fred clutched the stone, and mentally unraveled its invisible message from his son, the room mysteriously brightened and he looked up at his onlookers and silently mouthed, *I'm sorry…but I have a lot to be thankful for.*

It was at that precise moment he felt the warm touch of a thread-like family connection, as it penetrated his chest and began to spin around his hopeful heart.

It was good medicine.

Author's Note

Most of the previous pages have been fictionalized, except for the general references to the wondrous beauty and the mysterious idiosyncrasies of nature and portions of Little Turtle and Ben's prayers derived from the Great Spirit Prayer and Psalm 23, respectively. There is also an abundance of historical facts embedded here and there that may be compelling to the reader. Along with those, one of the most predominant historical facts presented in this story pertains to one of the two featured protagonists—Little Turtle.

This character was a real Native American who lived and walked upon this earth with dignity and respect during the period presented and well beyond as an adult. Even though his first warpath in this story is a part of what could have been, there were many more factual ones in his lifetime, which extended into the mid-1790s, fighting for the Miami people's effort to maintain their native territorial lands.

During their many struggles, he soon became a well-respected leader and an eventual tribal war chief in the early 1790s. He has been credited as one of the most famous Native American military leaders of his day.

Later in life, he became an important advocate to keep his tribe at peace once the much greater military forces of the American armies finally became successful in capturing vast quantities of their tribal lands found within the Michigan and Indiana territories, culminating with the notable signing of the Treaty of Greenville in

1795.

    It has been said in many ways that Little Turtle's gift as a great leader was one of persistently resisting against what he believed to be senseless foreign interventions, and later in life, as a faithful advocate for the honorable ending of the hostilities in the name of peace on behalf of his people, all for one simple reason: to save tribal lives and preserve their future heritage. His life was a heroic one, devoted to the Miami people first. Some of this fictionalized story tries to project that reality.

    Beyond that historical note, there are a great many books of reference that may satisfy further readings about our natural surroundings in general and our Native Americans in particular. This is all part of our recorded history that is available in libraries, bookstores, and online. Further information is ours to seek.

Geographical and Historical Maps

North American Tribes of the Great Lakes

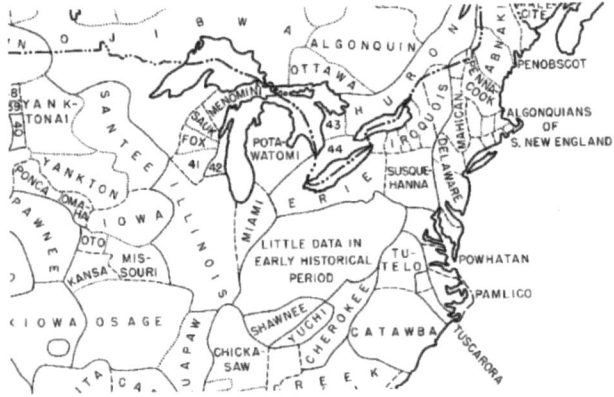

Source: Indians of North America, Harold E. Driver, 1961

Territories Held by France and Great Britain Prior to 1750

commons.wikimedia.org/File: Nouvelle_France.map_en.svg

About the Author

H. S. Dunham is a lifelong outdoor enthusiast. Be it nature photography, camping, landscaping, organic gardening or having cared for a wide variety of farm animals for most of his adult life - when it comes to plants and animals - he has played no favorites. He has been an enduring student of all that nature has made available to him, engrossed in learning and living in a natural way since early adulthood. Parallel in this interest in nature is the history of all Native Americans and their varied cultures. He is an ongoing learner in both interests and has a BS degree in Anthropology and a BA degree in Business used to further develop his organic Gills and Beaks game farm.

Among some other special highlights was his visit early in life to Walden Pond and the Henry Thoreau Lyceum in Concorde, Massachusetts, and then, to the Little Bighorn Battlefield National Monument in southeastern Montana. At both sites, first when walking along the famous pond's shoreline, and later, along the edge of the grounds of the renowned battlefield, the origin of *The Shaman's Stone* was born. Other contributing highlights include his wilderness camping trips to the Boundary Waters Canoe Area in northern Minnesota and several forays to our national park, ocean and desert areas exploring nature's vistas throughout the United States.

He is married, has five children, and currently lives in a small rural community in east central Wisconsin.

Acknowledgements

Bringing a story to life is not a one-person enterprise nor is it simply born by putting together numerous sentences and paragraphs. With this book there were many behind-the-scenes contributors, and I would be remiss if I didn't thank those who helped move this story along from start to finish.

First, to Joe Tesch, who initially challenged me to generate a pipe-dream idea into a story.

To Diane and Brad Ward, Scott MacFarlane and Katie Dunham for their initial reviews as beta readers and insightful suggestions to improve an undeveloped collection of chapters.

To Emily Dunham for her constructive analysis and initial editing details. Her comments changed the direction of the story and helped pull it together in a meaningful way.

To Carolyn Haley and Jessica Powers, both from Reedsy, for their professional edits (developmental and copy) and to Susan Hegedus for her proofreading skill. Thanks also for their literary encouragement, raising tough questions, eliminating gaps, and elevating the story's readability level to greater heights.

To Patricia Lewis, director of Van Velzer Press, for her strong faith in the story premise and an eye-catching development of the front and back cover designs. Her help preparing *The Shaman's Stone* for publication combined with her experienced overview of current publishing industry norms has been invaluable. In short, Patricia and her team's quality involvement has been superb.

To my wife, Jamie, for all her support throughout this lengthy process. She enabled my many hours spent at the keyboard. She has always been our family captain and it showed once again by filling in for me on so many occasions.

Finally, borrowing the words from one of my characters, Dr. Fred Nelson, who said he had a lot to be thankful for. Well, so do I.

H. S. Dunham
hdunham2@icloud.com

www.ingramcontent.com/pod-product-compliance
Lightning Source LLC
LaVergne TN
LVHW041738060526
838201LV00046B/855